THE PRIDE OF MINNESOTA

THE PRIDE OF MINNESOTA

THE TWINS IN THE TURBULENT 1960S

THOM HENNINGER

University of Nebraska Press

LINCOLN

Library of Congress Cataloging-in-Publication Data
Names: Henninger, Thom, author.
Title: The pride of Minnesota: the Twins in the turbulent 1960s /
Thom Henninger.
Description: Lincoln: University of Nebraska Press, 2021. |
Includes bibliographical references and index.
Identifiers: LCCN 2020041729
ISBN 9781496225603 (Hardback: acid-free paper)
ISBN 9781496227119 (ePub)
ISBN 9781496227126 (mobi)
ISBN 9781496227133 (PDF)
Subjects: LCSH: Minnesota Twins (Baseball team)—History. |
World Series (Baseball) (1965) | Baseball—Minnesota—
Minneapolis—History. | Major League Baseball (Organization)—
History—20th century.
Classification: LCC GV875.M55 .H46 2021 |
DDC 796.357/6409776579—dc23
LC record available at https://lccn.loc.gov/2020041729

Set in Scala OT by Laura Buis.

CONTENTS

ILLUSTRATIONS

18. Billy Martin
19. Ron Perranoski
20. Bert Blyleven
21. Even the Beatles' George Harrison has donned the "TC" of the Twins

PREFACE

Like so many boys growing up in St. Paul in the early 1960s, I spent most of my summer days at the local playground playing baseball. Two or three games a day were common, interrupted only by meals and rain. It was after a sunny afternoon at the playground—in June 1964—that I learned the Minnesota Twins had traded away two of my favorite players. I was ten years old, a loyal Twins fan since the team arrived from Washington DC four years earlier, and I was disheartened to hear my team had dealt fleet-footed center fielder Lenny Green and dazzling first baseman Vic Power to the Los Angeles Angels.

Green was on the field when the Twins played their first game at Yankee Stadium on April 11, 1961. He batted second between rookie Zoilo Versalles and young slugger Harmon Killebrew, but was the primary leadoff man for the first two years of Twins baseball. Green, who walked far more often than he struck out, ranked among league leaders in walks and runs in '61 and '62. He caught my attention for his speed and grace in the outfield, ranging far to chase down fly balls that seemed out of reach. Like Green, I was left-handed, and I wanted to play like him when I roamed the outfield at the playground. By late in the summer I would always be very tan, and I remember my mother once telling me I was "looking more like Lenny Green every day." She told me years later that I beamed with pride when she spoke those words.

Power came to Minnesota shortly before Opening Day 1962, acquired in a trade that moved Pedro Ramos—the starter and winning pitcher of that first Twins game—to Cleveland. Power was a slick-fielding first baseman who scooped balls out of the dirt effortlessly with a sweeping motion while blowing huge bubbles with his gum. And he caught everything one-handed, breaking the cardinal rule that every coach preached to me growing up: catch the ball with two hands. That, of course, is something almost nobody does today. Power, who grew up in Puerto Rico, was outgoing, gregarious, a mentor to Latin players such as Versalles and Tony Oliva, and a fan favorite who loved playing in Minnesota.

Seeing Green and Power depart didn't sit well with ten-year-old me. By then, I took a liking to first base, worked at digging low throws out of the dirt, and chewed a lot of gum. Even after Green and Power were long gone and the Twins were contenders later in the decade, I wished they had been able to play for the 1965 club that won the American League pennant. Both spent twelve seasons in the Majors; neither made it to a World Series. The Yankees represented the AL in all but three years of Power's career, and Power retired after the '65 season. Green came close more than once. He played for the Red Sox in '65 and '66, but joined the Detroit Tigers the following season, when Boston enjoyed its "Impossible Dream" run to the AL title. Green played his last six Major League games in June 1968 for the Tigers, who won the World Series that October.

That 1964 trade was an early lesson that change is a constant in life. The Twins, of course, emerged to dethrone the Yankees in 1965, beginning an era of success at a time when change was in the air on so many fronts and my interests were diversifying. The Beatles suddenly grabbed my attention, sparking an interest in music that didn't always garner parental approval. The national news was a fixture at home, and the budding civil rights movement and expanding Vietnam War were front and center. For the first time in history, television brought into our homes such events as the assassination of a president, Alabama state police attacking a group of peaceful protesters in Selma, the weekly footage of body bags coming home from a faraway war, and the challenges and ultimate victory of a decade-long pursuit to put human beings on the moon.

As a young person, it was a challenging time to make sense of the world. It seemed to be coming apart at the seams in 1968, when civil rights leader Martin Luther King Jr. and presidential candidate Robert Kennedy were assassinated two months apart in the midst of a divisive and eventful presidential campaign. Amid all the turmoil, with a young teenager's idealism and naivete, I was now riveted by the changes going on around me. At the same time, the Minnesota Twins, a constant as I grew up in the '60s, became an exciting team to follow through several dramatic pennant races.

ACKNOWLEDGMENTS

I offer a special thanks to two longtime and dear friends, Stuart Shea and the late Ron Thompson, both of whom reviewed the manuscript and provided helpful advice and editing. Stu's encouragement and support throughout the project's ups and downs mean so much to me, and I'll be forever touched that Ron tackled the manuscript when, unbeknownst to me, his illness had taken a turn for the worse and he had little time left. Thanks also to good friends Ken Goldberg and Chuck Miller, who weighed in on subject matter or provided statistical support along the way.

Taking on a historical project like this one was made much easier by such sources as Baseball Reference and Retrosheet. And it couldn't have been done without the beat writers of the era bringing Twins baseball to life. Growing up, I read *St. Paul Pioneer Press* beat writer Arno Goethel's coverage of the Twins religiously, and his insights and humor help tell this story. I'd also like to acknowledge the valuable work of his 1960s colleagues on both sides of the river: Tom Briere, Mike Lamey, Glenn Redmann, Patrick Reusse, Dave Mona, Jon Roe, Dwayne Netland, and columnists Dick Young, Sid Hartman, and the outrageous Don Riley.

The expertise and attention to detail of Rob Taylor, Joeth Zucco, Amanda Jackson, and other University of Nebraska Press staff that steered this project to completion are also appreciated. And I offer my heartfelt thanks to my wife, Kathy McMahon, and our wonderful daughter, Meara McMahon. They were always supportive during this often-lonely endeavor. It's because of them you'll find George Harrison wearing a Twins cap in these pages.

INTRODUCTION

A Contender Emerges in Troubling Times

The Minnesota Twins were an exceptional baseball team during one of the more turbulent times in our country's social and political history. Soon after the struggling Washington Senators moved to Minnesota for the 1961 season, the civil rights movement took flight and dozens of Brits arrived on American shores to turn the music world upside down. Amid the dramatic social change fueled by the civil rights struggle and the British Invasion, a war fought halfway around the world ignited an anti-war movement and divided the nation.

Assassinations marred the decade. In 1968, with the civil rights movement and the Vietnam War becoming increasingly contentious subjects in America, the killings of the Rev. Dr. Martin Luther King Jr. and Robert Kennedy in a two-month span severely tested the nation's psyche. King's assassination spurred riots in more than one hundred U.S. cities, and Kennedy's marked his family's second violent death of the 1960s. The killing of a president and presidential candidate ran counter to a democracy that prided itself in the peaceful and orderly transfer of power through elections. With cities burning and opposition to the war on the rise, America's democracy was at a difficult crossroad.

Life in the 1950s couldn't portend what the 1960s would bring. The postwar years in America were known for their booming economy. The gross national product more than doubled between

1945 and 1960, supported by a surge in government spending that built the Interstate Highway System, schools and infrastructure, and financed new technologies and a growing military. The schools and infrastructure were especially important as American women bore four million babies a year throughout the 1950s, a "baby boom" that spawned roughly 75 million baby boomers in the two decades following World War II. Wages were high, inflation and unemployment were low, and urban families flocked to the booming suburbs.

Despite America's image as the land of opportunity, certain segments of the nation didn't share in the wealth of the postwar years. In 1959, according to federal statistics, more than one in four American children lived in poverty. Men without a college education, people of color, families headed by women, and the elderly often struggled to make ends meet. Nearly 21 percent of American families lived below the poverty line. With African Americans lacking the same opportunities as white Americans, 54.9 percent of Black families were poor.

Jim Crow laws enforced America's Southern-style apartheid, which kept many African Americans poor and disenfranchised. In Montgomery, Alabama, on December 1, 1955, seamstress Rosa Parks was riding the bus home from work, sitting in the front row of the "colored" section at the back of the bus. When all seats in the "white" section were taken and a white man boarded the bus, bus driver James Blake ordered the four riders in the front row of the "colored" section to give up their seats. Three of them did, but Parks refused. Her arrest and conviction for violating segregation laws inspired the Montgomery Bus Boycott by African American residents, who made up 70 percent of the city's ridership. The boycott, an early milestone of the civil rights movement that brought the twenty-six-year-old King into the public eye, went on for a year, drawing national attention to living conditions in the South. In November 1956, the Supreme Court ruled that bus segregation was unconstitutional.

At the same time that the civil rights movement was taking root, white entertainers were discovering Black artists and covering their songs. Crooner Pat Boone had hits with Fats Domino's "Ain't That a Shame" and Little Richard's "Long Tall Sally" and "Tutti Frutti." When Little Richard sang the latter song live, it began "Tutti Frutti, good booty" with a host of sexual euphemisms to follow. Kevin Phinney, author of *Souled American: How Black Music Transformed White Culture*, wrote that "it took Pat Boone to bleach it white."

Then Elvis Presley burst onto the scene, oozing sexuality as he sang R&B. Presley had early hits with Otis Blackwell's "Don't Be Cruel" and "All Shook Up" and Arthur Crudup's "That's All Right." Unlike Boone, noted Phinney, Presley "didn't downplay the records' blackness. He amplified it." While most of white America wasn't ready for that in the 1950s, across the pond, young Brits were tuning in to Radio Luxembourg in the late-evening hours to hear American blues and R&B. The exciting, liberating music inspired a new generation of musicians. Many, like Mick Jagger, mail-ordered blues and R&B albums from the United States. The story goes that Jagger was carrying a copy of *The Best of Muddy Waters* when he and Keith Richards first met on a train.

Before they broke out in the United States, the Rolling Stones had big hits in Britain with Chuck Berry's "Come On," Bobby and Shirley Womack's "It's All Over Now," and Willie Dixon's "Little Red Rooster." The Beatles recorded Chuck Berry's "Roll Over Beethoven," the Marvelettes hit "Please Mr. Postman," Smokey Robinson's "You Really Got a Hold on Me" and "Twist and Shout," the Phil Medley-Bert Russell tune first made popular by the Isley Brothers.

Just as the notion that British moptops would take America by storm would have seemed unimaginable in the 1950s, so would the idea that the Twin Cities could secure a Major League Baseball team. There had been only sixteen teams in the two major leagues since 1901 and franchise shifts had been rare until the Boston Braves relocated to Milwaukee in 1953. A year later the St. Louis Browns headed east to Baltimore, and the Philadelphia Athletics departed for Kansas City in 1955. When the Brooklyn Dodgers and New York Giants moved to the West Coast in 1957, Giants owner Horace Stoneham had originally targeted Minneapolis, home to his team's Triple-A affiliate, but Dodgers owner Walter O'Malley convinced Stoneham to join him in California. The door had been opened, but the push to bring a Major League club to the upper Midwest didn't take shape until late in the decade.

Perhaps even more absurd would have been any thought that Minnesota would soon host a World Series. The New York Yankees had dominated the American League since Casey Stengel became their manager in 1949. He was at the helm for five straight World Series titles, beginning in '49, and only the Cleveland Indians (1954) and Chicago White Sox (1959) interrupted New York's run of fourteen AL pennants in sixteen seasons through 1964. Stengel's hiring had been a surprising move by the architect of the Yankees' dynasty, George Weiss, a stuffy, humorless man who rivaled Twins owner Calvin Griffith in the fine art of penny-pinching when negotiating contracts.

Weiss's choice shocked more than a few baseball executives and players. Stengel, who had never managed a big league team to a first-division finish in nine seasons with the Brooklyn Dodgers and Boston Braves, was widely seen as a clownish figure who couldn't be taken seriously running the legendary Yankees. He was best known for his antics as a player. During a spring training game in 1912, Stengel climbed into a manhole in center field and popped out in time to make a catch. He delighted in catching easy fly balls behind his back and once took batting practice with his uniform on backward.

While Stengel charmed fans with his eccentric ways, he was a thorn in the side to nearly every owner for whom he played. He regularly held out for bigger paychecks and complained about what he was paid. A man who never endeared himself to management was now taking over the reins of the staid Yankees. Stengel may have confirmed his critics' worst fears when he was introduced as the manager. At the 1949 press conference, he had this to say about his appointment: "This is a big job, fellows, and I barely have had time to study it. In fact, I scarcely know where I am at."

Stengel clearly knew where he was at, and Weiss had recognized Stengel's rapid-fire ability to execute good baseball decisions. He believed in his new skipper's use of platoons, a managerial technique deftly manipulated by legendary New York Giants manager John McGraw, for whom Stengel played in the 1920s. The new Yankees manager didn't make decisions strictly by the book, but usually made the right ones.

It didn't hurt that Stengel had one of the game's most potent lineups for more than a decade. He was at the helm for the best years of Mickey Mantle, Whitey Ford, Yogi Berra, Hank Bauer, Allie Reynolds, Eddie Lopat, and Gil McDougald. Even Joe DiMaggio was there at the start of Stengel's tenure, closing out his career in 1951, the same year Mantle debuted as his replacement. In Stengel's twelve seasons in the Bronx, he directed the Yankees to ten first-place finishes and seven World Series titles between 1949 and 1960. His last World Series in 1960, however, didn't end well. New York batted .338 and outscored the Pittsburgh Pirates 55-21, but the Pirates took home the big prize when Bill Mazeroski abruptly ended a dramatic Game Seven with a lead-off ninth-inning home run off Ralph Terry in Pittsburgh.

New York's return to the World Series in 1960 marked the first of five straight appearances in the Fall Classic. But two days after Maz's big fly, Stengel was cut loose to make room for Ralph Houk, the highly regarded managerial prospect who the Yankees feared would leave were he not promoted. Yankees owners Dan Topping and Del Webb called a press conference and forced Stengel to read an announcement of his retirement. In a massive public relations blunder, Topping cited Stengel's age as the reason for his release, to which Casey replied bitterly, "I'll never make the mistake of being 70 again."

When Calvin Griffith picked up stakes and moved the Washington Senators to Minnesota in 1961, the franchise had finished in the top half of the American League standings just four times since winning its last pennant in 1933. The Senators plunged to seventh place in '34, setting the tone for nearly three decades of uninspiring baseball.

The franchise's fortunes began to turn just prior to departing the nation's capital. Homegrown talents Harmon Killebrew and Bob Allison blossomed into premier sluggers, and Camilo Pascual and Jim Kaat became effective starters around which to build a pitching staff. In a key trade a year before the move to Minnesota, Griffith dealt power-hitter Roy Sievers, in his mid-thirties and soon to decline, to the Chicago White Sox for two promising young players, catcher Earl Battey and first baseman Don Mincher. During the inaugural season of Twins baseball in 1961, Zoilo Versalles emerged as the first of several impact rookies to join the club.

On April 11, 1961, the transplanted Washington franchise made its Twins debut at Yankee Stadium. Minnesota manager Cookie Lavagetto, who moved from Washington with the club, called on Cuban-born Pedro Ramos to start Minnesota's inaugural game. Ramos had already made quite a first impression on Twins fans. With Cuban-U.S. relations quickly deteriorating that spring, the flamboyant and outspoken Ramos livened the final days of spring training by announcing to the world that he might return to his homeland to fight Fidel Castro's revolutionary government. Days later, he settled for whipping the Yankees at the home of the reigning AL champions.

The right-hander tossed a three-hitter and quieted the New York faithful with a 6–0 shutout. He outdueled Whitey Ford—the Cy Young Award winner that year—and Allison broke up the scoreless match by drilling a Ford fastball for a seventh-inning home run, the first in Twins history. Ramos later ambushed the *Yanquis* with a two-run single of his own. Soon after, Ramos announced that he intended to keep his day job and took himself out of the running for war duty. "I'm a baseball player," he quipped, "not a fighter."

The Twins victory certainly didn't set the course for the Yankees' 1961 campaign. Mickey Mantle and Roger Maris flirted with Babe Ruth's home run record; Maris topped it with 61. Whitey Ford finished 25-4 and the Yankees won 109 games and a five-game World Series over the Cincinnati Reds. Meanwhile, the Twins went 70-90, though this was an improvement for a franchise that had averaged 93 losses a year in its final six seasons in Washington, complete with four last-place finishes.

At the core of the young Twins' emergence was the franchise's version of Mantle and Maris, the power duo of Allison and Killebrew. Allison was a toolsy player in the mold of Mantle, a combination of power and speed with a terrific arm, though it took some time for his bat to come around in the Minors. He excelled at both football and baseball at the University of Kansas, just fifty miles from his hometown of Raytown, Missouri, drawing the interest of the Yankees and Senators as well as the NFL's San Francisco 49ers. The athletic, six-foot-three Allison played baseball with a football mentality, running into fences and scaring infielders when he charged into bases, but off the field, the man with the matinee-idol looks was as soft-spoken as his slugging teammate.

"Bob was more of a social guy than I was," noted Killebrew, who mostly let his bat do the talking. It spoke loudly when Washington scout Ossie Bluege traveled to Payette, Idaho, to watch the seventeen-year-old, four-sport letterman in 1954. Killebrew slugged a 435-foot home run into a nearby beet field. The youngster had a football scholarship lined up at the University of Oregon, where he intended to play baseball as well, but as graduation day approached, the Senators and Boston Red Sox turned up the heat.

Killebrew's family was in touch with Boston scout Earl Johnson, who asked the seventeen-year-old prospect to get back to him before agreeing to a contract. When Killebrew informed Johnson of Washington's offer—a three-year deal for $6,000 a year with an annual bonus of $4,000—Johnson told him he should take it. "When I went to Fenway Park and saw how close that fence was there, I had second thoughts," Killebrew said in a 2004 interview. "Griffith Stadium was huge—biggest park in baseball. It was 405 feet down the left-field line." His place in the game's home run annals might be loftier if he had spent most of his career calling Fenway Park home.

Just days after graduation he was with the Senators, a bonus-baby signing. By the rules of the time, he was required to spend his first two pro seasons in the Majors, and he quickly learned there was no such thing as a cheap home run in Washington's home park. Well, except for his first Major League homer on June 24, 1955, with the Senators trailing the Detroit Tigers, 13–0 in the fifth inning. Fifty years later, Killebrew told the story to the *Denver Post*'s Adam Schefter:

> I came to the plate, and it was against a left-handed pitcher by the name of Billy Hoeft, and the catcher was Frank House. When I stepped to the plate, Frank said, "Kid we're going to throw you a fastball." I didn't know whether he was telling me the truth or not, I was so young and naïve. I wasn't quite sure, but sure enough, here came a fastball, and I hit it 476 feet— probably the longest home run I ever hit in Griffith Stadium. . . . As I was coming around the bases, I stepped on home plate and Frank House said, "Kid, that's the last time we're ever going to tell you what's coming." And sure enough, it was. Nobody ever told me what was coming after that.

Killebrew lost key development time sitting in the Senators dugout instead of playing in the Minors, but finally got to play regularly in 1956 at Class-A Charlotte, where he and Allison were roommates. They were as close as brothers by the time they had passed through Double-A Chattanooga the following summer and reached Washington to stay in 1959. They quickly emerged as middle-of-the-order sluggers.

The twenty-four-year-old Allison drilled 30 home runs, legged out a league-leading nine triples, and earned Rookie of the Year honors. Without the assistance of opposing catchers, Killebrew, just twenty-three, won the AL home run title in his first full season in the Majors, pounding 42 to share honors with Cleveland's Rocky Colavito. Playing at cavernous Griffith Stadium, Killebrew didn't hit many cheapies. His majestic blasts inspired Paul Richards, the Orioles manager at the time, to quip: "Killebrew can knock the ball out of any park, including Yellowstone."

Both Killebrew and Allison topped 100 RBIS in the first two seasons of Twins baseball. In an eleven-run first inning against Cleveland on July 18, 1962, the slugging duo became the first teammates to stroke grand slam home runs in the same inning, connecting off future teammate Jim Perry. The duo's power strokes earned them nicknames. Killebrew, who often hit long, arching home runs deep into the seats, was dubbed "Mr. Upstairs." Allison, who more often hit line shots that headed for the seats like ballistic missiles, was "Mr. Downstairs."

Allison and Killebrew anchored a Twins lineup that became increasingly dangerous when rookie center fielder Jimmie Hall arrived in 1963. Hall slugged 33 homers to give the Twins one of the game's most powerful outfields. With Killebrew in left and Allison in right, the trio produced 113 home runs and all three ranked among the league's top ten in extra-base hits and total bases in '63. Then Tony Oliva broke out in '64, stroking 32 homers and winning the AL batting title with one of the best Major League debuts in history. Oliva's emergence forced Allison to first base.

Minnesota's pitching also was on the upswing. Ramos and fellow Cuban Camilo Pascual had anchored the rotation in those final dreadful years in Washington. While the Twins dealt Ramos to Cleveland before the 1962 campaign—for dazzling first baseman Vic Power and Minnesota native Dick Stigman—Pascual blossomed into an ace. He threw one of the era's best curveballs, but struggled to locate his fastball effectively in his early years. The right-hander couldn't throw enough fastball strikes to make the most of his devastating breaking pitch. Pascual endured on-the-job training for Washington clubs desperate for pitching, but it all came together when he became Minnesota's first twenty-game winner in 1962.

Jim Kaat, who made his Major League debut with the Senators in 1959, won eighteen games and led the league with five shutouts in 1962, when the Twins flirted with a pennant race for the first time. That summer, at age twenty-three, the lanky lefty began a run of twelve straight seasons of double-digit wins for Minnesota. Kaat averaged 233 innings and 15 wins a season during this stretch, pairing with Pascual in a lefty-righty combination that helped the club become competitive. After capturing 18 wins for the 1965 AL champions, Kaat pitched a career-high 304 2/3 innings and won a league-high twenty-five games in 1966.

For all their youth, the Twins became legitimate contenders in 1965 only after picking up Al Worthington and Johnny

Klippstein, castoffs who had bounced from team to team into their mid-thirties. Minnesota purchased the thirty-six-year-old Worthington from the Cincinnati Reds in June 1964. Three days later the Twins picked up Klippstein, also thirty-six, from the Philadelphia Phillies. They were at their best a year later, anchoring the bullpen of the 1965 AL champions.

While the Twins were on the rise, an aging Yankees club that had won 109 games in 1961 was showing signs of decline. The game's most dominant franchise for more than a decade, New York won its final World Series in 1962, when the outcome might have been different if Willie McCovey's Game Seven-ending liner had been hit a foot or two in either direction from Yankees second baseman Bobby Richardson. By then, most of the 1950s Yankees had retired. Mantle, wracked by injury at age thirty-one, had just one good year left in him—1964. Ford, three years older than Mantle, remained the ace through '64, the last year of the dynasty, but a circulatory problem in his throwing shoulder forced him to retire in 1967. Injuries also sabotaged the careers of younger New York stars, such as Jim Bouton, Tom Tresh, and Tony Kubek.

The Yankees still won 104 games in '63, but the farm system no longer developed the premier talent that fueled Weiss's dynasty. Weiss was shown the door soon after Stengel, and author Peter Golenbock, in *Dynasty: The New York Yankees, 1949–1964*, maintained that Weiss shares the blame for the team's mid-1960s crash. While other Major League clubs began employing the best African American players following Jackie Robinson's arrival, the arrogant Weiss resisted change. As good as the Yankees were in the 1950s, they had lost out on a substantial infusion of gifted young players, including several future Hall of Famers who thrived in the 1960s.

The Griffith family, on the other hand, tapped into talent-rich Cuba as early as the 1930s, initially signing light-skinned players prior to the game's integration. The family turned to Italian-born entrepreneur Joe Cambria, who owned a lucrative laundry business in Baltimore, bought a few baseball teams including the Negro leagues' Baltimore Black Sox, and as a scout signed more than four hundred Cuban players while working in and around Havana for three decades. By the time the Twins became competitive in the mid-1960s, Pascual, Versalles, and Oliva were franchise cornerstones.

Cambria, affectionately called "Papa Joe" by the players he signed, was the only full-time scout working the island for most of those years, giving the Senators nearly exclusive access to a wealth of cost-effective talent. The stocky man with a Panama hat and ever-present cigar was no more likely to offer a promising player a bonus than was the owner for whom he worked; this caused Cuban sportswriter Jess Losada to brand Cambria the Christopher Columbus of baseball for pillaging the island's treasures. The players he signed, however, appreciated his ability to facilitate annual visas and bureaucratic snafus, particularly after Cuban-U.S. relations suffered at the start of the 1960s.

By the time the Senators relocated to Minnesota, more than thirty Cubans populated the Twins' Minor League camp each spring. And most of Cambria's biggest finds benefited the Twins more than the Senators. Pascual and Ramos were fixtures in Washington's rotation before Pascual emerged as the Twins' ace. Defensive whiz Versalles emerged as a big league regular in 1961 and won AL Most Valuable Player honors in '65.

Cambria's last big signing was Oliva, who arrived in the United States in the wake of the CIA-directed Bay of Pigs invasion in April 1961. Oliva's skills were so raw that the Twins decided not to sign him at the close of spring training in '61, but when the failed attempt to overthrow Fidel Castro led to the closing of borders between the two countries, Oliva stayed in the United States and cashed in on his second chance. In 1965 he and Versalles were the leading MVP candidates and Cuban-born rookie Sandy Valdespino also contributed to Minnesota's pennant push.

The Twins took their first run at the Yankees in 1962. With Killebrew delivering league highs in homers and RBIs, and Pascual winning twenty games, the Twins stayed close to New York all season in what initially was a four-team race that included the Cleveland Indians and Los Angeles Angels. Minnesota had a key opportunity to make a move on first place when the AL champion Yankees arrived at Metropolitan Stadium for three July contests to close out the first half. At the time the surprising Angels, an expansion team playing its second season, topped the standings. New York and Cleveland trailed by a half game with the Twins two games back.

Twins skipper Sam Mele turned to Pascual and lefties Jack Kralick and Kaat to pitch the weekend series. Before nearly forty thousand fans each day, the Yankees throttled all three starters and swept the series to take over first place while the Twins fell 4½ games behind the new front-runner. With New York in the midst of winning thirteen of fifteen, the Twins never recovered. They inched within two games on August 29, but were done playing the Yankees after losing eleven of eighteen matchups with them. That was as close as the Twins would come down the stretch; they finished five games back at 91-71.

Although the Twins won ninety-one games again in 1963, the Yankees ran away from the pack to capture their fourth straight pennant. Despite missing Mickey Mantle and Roger Maris for long stretches due to injuries, the Yankees still scored with ease. With twenty-game winners Whitey Ford and Jim Bouton leading the way, the Yankees finished 10½ games up on second-place Chicago, with the third-place Twins thirteen games back.

The Yankees posted a winning record against every AL opponent in 1963 and finished second in league scoring behind the Twins, but tallied just four runs in a four-game World Series sweep at the hands of Sandy Koufax and the Los Angeles Dodgers. The Yankees' quiet exit in October fueled hope for AL clubs heading into 1964. Coming off back-to-back ninety-one-win seasons, the Twins were optimistic when they gathered in Orlando for training camp.

The bats didn't disappoint in '64. The Twins again topped the league in scoring and led all Major League clubs with 221 homers—the third-highest single-season total in big league history to that point. Six Twins powered at least 20 home runs, a remarkable feat in the pitching-dominant 1960s. Killebrew, with 49, handily won the AL home run crown for the third straight year. Oliva, enjoying one of the all-time greatest rookie seasons, stroked 32, and Allison matched his total. Jimmie Hall (25), Don Mincher (23) and Versalles (20) rounded out the group of six.

But all that firepower wasn't enough, as the Twins stumbled and bumbled to a sixth-place tie with Cleveland at 79-83. Minnesota's young position players experienced a defensive collapse and the bullpen pitched poorly during the first half, when the Twins struggled to stay above .500. Adding Worthington and Klippstein patched up the pen, but all season long, fielders gave opponents extra outs.

Although the Twins weren't in the mix, 1964 was no pleasure cruise for the Yankees. They got off to a slow start under first-year manager Yogi Berra, who took over when Ralph Houk was promoted to general manager. Mantle and Maris were hobbled by spring injuries while other regulars provided little first-half offense. Lefty Al Downing and Bouton, a twenty-one-game winner in 1963, battled health issues near midseason, and Ford's throwing shoulder became increasingly problematic. Down the stretch they fought for the pennant with the Orioles and White Sox. While these Yankees lacked the power and rotation depth of recent New York squads, they closed with a 23-7 surge to win the flag by a single game over Chicago.

Key to New York's stretch-run success was Pedro Ramos, who had started the first game in Twins history three years earlier. Traded to Cleveland in 1962, the right-hander was dealt to the Yankees in early September 1964. Ramos sometimes had trouble controlling his heater, but now ten years into his Major League career, was at his best in a dramatic pennant race. Pitching in relief, the right-hander ceded just three earned runs and didn't allow a single walk in 21⅔ innings. He converted all seven of his save opportunities, four during an eleven-game winning streak in late September.

Still, the Yankees wouldn't have done it without Mantle, who stroked 35 home runs, drove in 111 runs and posted a league-high 1.015 ops in his last great season. Mantle hit three more homers in the World Series, but Bob Gibson and the St. Louis Cardinals topped the Yankees in seven games. When the AL champions succumbed to Gibson for a second time in the finale, the New

York dynasty that had begun in 1949 with the hiring of Casey Stengel was on life support.

The dynasty began when Bing Crosby and Perry Como were pop music stars and the biggest names in entertainment included Bob Hope, John Wayne, Betty Grable, and Abbott and Costello. In the dynasty's final days, with the Twins poised to become an elite team, the Beatles were all the rage, the civil rights movement and the U.S. space program were gaining traction, and President Lyndon Johnson was contemplating an American ground war in Vietnam. These were the events that touched this writer as a teenager in the 1960s. Historic hallmarks of the decade, they reached a feverish pitch during the best years of the 1960s Twins. Together, they made it a compelling time to come of age in Minnesota.

THE PRIDE OF MINNESOTA

ONE

A New Day

I n the American League, not much changed in 1964. The
Yankees won their fifth straight AL pennant and appeared
in their fourteenth World Series in sixteen seasons. Though
vulnerable, they had again found a way to play October baseball
before losing a seven-game World Series to the St. Louis Cardinals. Away from the diamond, however, one of the most tumul-
tuous and divisive decades in American history was already in
full swing.

The prosperity of the 1950s had failed to benefit many Americans and nearly 20 percent of the nation lived below the poverty
line by the early 1960s. The state of the poor and racial segregation had inspired the budding civil rights movement, which
increasingly drew national attention after Martin Luther King Jr.
delivered his "I Have a Dream" speech at the Lincoln Memorial
in August 1963. In early 1964, just six weeks after the assassination of John F. Kennedy, President Lyndon Johnson launched his
"war on poverty" during his first State of the Union address. That
July he signed the Civil Rights Act of 1964, the most sweeping
civil rights legislation in the nation's history, which prohibited
all forms of racial discrimination in employment, housing, and
public places. Implementing the new law proved to be a polarizing struggle, and the nation endured years of protests, riots,
and racially motivated violence.

Civil rights legislation and the concomitant effort to lift tens of thousands of Americans above poverty level were integral to LBJ's legacy. But so was the Vietnam War. Soon after passing the civil rights bill, Congress gave Johnson sweeping powers to wage war in Asia. The president dispatched more military advisors to Vietnam, increasing the total to twenty-one thousand, and full U.S. involvement in the war was soon to come. In May 1964, nearly one thousand students waged the era's first anti-war protest at New York's Times Square; ten days later, twelve young men became the first to publicly burn their draft cards. The anti-war movement was underway, months before American soldiers were shipped off to fight in March 1965.

Arguably the biggest newsmakers of 1964, however, were four Liverpool lads who quickly took America by storm. By then, the Beatles—John Lennon, Paul McCartney, George Harrison, and Ringo Starr—were already a phenomenon in Britain, releasing their first single, "Love Me Do," in late 1962. They had a string of hits at home with Parlophone Records, yet Capitol Records, the U.S. subsidiary of EMI that also owned Parlophone, refused to release their debut album, *Please Please Me*, and the early singles in the United States. Vee-Jay Records, a small label based in Chicago, stepped up and released the group's first American album, *Introducing . . . the Beatles*, in January 1964.

Capitol's folly couldn't slow Beatlemania, even with the record company failing to release "I Want to Hold Your Hand" until the final days of 1963. Although no Beatles music was played on a New York City radio station until early in the New Year, the song sold more than one million copies and reached number one by mid-January. By then, Capitol had issued *Meet the Beatles*, the group's second American LP, and the British Invasion was officially on when the Beatles stepped off a plane at New York's John F. Kennedy International Airport on February 7, 1964. A crowd of nearly five thousand screaming fans provided an early warning of what awaited them in the United States. "So this is America," said Starr upon the group's arrival. "They all seem out of their minds."

That was only the beginning. Two days later, seventy-three million television viewers tuned in to *The Ed Sullivan Show* to see the Beatles' first American performance. To the delight of shrieking teenage girls in the audience, the group opened with "All My Loving," followed by "Till There Was You," "She Loves You," "I Saw Her Standing There," and "I Want to Hold Your Hand."

Steven D. Stark, author of *Meet the Beatles: A Cultural History of the Band That Shook Youth, Gender, and the World*, called "I Want to Hold Your Hand," the group's first hit in the U.S., the "record that altered everything in America." He recounted the story of Bob Dylan first hearing the song while driving up the California coast in January 1964. "He practically jumped out of the car," a Dylan friend said, explaining the song's immediate impact. Dylan couldn't stop dropping f-bombs raving about the song. "They were doing things nobody was doing," Dylan said years later. "Their chords were outrageous, just outrageous, and their harmonies made it all valid." When 1964 came to a close, the Beatles had enjoyed six number-one hits nationally.

For all the budding political upheaval and social change underway, in spring 1965, the challenge for the Minnesota Twins was the same as it had been since the franchise had moved from Washington to the Upper Midwest four years earlier. How do you dethrone the mighty Yankees?

While the old Senators hadn't been contenders for nearly three decades, the franchise's outlook began to change in Minnesota with the emergence of cornerstone players Harmon Killebrew, Bob Allison, Earl Battey, Camilo Pascual, and Jim Kaat. Then a steady stream of rookies plugged into the Minnesota lineup, beginning with twenty-one-year-old shortstop Zoilo Versalles in 1961. Infielders Rich Rollins and Bernie Allen turned in solid debuts in '62, and Jimmie Hall posted impressive power totals in '63.

After the Twins won ninety-one games in both '62 and '63, expectations ran exceedingly high in spring 1964. Despite the breakout Rookie of the Year season from Tony Oliva that summer, the young, error-prone Twins stumbled to 73 wins and a sixth-place finish. So, expectations were tempered a year later when the club assembled in Orlando to prepare for the 1965 campaign. In a *Minneapolis Tribune* poll of area baseball fans, roughly half predicted the Twins to finish between third and fifth place in the ten-team American League. Only 3 percent believed the Twins would win the American League pennant.

Twins fans were absorbed by more pressing matters that spring. While the first U.S. Marines came ashore that March at Da Nang, South Vietnam, and civil rights protesters clashed with police in Montgomery, Alabama, news of extreme weather conditions dominated the airwaves in Minnesota and bordering states.

Midwesterners had endured a bitter, cold winter, punctuated by a steady blast of snow that continued deep into spring. A late thaw delayed the inevitable destruction, and by early April, waters rose to dangerous levels all across the eastern part of the state. The Vermillion River near Hastings was the first to overrun its banks. Soon after, communities along the Minnesota, Blue Earth, Crow, St. Croix, and Mississippi rivers were focused on piling sandbags and building dikes to counter climbing water levels. Some towns were deluged by floodwaters from more than one source, and at least twenty-two thousand Minnesotans were forced from their homes.

In the Twin Cities and most surrounding areas, floodwaters crested at record levels the weekend of April 18. Distressed city officials in both Minneapolis and St. Paul anxiously awaited the Mississippi's high-water peaks, hoping to keep damage to the downtown areas to a minimum. Extensive water damage to the business districts was avoided. St. Paul and communities to the south of the capital escaped a bigger hit because the Mississippi and Minnesota rivers did not crest at the same time.

President Lyndon Johnson flew into the Twin Cities on April 14 to view the flood damage. He stood on a wooden platform off Shepard Road in St. Paul, looking down the river in a driving rainstorm with cold rainwater running down his face. Mother Nature had set an appropriate mood for his visit, after which he pledged federal funds for flood relief.

The mighty Mississippi wreaked havoc for weeks, but that wasn't the end of Minnesota's extreme weather. With thousands of area residents still working to salvage homes and property, tornadoes and heavy thunderstorms ripped through the Twin Cities' northern and western suburbs on May 6.

Seventeen people were killed and nearly seven hundred were injured during a six-hour assault from six major tornadoes. During those scary hours, at least a dozen funnel clouds were spotted on radar by the U.S. Weather Bureau at Minneapolis-St. Paul International Airport. The destruction began southwest of Minneapolis in Carver County, when the first funnel cloud touched down just east of the small town of Cologne soon after 6:00 p.m. It was on the ground for thirteen miles, laying waste to everything in its path as it traveled northeast into western Hennepin County.

Other tornadoes began their assault near Lake Susan in Chanhassen, and near New Auburn and Green Isle in Sibley County. Shortly after 7:00 p.m., the fifth major tornado struck Fridley in Anoka County. And barely more than an hour later, the most destructive one touched down first in Golden Valley, cut through eighteen miles of Hennepin, Ramsey, and Anoka counties, and claimed at least six of the seventeen fatalities.

Hundreds of homes and businesses were destroyed in more than a dozen suburbs. It wasn't until the following day that the breadth of the damage was known, though the area wasn't quite finished facing extreme weather. Heavy rains and hail fell in parts of the Twin Cities area that day, and some residents had reason to believe aftershocks were a part of the tornado phenomenon. That evening, a new tornado was sighted at Le Sueur, roughly sixty miles southwest of Minneapolis. A few hours later, according to a *Minneapolis Tribune* report, "a tornado whirled down Main St. in Waterville, Minn., 65 miles southwest of the Twin Cities. It bowled over a car and toppled the Post Office chimney."

So, to no one's surprise, baseball was far from the minds of most Minnesotans that spring. While residents living along the state's waterways awaited the onslaught of floodwaters, the Twins trained in sunny Florida, hoping to rebound from a disappointing 1964 season. The only major storm brewing in Orlando was a run-in between Zoilo Versalles and Twins manager Sam Mele.

The skipper pulled the shortstop from a spring training game after Versalles mishandled a routine ground ball. Mele believed his infielder hadn't given maximum effort on the play, which led to two runs by the New York Mets.

Versalles headed to the outfield to complete his postgame running regimen, but when he returned to the dugout, Twins third base coach Billy Martin, who had been working with him all spring to make him a more consistent performer, confronted the young veteran. Mele stepped in and told Versalles to sit on the bench in the chance he might learn something, and Versalles angrily replied that he would sit on the bench for Martin, but not for his manager. Mele levied a $100 fine on the spot, and the encounter quickly resembled an auction, according to *St. Paul Pioneer Press* writer Arno Goethel:

"Why not make it $200?" Versalles countered.

"Okay," said Mele. "It's $200."

Versalles persisted. "Why not make it $300?"

"That's what it is," Mele agreed.

Soon Versalles was $300 poorer. For the Twins, however, the young shortstop's blowout with Mele and his depleted wallet wouldn't be omens for the baseball season to come.

Overtaking the New York Yankees, coming off five straight World Series appearances, was a tall order, but in 1965, Sam Mele won with essentially the same roster he managed during Minnesota's disappointing '64 season. He steered the 1965 club through a maze of injuries—perhaps more than any other team in the league—to the franchise's first first-place finish since 1933. It was Mele's finest moment as a big league manager.

Injuries took down the club's stars for notable stretches. Twins ace Camilo Pascual tore a muscle in his back in late July and was out until September. Harmon Killebrew went down in August with a dislocated and fractured elbow and missed forty-eight games. Bob Allison missed time when he fractured a small bone in his wrist, and backstop Earl Battey was sidelined thirteen times by assorted injuries in an All-Star season. The breadth of injuries plaguing the Twins was not limited to the typical on-field ailments; rookie hurler Dave Boswell missed a month with mononucleosis.

One notable difference in 1965 was how role players stepped up and performed exceptionally well in the heat of a pennant race. Right-hander Jim Perry and slugging first baseman Don Mincher played major roles when Pascual, Boswell, and Killebrew were lost to injury for long stretches.

Perry, rumored to be traded or released that spring, was effective in relief and provided a huge lift when he joined the rotation on July 5. He blanked Boston 2–0 on seven hits, which allowed the Twins to maintain a slim lead in what was then a five-team AL race. As a starter, Perry won seven games and posted a 2.45 ERA in nineteen outings, and a lack of run support cost him several more victories.

Mincher had stroked 23 home runs in just 287 at-bats in 1964. He offered to work out at other positions the following spring, yet didn't make his first 1965 start until May 19. His playing time picked up in mid-June, when Killebrew, in his typically unselfish manner, moved to third base to get Mincher's bat into the lineup. Within a week, Mincher responded with two homers in a four-game set with Detroit, including, on June 27, a two-run shot off the Tigers' Fred Gladding, which snapped a 4–4 tie and gave Minnesota a 6–4 victory.

Mincher's power surge carried into the second half. After Killebrew suffered his elbow injury in early August, Mincher led the team with eight homers and 34 RBIs in the forty-eight games the Twins played without their top slugger. By season's end, Mincher had collected 22 homers and a team-leading .509 slugging percentage in 346 at-bats—the third of three straight years that he slugged higher than .500 as a part-time player.

The bullpen's old hands, Al Worthington and Johnny Klippstein, were exceptional in '64 and every bit as dependable in '65. They combined for 19 wins and 26 saves, and easily posted the lowest two ERAS on the staff for a second straight season during Minnesota's championship run. But they didn't have to do it by themselves in '65. The bullpen went 38-24, securing more wins than any other big league pen while recording a 2.92 ERA that ranked third in the league. Perry excelled as a reliever and left-hander Billy Pleis was terrific all season, posting a 2.18 ERA in thirty-nine relief appearances. He stepped up to make two emergency starts in June, during which he allowed nearly half of the 17 earned runs he allowed all season. Three other lefties, Minnesota native Dick Stigman, Garry Roggenburk, and Mel Nelson, pitched effectively in relief down the stretch.

Several rookies provided key contributions as well. Boswell and Jim Merritt plugged holes in the rotation created by injury. Boswell won twice during a nine-game winning streak to open July, which made Minnesota the team to beat during the second half. After mononucleosis sidelined Boswell, Merritt joined the rotation in August and won four of his first six big league starts. Another rookie, southpaw reliever Jerry Fosnow, held left-handed hitters to a .145 average in twenty-nine games.

Young outfielders Sandy Valdespino and Joe Nossek were on the roster all year. By season's end, they had worked their way into platoon roles that afforded them starts in the World Series. The right-handed-hitting Nossek replaced lefty-hitting Jimmie Hall in center field when the Twins faced southpaws, including Dodgers starters Sandy Koufax and Claude Osteen that October. Against some right-handers, the left-handed-hitting Valdespino took starts from Allison in left field. The twenty-six-year-old rookie collected hits off both Koufax and right-hander Don Drysdale in the World Series.

Frank Quilici arrived near midseason and shared second base with veteran Jerry Kindall down the stretch. In Game One against the Dodgers in October, Quilici delivered two hits off Drysdale—in a single inning—to tie a World Series record. César Tovar, who became an effective leadoff hitter for the Twins teams that won the first two American League West titles at the end of the decade, spent most of the season in the Minors. But he was on the Opening Day roster and nearly donned the goat horns in an extra-inning affair.

As fate would have it, the Twins opened the 1965 season at Metropolitan Stadium against the New York Yankees, the five-time defending American League champions. The 1964 wins leaders for the two clubs, Jim Kaat (17-11) and Jim Bouton (18-13), squared off on a typically blustery early April day. Temperatures were near freezing and high winds made it seem colder.

If those conditions weren't challenging enough, floodwaters created an unforeseen obstacle for Kaat, starting third baseman Rich Rollins, and Stigman. Living in an apartment complex in nearby Burnsville, they discovered that the bridge on their route to the Met was under water. With other travel options also off limits because of flooding, Kaat's Opening Day start hung in the balance. He contacted Paul Giel, a former teammate and University of Minnesota great in both baseball and football, who was working for wcco radio after retiring from baseball. The station had rented a helicopter to cover the flooding, and Kaat arranged a flight for himself and his teammates. After landing in a schoolyard near the stadium, a quick ride to the park guaranteed their arrival before game time.

The Twins defeated the Yankees in their first 1965 showdown, 5–4 in eleven innings. The game featured eight errors, five by New York. Tovar, debuting at third base and fighting a brisk wind, dropped a lazy fly hit by the Yankees' Joe Pepitone with two outs in the ninth and Minnesota up by a run. The error allowed the Yankees to tie the game off Kaat, but Tovar made amends in the eleventh.

New York's rookie left fielder, Art López, a pinch runner for Mickey Mantle in the ninth, misjudged a Bob Allison fly ball to open the Twins' half of the eleventh. After Allison reached third base on the error, Yankees manager Johnny Keane had former Twin Pedro Ramos intentionally walk pinch hitters Rich Reese and Sandy Valdespino to load the bases to set up a force play at home. Ramos induced a short fly from Zoilo Versalles and fanned Jerry Kindall before Tovar drilled a 1-2 pitch into center field. New York's Tom Tresh dove for the sinking liner but could only trap it, and Allison scored the winning run.

Ramos took the loss that day. On Opening Day four years earlier, he was on the mound for the Twins in their Minnesota debut. Before a small crowd of 14,607 at Yankee Stadium, the Cuban right-hander had shut out New York on three hits, though the Twins would have little success against the AL champions in the years that followed. They won only four of eighteen match-ups in 1961 and lost the season series with New York in each of the first four years in Minnesota. Heading into the 1965 opener, the Twins had gone 25-46 against the Yankees.

A week after winning the 1965 season opener, Minnesota claimed two more victories over New York at Yankee Stadium. The Bronx Bombers drew 39,082 for their home debut, their largest Opening Day crowd since 1952, but Yankee fans went home disappointed when Tony Oliva, Rollins, and Hall powered two-run homers in a 7–2 Twins romp. Oliva, off to a slow start after winning the batting title as a rookie in 1964, drilled two more homers the next day in an 8–2 thumping of the Yankees.

Sandwiched between Oliva's two homers was a ninth-inning, inside-the-park home run by Versalles, who stroked a pitch from Ramos into the left-center-field gap. The speedy Versalles raced around the bases as New York outfielders Mickey Mantle and Tom Tresh gave chase. Versalles capped his daring run with a dazzling hook slide, just ahead of the throw to Yankees catcher Bob Schmidt.

The tide had turned. The Twins claimed thirteen of eigh-teen games from the Yankees, who stumbled along near .500 all season in 1965. While the Yankees were never in the mix, the Twins, in the thick of the pennant race from the start, faced stiff competition from several other AL clubs.

TWO

The Fast Start

I n March 1965, just weeks before the Minnesota Twins opened the season with an eleven-inning victory over the New York Yankees, the United States dispatched 3,500 Marines to South Vietnam, marking the beginning of the American ground war. By year's end, 184,000 American soldiers were fighting in Vietnam, and more than 2.5 million Americans would do tours of duty there.

The war quickly escalated while the Twins got off to a fast start in '65, which proved to be a good buffer against the host of injuries the team suffered throughout the campaign. But the 1965 club had more than just a powerful lineup, a solid pitching staff, and effective role players in the dugout. Two additions to manager Sam Mele's coaching staff that spring were key to Minnesota's contender status.

Billy Martin, the former Yankee who had retired as a player after handling second base for the Twins in 1961, took over as third base coach. Johnny Sain, who had teamed with Hall of Famer Warren Spahn as the aces of the postwar Boston Braves and played with Martin in New York in the mid-1950s, joined the staff as pitching coach. Sain, a four-time twenty-game winner, pitched in four World Series and coached in five.

Martin played a pivotal role in refining the skills and boosting the confidence of Zoilo Versalles, who had shown flashes of brilliance but could be wildly inconsistent. "Zoilo Versalles can win the Most Valuable Player Award," the demonstrative Martin declared that spring. "He has all the tools. Someone just has to teach him." Martin had Versalles bunting regularly in camp, looking to have the young veteran taking advantage of his outstanding speed. Martin worked with him on the mental tool of thinking ahead and anticipating plays before they happen, and coached him on positioning himself successfully in the infield.

The teacher also inspired a more even performance from his former double-play partner. Versalles had slumped in the second half of each of his previous four seasons, but the coach's fire and morale-boosting efforts spurred his pupil to improve on his first-half production after the All-Star break. A baseball season is a six-month marathon in which staying completely focused on a daily basis is a challenge, and Versalles was an offensive catalyst and run producer throughout the 1965 club's pennant push.

The new third base coach made the Twins more aggressive on the bases. His penchant for stealing and taking the extra base gave the power-laden Twins an added dimension, and Martin was remarkably successful at reading plays in the outfield and knowing when to advance base runners. "Casey Stengel taught me to always size up the position of the outfielders *before* a play," Martin told *Sporting News* during a 1965 interview. "Then, when you see the ball in the air, you can make up your mind quickly."

Martin's running approach also required some unanticipated work in Florida that spring. Players endured sliding practice in spring training for the first time since the franchise shift to Minnesota. Pitchers were not exempt. Relievers Billy Pleis and Mel Nelson, a former outfielder, had it down. Many others, including the bullpen elders Al Worthington and Johnny Klippstein, struggled. Worthington, thirty-six, said he hadn't even attempted a slide in six years.

Another change in Florida began the first day of batting practice. On a player's last swing in the batting cage, he was expected to run to first base at full speed. He stayed there for the next hitter and sprinted to third on the first ball put in play, regardless of where it went, because Mele was looking to have runners go first to third more frequently on balls hit to the outfield. The manager used the hit and run regularly in spring games, and the running game was in full swing by the end of camp.

Once the season started, the Twins used the hit and run relentlessly, even with their sluggers. With Martin perched in the third base box, four times that year Versalles scored from first on hits that started simply as singles to left field. Even Harmon Killebrew and Earl Battey were scoring on plays that were high-percentage risks, as Martin constantly forced the opposition to execute the perfect relay throw. Those little-ball aspects benefited the Twins when Killebrew was lost to injury for six weeks in the second half; the Twins kept scoring and winning.

Martin brought fire and energy to the Twins, which players quickly discovered in spring training. He was always chattering, barking instructions and encouragement. One minute he was hitting grounders to infielders; the next he was pitching batting practice or working with middle infielders at second base. As a teacher, Martin put in long hours. That intense drive sometimes led to trouble, both on and off the field, and no one would deny that having Billy around might lead to an adventure. That was Mele's discovery late in spring training, when the pair rented a rowboat and went fishing. They get the boat in the water and, as *Sporting News* columnist Dick Young recounted, "The next thing you know, Mele was thrashing around in the water with the fish."

"I wanted to cast to the other side of the boat," Mele told Young, "and I told Billy to bend down. I lost my balance and . . . splash." Martin joked that he expected a fellow Italian to be a good fisherman. When a reporter asked Martin what he did when he saw his manager in the drink, Mele jumped in: "He started rowing away."

Mele and Martin laughed about the skipper's unanticipated dip, though Young noted that some observers viewed the event as symbolic. From the start of spring training, there was buzz that Martin was hired as a potential replacement for Mele, whose managerial future after a dismal 1964 campaign seemed to hinge on a good start in 1965. Both had to address the issue occasionally in Florida. Mele simply agreed that the team had to win, while Martin had a pat speech in which he made it clear that he was embarrassed by the talk.

The team's fast start ended speculation that Mele was on his way out. It's hard to imagine owner Calvin Griffith was seriously thinking of replacing Mele, who took over for Cookie Lavagetto in June 1961, a few months after the move to Minnesota. In his first full season as a big league manager in '62, Mele led the young Twins to 91 wins and a second-place finish, five games behind the Yankees. Then the Twins repeated that win total in '63. Not bad for a franchise that hadn't won ninety games since 1933— the last time the Senators had appeared in the World Series.

Mele, an outfielder who played ten seasons and became a lifelong friend of Ted Williams during a short stint with the Red Sox, was mild mannered, commanding the respect of his players without fanfare or histrionics. Griffith thought Mele was too soft when the team struggled, and Martin's fire-and-brimstone approach might have looked attractive had the team not competed from the start in 1965.

Sain, the other critical staff addition, departed as Yankees pitching coach after Yogi Berra was named New York's manager in 1964. Sain said he deliberately priced himself out of the job during contract negotiations because he doubted that Berra could manage his former teammates. If instead Sain was fired by Yankees general manager Ralph Houk after the 1963 season, as was reported, his release followed three AL pennants and two World Series victories in three seasons as pitching coach.

Jim Bouton, who won twenty-one games for the Yankees in 1963 under Sain's tutelage, called Sain "the greatest pitching coach who ever lived." When Bouton heard the Yankees weren't willing to pay what Sain demanded, he offered to pay the difference out of his own pocket. The coach went home to his Arkansas farm, but soon Griffith came calling. The Twins owner, desperate to give his potent lineup the pitching necessary to compete for the pennant, gave in to Sain's asking price. "I have never paid a coach so much in my life," Griffith complained soon after signing Sain.

Equally surprising, notes Sridhar Pappu in *The Year of the Pitcher*, was having "one of the most conservative owners in sports hiring one of the most progressive coaches." Sain defied many of the era's conventions of pitching instruction—and created a few that live on today. He was the first coach to have the next day's pitcher chart opposing hitters from the dugout. He focused on the mental side of the game—nearly unheard of at the time—and shared self-help and motivational books with his pitchers. And Sain didn't buy into the conventional wisdom that a running program was critical to good pitching. That made more than a few Twins pitchers happy and nearly everyone on the staff was a better pitcher in 1965.

The coach was so committed to his methods that he wanted autonomy over the pitching staff and didn't want other coaches—or even the manager—to interfere with his pitchers' work. He often clashed with fellow coaches and management—and frequently changed jobs. On the Fourth of July in 1965, Sain and Martin had a falling out after rookie reliever Jerry Fosnow tossed an intended pitchout too close to the plate and Kansas City's Mike Hershberger executed a suicide squeeze in a 5–2 Twins victory. When the Twins came off the field, Martin exclaimed that such a mistake could cost the team the pennant. Sain, bothered that Martin would call out Fosnow in front of the entire team, defended his pitcher. Both coaches avoided escalating the exchange in the dugout, but had it out after the game. Mele stayed out of the fray, after which Sain moved out of the coaches' room and dressed with the players the rest of the season.

Despite such run-ins, Sain developed believers and disciples everywhere he worked. Terry Forster, a hard-throwing reliever who debuted in 1971 with Sain as his coach with the White Sox, once said the pitching coach "saw pitchers as snowflakes" and "no two were alike." Sain didn't preach one philosophy to all pitchers; he took a different approach with each member of his staff. The instruction a power pitcher needed to refine his game invariably was different than what could help a finesse pitcher or knuckleballer.

Sain wasn't a preacher who expected his student to sit quietly and absorb his lessons. "I actually learn more from the pitchers as a coach than they do from me," he told *Sporting News* that summer. "You work with a pitcher and you pick up ideas. About all I do as a coach is pass along ideas that I have accumulated." Armed with ideas gathered over a long career, Sain found particular adjustments that allowed nearly all of his pitchers to work more effectively, including the 1965 team's oldest player, John Klippstein. "I pitched for six other major league clubs before coming here last year," the thirty-seven-year-old reliever said in a *Life* magazine feature on Sain that summer. "But John has so many new ideas I wonder if I've been spinning my wheels somewhere. . . . He understands pitchers."

Sixteen pitchers won twenty games in Sain's fourteen seasons coaching for the Yankees, Twins, Tigers, White Sox, and Braves. Several big league starters, including Bouton, Jim Kaat, and Wilbur Wood, credit Sain with turning their careers around. Bouton posted his only twenty-win campaign at age twenty-four, in his first full season as a big league starter. Soon after, his budding career was sidetracked by major arm troubles. At the same time Sain was assisting Bouton, he was teaching staff ace Whitey Ford a slider that helped rejuvenate his career. In 1963, Sain's final year as New York's pitching coach, the thirty-four-year-old Ford went 24-7.

"He meant more to my career than anybody I met in baseball," Kaat told the *Chicago Tribune* in 2002. When Sain joined the Twins, Kaat had already pitched four seasons in the Majors and was always looking for ways to gain an edge over hitters. Sain provided insightful ideas on both mental and physical aspects of pitching, and Kaat plugged into them. The left-hander reached the twenty-win plateau for the first time and won a career-high twenty-five games in 1966, Sain's final year with the Twins. He won twenty twice more during his career, both times with Sain and the White Sox in the mid-1970s.

Other well-known pitchers upped their game with Sain's assistance. Right-hander Earl Wilson finished 22-11 with Detroit in 1967, posting his only twenty-win campaign after Sain had hooked

up with the Tigers. That same summer, the pitching coach taught
Denny McLain a devastating sidearm slider to go with his heat,
and a year later he turned in his historic 31-6 season. In 1971,
knuckleball specialist Wood converted from reliever to starter;
Sain convinced White Sox manager Chuck Tanner that the left-
hander's easy motion and use of the knuckler would allow him
to pitch more frequently than others in the rotation. Beginning
in '71, Wood made more than 40 starts a year for five straight
seasons and claimed 20 or more wins in the first four of them.
He even started both ends of a doubleheader in 1973.

Jim "Mudcat" Grant, Minnesota's ace in 1965, went 21-7 in the
best year of his career. Grant remembers Sain always emphasiz-
ing movement, finding ways to alter the trajectory of pitches to
fool hitters and mess with their timing. Movement was one of
the few tenets that applied to nearly every pitcher Sain assisted,
as he insisted that velocity alone rarely succeeded. His alteration
to add movement to a pitcher's arsenal might be as simple as
changing finger pressure or a pitcher's grip. In Florida in '65,
Sain convinced Grant to abandon a slider and take up a sinker
and a short, faster curveball, pitches that were game-changers
in his lone twenty-win campaign.

Grant wasn't the only Twins hurler to pick up Sain's "fast curve"
that summer. After Sain discovered Jim Perry had less spin on
his pitches than anyone he had ever seen, he worked with the
veteran right-hander to add the pitch to his arsenal. Perry mastered it and was terrific in 1965. "The main thing is to get spin,"
Perry told *Life*, a clear sign he had bought into Sain's approach.

With Martin and Sain on board, the Twins were more consistent both offensively and defensively. The hitters drew the
most attention, but Grant and Camilo Pascual fueled the club's
fast start. Neither starter took a loss until June. With Pascual
usually following Grant in the rotation, Minnesota was a good
bet to post consecutive wins on those days, no matter how the
bats were doing. During a five-week streak in May and June, the
right-handers won 14 of their 18 combined starts. Grant started
5-0 before losing on June 7. Pascual was 8-0 when he took his
first "L" two weeks later.

The Twins and Chicago White Sox were the American League's fast starters. The early contenders contrasted markedly in style. The slugging Twins had led all Major League teams in home runs the previous two seasons. They rarely struggled to push across runs, a task that by the mid-1960s had become increasingly difficult for the light-hitting White Sox. Featuring strong pitching and defense, they led the league in team ERA in both 1964 and 1965.

Minnesota won six of its first seven games, including those three early matchups with the AL champion Yankees. Pascual quickly flashed midseason form when he limited New York to two runs in a 7–2 victory at Yankee Stadium on April 21. In his next start, the Cuban native worked a masterful two-hitter against Cleveland and delivered a first-inning grand slam off reliever Stan Williams in an 11–1 romp. The right-handed-hitting Pascual tucked a 320-foot shot just inside the right-field foul pole to give the Twins a 7–0 lead. "I'm starting to pull the ball a little better now," Pascual quipped after the game. In 1960, his first of two career grand slams pinged off the right-field foul pole at Yankee Stadium. "This one I pulled inside the pole."

Grant, however, had failed to go more than three innings in either of his first two starts when he took the mound to face the first-place White Sox on April 30. The Twins trailed the Sox by a half game, and the four-game set was the first of several showdowns with first place on the line. In the Friday night opener at Comiskey Park, the winless Grant squared off against left-hander Gary Peters, who had won twenty games in 1964 and was 2-0 so far in '65.

Taking the mound with a nasty headache that had plagued him all afternoon, Grant dominated the White Sox, blanking them 7–0 on three hits to end a five-game Chicago winning streak. He mostly called on his fastball and his new curve, which he threw for strikes consistently for the first time. Effectively locating his stuff low in the zone, he allowed just seven balls to be hit beyond his infielders. With his first of a league-leading six shutouts in 1965, Grant gave American League hitters a disheartening glimpse of what to expect. On top of that, the Twins were in first place, though not for long. The clubs split four games, so Chicago maintained its half-game lead when the Twins left town.

The next time through the rotation, Grant and Pascual claimed complete-game wins in back-to-back games against the Baltimore Orioles at Metropolitan Stadium. Temperatures were on the cool side for the first two night games of the season, with fewer than ten thousand fans on hand each night. Neither ace seemed to mind. In a 7–3 win on May 4, Grant allowed just four Orioles hits and located his breaking pitches so effectively that he was throwing them consistently for first-pitch strikes. The following night Pascual scattered six hits in a 9–2 victory. He flashed his two curveballs—the off-speed bender and the hard, sharp-breaking version that was among the best in the game—but opposing managers were praising his changeup in postgame interviews.

The Twins dropped the series finale to the Orioles the following afternoon, just hours before at least six tornadoes claimed seventeen lives and laid waste to hundreds of homes, businesses, and schools across a fifty-mile span and several Minnesota counties. Combing through the destruction took days, but news sources soon identified the dead as residents of Norwood in Carver County, roughly fifty miles southwest of Minneapolis; Mound, on the west side of Lake Minnetonka; and the northern suburbs of Spring Lake Park, Anoka, Fridley, Blaine, and Mounds View. Then heavy rain and hail pelted parts of the Twin Cities the following day.

In the midst of the inclement weather, Grant and Pascual continued to win. With Chicago following Baltimore to the Met, both hurlers limited the White Sox to a single run in a weekend series. In a 4–1 victory on Saturday, May 8, Grant stalled a five-game Chicago winning streak for the second time in ten days, again besting Gary Peters. The two dueled through five scoreless innings before each team tallied a sixth-inning run. A sacrifice fly by Zoilo Versalles in the seventh and a two-run homer by Jimmie Hall in the eighth secured Grant's third victory. After the game, White Sox hitters marveled at how effective Grant had been changing speeds and throwing breaking stuff.

"This isn't the Grant I used to catch," said White Sox catcher John Romano, batterymates with Grant in Cleveland. "He's pitching low rather than high, with good control. He used to challenge you with the high fastball. Now he's throwing curves and sliders." Grant played down the differences, saying he was the "same old Grant," but that was to be expected. A pitcher prefers to keep opponents in the dark about a new pitch or approach.

The next day was Mother's Day, Pascual's turn to take the mound. If you made the trip from St. Paul to Metropolitan Stadium for the afternoon affair with the White Sox, you may have arrived surprisingly early. St. Paul had gone on daylight savings time in the early morning hours, moving the clock ahead an hour, while Minneapolis did not. The two cities could not agree on when to sacrifice that hour of sleep, and Minneapolis and most of the rest of the state chose to push clocks ahead two weeks later on May 23. With Minneapolis falling an hour behind its neighbor on the other side of the river, confusion ensued and a host of workers arrived early or late to jobs at the start of the workweek. Most St. Paul businesses moved their clocks ahead, but some stayed on standard time. So did state and federal offices, and the telephone company's time-of-day number, then a popular way to get the time, provided callers with standard time.

Early or not for the Twins' Mother's Day matinee, a crowd of 17,644 was on hand to see Pascual belt his second homer of the season and go the distance in a 6–1 win. By improving to 4-0, the twelve-year veteran evened his career record at 132-132. He had joined the Washington Senators as a twenty-year-old in 1954, before he was Major League-ready, but struggled to find his way pitching for a dreadful team that averaged 93 losses a year in its final seven seasons in the nation's capital. Lacking the fastball command that would maximize the use of his elite curveball, he posted double-digit losses in his first five full seasons before breaking out with 17 wins, a 2.64 ERA, and a league-leading six shutouts in 1959.

Still, Pascual left Washington with a 57-84 record. He recorded twenty-win seasons in 1962 and '63, when he also led the American League in complete games, and he topped the league in strikeouts three consecutive years through Minnesota's ninety-one-win campaign in '63. After defeating the White Sox on Mother's Day 1965, he never slipped below .500 again. Even with a late-1960s return to Washington for a three-year stint with the equally inept "new" Senators, Pascual finished his career with a 174-170 record.

After Pascual's victory, the Twins defeated Chicago on Monday, May 10, to take over first place in the American League. Arguably the league's biggest story, however, was the failing health of Yankees star Mickey Mantle, sidelined with two pulled muscles in his right leg. The Yankees were already missing catcher Elston Howard, out following surgery on his throwing arm, and Roger Maris, nursing an ailing hamstring. On top of that, the Yankees were five games under .500 and lodged in ninth place, though their six-game deficit in the standings wasn't insurmountable.

Although the season was young, colorful *St. Paul Pioneer Press* columnist Don Riley slapped a tombstone on the dying Yankees dynasty with the kind of sardonic rant that was his trademark. "I told you neophytes six weeks ago the Yankees have had it," Riley wrote in a May 9 column. "Elston Howard is at an age where his clutch has got to slip. Mantle's gear box is shot. (Whitey) Ford's differential is rusty. . . . When a team which relies so greatly on three or four super-stars to embellish the trophy case sees them all wither together, it's an emotional jolt as well as physical. . . . The Yankees still have that tradition. At the moment, they don't have a helluva lot more."

Riley was right about the 1965 Yankees, but the Twins faced stiff challenges from several AL clubs. In May, California, Cleveland, Baltimore, and Detroit joined the Twins and White Sox in the hunt. The Twins often looked like a team of destiny, however, frequently executing late-inning rallies to win key games. Late comebacks became familiar to Twins fans. After the Twins claimed the top spot by topping Chicago three times on Mother's Day weekend, they extended their winning streak to five games with a pair of one-run, come-from-behind victories over the visiting Angels.

On May 11, the Twins trailed the Angels 2–1 with two outs in the sixth when reigning batting champion Tony Oliva, off to a slow start in his sophomore season, took reigning Cy Young Award winner Dean Chance deep to tie the game 2–2. Chance was still on the mound in the ninth with one out and Oliva, who had doubled, perched at third. Up stepped Harmon Killebrew, who hadn't hit the ball out of the infield in three trips. The ball stayed in the infield again as he lined an 0-1 pitch off Chance's left leg. Oliva dashed for home as the ball caromed halfway back toward home plate, and the pitcher's backhanded flip to catcher Buck Rodgers was too late. Minnesota's 3–2 victory stuck Chance with his first loss in seven starts.

Killebrew was the late-inning hero again the following night at the Met. After tying the game in the sixth with a solo shot off Angels lefty Rudy May, Killebrew erased a 3–2 deficit in the eighth with a two-out, two-run bomb that traveled 453 feet to straightaway center. This time he connected off Bob Lee, one of the game's better relievers, to secure a 4–3 win.

Two nights later in Kansas City, the Twins were losing 3–0 heading into the eighth. Bob Allison powered a three-run homer off Athletics starter John O'Donoghue to the tie the game before the Twins pushed across two unearned in the ninth for a 5–3 victory. The key play was a ninth-inning bunt by backup catcher Jerry Zimmerman. After Jerry Kindall opened the inning with a single, Zimmerman laid down a bunt that traveled less than ten feet down the first base line. It might have set up an easy force play at second base, but when A's catcher Rene Lachemann collided with Zimmerman while fielding the ball, home plate umpire Al Salerno called interference and awarded Zimmerman first base. Moments later Zoilo Versalles singled home Kindall, and the Twins tacked on another run on John Wyatt's wild pitch.

In all, the Twins claimed 16 wins in 1965 when they trailed at some point after the seventh inning, victimizing the Tigers, Angels, Senators, and Yankees three times each. Nine of those late come-from-behind victories came on the road and four were walk-off wins, including two against the defending AL champion Yankees.

THREE

Taking Flight on a Bumpy Ride

While Vietnam and the civil rights movement were the dominant news stories of 1965, the space program took monumental steps that year. Four years earlier, in May 1961, a month after the Soviet Union had sent the first man into space, President John Kennedy announced to Congress his goal to accelerate the U.S. space program and send an American to the moon by the end of the decade. The initial steps were small—sending Alan Shepard, Virgil Grissom, and John Glenn on short solo missions—but soon after Kennedy's assassination, the Gemini program began.

A two-man spacecraft was the cornerstone of the program, with the goals of studying how astronauts were affected by long periods of space travel, mastering the docking of spacecrafts to orbiting objects, and perfecting entry and reentry maneuvers into Earth's atmosphere. With NASA focused on improving the spacecraft's heat protection upon entry and reentry, the first two Gemini missions were unmanned, including *Gemini 2* in January 1965. Two months later, the first manned flight of the program, *Gemini 3*, carried Grissom, making his second trip into space, and John Young.

In all, six Gemini missions took flight in 1965, advancing the space program markedly in a very short time. In August 1965, the *Gemini 5* crew of L. Gordon Cooper Jr. and Charles "Pete"

Conrad spent a record-setting eight days in space, matching the time necessary to fly to the moon, land, and return to Earth. The small size of the Gemini capsule, roughly the equivalent of the front seats of a Volkswagen Beetle, inspired Conrad to label the mission "eight days in a garbage can." Their extended stay in the "garbage can" was made possible by new fuel cells developed by NASA prior to the *Gemini 5* flight, which set the stage for traveling greater distances into space.

New technology didn't always cooperate, however, during what was the most ambitious space flight to that point. Cooper and Conrad were forced to adjust to twelve different equipment failures. A trip to the moon would require rendezvousing and docking different elements of the spacecraft, and Cooper and Conrad were expected to practice a rendezvous with a "pod" deployed by their spacecraft. Electrical problems with the "pod" forced a "phantom rendezvous" in which the Gemini craft maneuvered to a predetermined place in space as if the two units were going to dock. It had never been attempted before, but the astronauts executed the "phantom rendezvous" successfully.

Among the program's most memorable missions was *Gemini 4* that June, during which astronaut Ed White, partnered with Commander James McDivitt, floated out of the capsule for a twenty-three-minute spacewalk, the first by an American. Russian cosmonaut Alexei Leonov had been the first to venture into the great unknown, stepping outside the capsule of *Voskhod 2* nearly three months earlier on March 18. Yet, White's trek was a key step in the U.S. space program's goal to put a man on the moon.

With the *Gemini 4* craft traveling seventeen thousand miles per hour, White—attached to it with a twenty-five-foot umbilical cord—exited with a hand-held gas-jet device to maneuver through the void. When the newly developed toy ran out of fuel a few minutes later, White got around by twisting his body and pulling on the cord. No amount of training could fully prepare anyone for that first spacewalk. This was uncharted territory, but White said the spacewalk was the most comfortable part of the entire mission.

With the incomparable beauty of the blue Earth as a backdrop, White was absolutely taken by the thrill of the moment. He and McDivitt bantered about it via radio, and in time, McDivitt had to coax his partner back to the capsule. When White admitted that he hated to end the walk, McDivitt responded, "Ed, come on in here. . . . Come on. Let's get back in here before it gets dark." "I'm coming back in," White replied, "and it's the saddest moment of my life."

Back on solid ground, things weren't going as smoothly for the fast-starting Minnesota Twins. Despite a May run of late-inning dramatics, the Twins soon stumbled, losing a season-high four straight games during a mid-May road trip. Meanwhile, the White Sox ran off nine straight victories to take a 4½-game lead over the Twins on May 18. Minnesota stopped its skid the following day by sweeping the Angels in a midweek doubleheader that concluded the trip, but by then, the clubhouse began to resemble a MASH unit. Catcher Earl Battey didn't miss a start on the road trip but was fighting a virus. Zoilo Versalles, who hadn't missed a game all season, was playing with a pulled groin muscle. In a loss to Kansas City at the Met on May 22, center fielder Jimmie Hall took a knee to the head while trying to break up a double play at second base and spent the night in a Minneapolis hospital.

Tony Oliva stayed in the lineup despite a bruised right knee and a chronic knuckle problem in his right middle finger, suffered during his breakout rookie season. Almost exactly a year earlier, twenty-seven games into the 1964 campaign, he attempted to turn on a fastball from Red Sox fireballer Dick Radatz and lost control of his bat. The knob struck the big knuckle of his right middle finger, causing the joint to rapidly swell. The pain was instantly severe and lingered all season. Twins trainer Doc Lentz taped a piece of rubber around the knuckle to absorb some shock when Oliva swung. He discovered that making contact was far less painful than swinging and missing, an added incentive to make contact on his way to the 1964 AL batting title. Despite a quiet off-season, which Oliva hoped would heal the injury, the pain returned in spring training and he kept playing with the tender knuckle.

The banged-up Twins went back on the road for games in Boston, Washington, and Baltimore, stopping first on Tuesday, May 25, at Fenway Park. On that same night, just up the road from Boston in Lewiston, Maine, twenty-three-year-old Muhammad Ali went toe-to-toe with grizzled former champion Sonny Liston in a rematch for the heavyweight championship of the world. In a major upset in February 1964, Ali—who at the time still went by Cassius Clay—had claimed the heavyweight boxing crown from Liston, a ferocious and menacing fighter with a string of early-round knockouts on his record. The brash, nonstop-talking challenger had taunted the champion from the moment the first matchup was announced. Although observers thought Clay's behavior betrayed a fear of Liston, the quick, elusive challenger avoided Liston's powerful punch and won the title when Liston didn't answer the bell for the seventh round. When the fight was called, Ali barraged the crowd with chants of "I am the greatest!" the first of many times that fight fans would hear the boast from the heavyweight champion of the world.

The highly anticipated rematch in Lewiston didn't last long. A minute into the fight, Ali clocked Liston with his first punch, a short right that put the former champ on the canvas. Ali stood over the prone Liston and shouted abuse at him, documented in the famous photograph by ringside photographer Neil Leifer. Liston eventually rose to his feet and the fight resumed momentarily, but the timekeeper had counted out Liston and the fight was quickly stopped. "It was lightning and thunder," Ali said of the punch that made quick work of Liston. "Fast as lightning and booming as thunder from the heavens." Ali had successfully defended his title for the first of nine times, beginning an astounding run as one of boxing's elite heavyweights.

The Twins had been lacking punch when they faced the Red Sox that same evening. Struggling to score runs, the Twins followed Ali's lead and roughed up Boston pitching for 20 hits in a 17–5 romp. Each position player in the lineup collected two or more hits and Grant went the distance for his fifth win without a loss. The lopsided victory was Minnesota's first of 17 wins in eighteen games against the Red Sox in 1965, and the first of ten Twins wins in a twelve-game stretch that moved them back into first place.

The twelve-game surge was a prelude to Minnesota's second half, when Versalles and Oliva sparked the club's push to the pennant and became the top candidates for American League MVP honors. Versalles scored 15 runs in those twelve games and wasn't just playing little ball. The Twins leadoff man powered five doubles and three homers and drove in 15 runs. After opening the 17–5 onslaught with a double and scoring three runs, Versalles delivered another leadoff double the following night, igniting a four-run first inning and a 9–7 victory.

These high-scoring affairs marked a turning point for the slow-starting Oliva, who headed to Boston in a 5-for-38 slump that had whittled his average to .227. He had bypassed winter ball for the first time to rest his ailing knuckle. Winter ball had allowed him to maintain his timing at the plate, and it took him several weeks of the 1965 season to find his groove after leading the American League in hitting for nearly all of 1964. It didn't help that Oliva's painful knuckle swelled after a March 1965 spring training game. That's when a bone chip made its first appearance on an X-ray. Surgery to remove the chip would have sidelined Oliva for ten weeks, so he held off on the procedure until after the season and won his second straight batting title.

Repeating as the league's batting champion seemed far-fetched, as Oliva trailed the leader, Detroit's Willie Horton, by 133 points. Nearly fifty AL regulars had higher batting averages, but Oliva began his ascent in Boston. In the seventh inning of the 17–5 victory, Oliva smashed a two-run shot into the screen above the Green Monster off Red Sox reliever Jack Lamabe. The following night he ripped a shot off Boston starter Earl Wilson that landed in the right-field bullpen. Oliva was starting to spray the ball all over the field again, a sign that his timing was coming around. He hit .371 in Minnesota's eight-game East Coast swing and in time reentered the batting race.

Suddenly things were going Minnesota's way again, even when they weren't going the way Sam Mele wanted. On May 30, with first place on the line, the Twins looked to complete a weekend series sweep in Washington. They were leading the Senators 1–0 in the fourth inning with runners on first and third, one out, and Versalles at the plate. Mele wanted Versalles to lay down a bunt. "I was hoping third base coach Billy Martin might get Versalles' eye," Mele said to beat writers after the game, "because second baseman Don Blasingame was playing Versalles over close to second base. I thought we could tell Versalles to push a hard bunt to normal second base position past the pitcher. I was ready to settle for one run from third base." But Martin failed to get Versalles's attention and the shortstop instead turned on a high, inside fastball and powered a three-run homer. After Camilo Pascual had scattered four hits in a 6–0 victory for his sixth win without a loss, Mele had to admit "it's like that when things are going right."

The surging Twins had regained first place and were in Baltimore playing the Orioles on May 31 when the skies opened over the Twin Cities, pelting the area with eight inches of rain in two days. Area residents had already endured an extremely harsh winter, massive spring flooding, and deadly May tornadoes. Nearly twenty inches of precipitation had fallen in the first five months of 1965—quickly approaching the yearly average of twenty-five inches—and the latest deluge flooded hundreds of basements, closed highways, and forced six hundred people to evacuate their homes in nearby Spring Valley, Wisconsin, where the Eau Galle and Kinnickinnic rivers rushed over their banks.

The following day, the Twins returned home as area residents began to clean up the mess left by the storm. Sporadic rain continued over the next several days and one game was rained out, but the Twins defeated the visiting Red Sox twice and then took two more from Washington to move 3½ games up on Chicago on June 6. In an 11–2 win over the Senators that Sunday afternoon, two unlikely heroes emerged with a crowd of 30,665 on hand at the Met for Bat Day.

Backup catcher Jerry Zimmerman, in his 556th plate appearance over five big league seasons, blasted his first Major League home run, a 402-foot shot off Phil Ortega. In the clubhouse after the game, Billy Martin quipped that Zimmerman should appear for running practice the next day because the thirty-year-old catcher didn't know how to run out home runs. But the laid-back Zimmerman took the sudden attention casually. "First homer in the Majors, sure," he told *Minneapolis Tribune* writer Tom Briere, "but I hit some in the Minors." The long blast inspired Arno Goethel to note in the next day's *St. Paul Pioneer Press* that Zimmerman's homer "left him 713 behind Babe Ruth."

Lefty reliever Bill "Shorty" Pleis also starred, working five scoreless innings in relief of rookie starter Dave Boswell, who had been bothered by a blister on his middle finger. With the Twins up 5–2, Pleis entered in the fifth and allowed just three singles and struck out seven. The morning after Pleis claimed his third win, *Minneapolis Tribune* columnist Sid Hartman reported that Pleis had been offered to the Cincinnati Reds in a trade two weeks earlier. Hartman wrote that the deal fell through when the Reds wouldn't part with twenty-four-year-old second baseman Pete Rose, who went on to have a breakout 1965 season, batting .312 and leading the National League in hits.

Minnesota's surge hit a snag on June 7, when Cleveland came to town for the first time in 1965. Luis Tiant, a twenty-four-year-old, second-year pitcher with an explosive fastball, outpitched Mudcat Grant in a 2–1 decision that stuck the Twins right-hander with his first loss. The Twins managed just two hits, which set the tone for the next few weeks.

A sudden drop in run production spurred a June swoon. Nearly every Twins regular struggled at the plate as the team closed the month dropping twelve of twenty-three games. Pascual secured his eighth straight win the night after Tiant's masterpiece, but Cleveland soon made its move with a ten-game winning streak, and Detroit and Baltimore inched closer to first place when the Twins struggled. The White Sox were in it, too, making it a five-team race as the season neared its midpoint.

During the Twins' struggles, one win seemingly slipped through a small hole in Jim Kaat's sleeve on June 9. Kaat was working a masterpiece that evening and took a 1–0 lead into the ninth against Cleveland. The southpaw was wearing a familiar sweatshirt under his jersey, one with a hole in the sleeve, which was technically a rule infraction. He had been wearing it for weeks, including when the Twins had played in Cleveland in late April, but Cleveland manager Birdie Tebbetts brought it to the attention of plate umpire Bill Haller after Kaat had fanned Chuck Hinton to open the ninth and started 2-1 on Rocky Colavito.

Haller hadn't noticed the hole, but when Sam Mele caught wind of what Tebbetts was discussing with Haller, he headed to home plate and unloaded on both parties. "I called Tebbetts a *lot* of names when he was standing at home plate," Mele said after the game. "He probably is the only manager who would do something like that—wait nine innings to call it." No Cleveland hitter had complained about the hole, but before play resumed, Kaat's sleeves were trimmed to remove it. Then Kaat walked Colavito, gave up a line-drive home run to Max Alvis, and took a 2–1 loss. Did Tebbetts's move upset Kaat's rhythm or focus? Kaat wasn't buying it: "Alvis would have hit that pitch if I was wearing ten sweatshirts," he said. "It went right down Broadway."

On June 16 at Comiskey Park in Chicago, Pascual finally took his first loss, a 3–1 defeat in which rubber-armed knuckleballer Eddie Fisher, making his thirty-second appearance in Chicago's fifty-seventh game, saved a win for John Buzhardt by extinguishing a late Twins rally. Pascual's loss allowed the Sox to move within a half game of first-place Minnesota; Baltimore, Cleveland, and Detroit were within four games of the top.

The best thing that could be said about the struggling Twins is that they were always winning when first place was on the line. The day before Pascual's first loss, Grant had blanked the White Sox 4–0 to keep the Twins from falling behind them in the standings. For Grant, who had posted a 3-16 record against Chicago while pitching for Cleveland, it was his second shutout of the White Sox in 1965 and his fifth straight win over them since joining the Twins in June 1964.

The day after Pascual lost in Chicago, Kaat kept the Twins in front by pitching a four-hitter in a 3–1 win over the White Sox. Then Grant turned the trick again on June 23, with both Chicago and Cleveland a half game behind Minnesota. A day earlier, the Tribe had rallied for their tenth straight victory—on a Chuck Hinton tenth-inning home run off Twins reliever Al Worthington—but Grant's pitching and home runs by Jimmie Hall, Bob Allison, and rookie Sandy Valdespino produced a 6–4 victory that stalled Cleveland's winning streak and kept the Twins in first place.

The Twins lost two of three in Cleveland, and the series proved particularly costly. Catcher Earl Battey suffered a dislocated finger that sidelined him for ten days. Pascual, who had lost for the second time in two starts against Cleveland, removed himself from the series finale on June 24 with a pulled ribcage muscle. The Twins were without both players when Detroit and Chicago came to the Met for key series.

The next night, with the Tigers opening a Twins home stand at the Met, the home team executed a late-inning comeback to maintain their half-game edge over Chicago and Cleveland. The Twins trailed 3–2 and were down to their final out in the ninth. Both Chicago and Cleveland had already won, and *twice* the Twins were within one pitch of losing and giving up first place. But both Harmon Killebrew and Don Mincher drew full-count walks off Detroit starter Dave Wickersham to set the stage for oft-injured second baseman Bernie Allen, making just his fourth appearance of the season after starting the year on the disabled list.

Tigers manager Chuck Dressen countered with Fred Gladding, who served up a 2-1 pitch that Allen laced into center field with the base runners in motion. Grant, pinch running for Killebrew, came around to score the tying run while Mincher motored around second and headed for third. Al Kaline, playing center field for the Tigers, anticipated the play and rifled a strong throw to third baseman Don Wert. The slow-footed Mincher didn't beat the relay, but displaced the ball from Wert's glove with a hard slide while Allen moved into second.

With first base open, Gladding intentionally walked Rich Rollins. That brought up twenty-four-year-old rookie utility man Joe Nossek. The speedy Nossek dribbled a slow roller just past Gladding. The ball stopped dead just before second baseman Jerry Lumpe made an impressive stab-and-throw, but Nossek beat the ball to the bag and Minnesota had a 4–3 win. The dramatic victory was the Twins' fortieth of the season and the fourth time they had come from behind in the ninth.

Thanks to more late-game dramatics, the Twins took both ends of a Sunday doubleheader with Detroit on June 27. Although Chicago and Cleveland also swept twin bills that afternoon, the Twins stayed a half game ahead of both clubs. Mincher drove a two-run homer off the right-field foul pole in the eighth for a 6–4 win in the opener, and in the nightcap Nossek singled in the tenth to deliver a 6–5 triumph. But Minnesota lost its hold on first the next day when Chicago arrived at the Met and erupted for 19 hits in a 17–4 rout. When the bloodbath was in the books, the Twins' twenty-nine-day reign atop the AL was over. They fell a half game behind Chicago and Cleveland, which also won big at Fenway Park.

On June 30, the struggling Twins managed only two singles off twenty-three-year-old Angels right-hander Fred Newman, who induced a plethora of weak grounders in a 5–0 decision. The Twins were unsure where their season was heading as the calendar flipped to July. They had an ailing ace, an overworked bullpen and a sputtering offense. Players apparently weren't losing sleep over the team's prospects, however. In the early morning hours before Twins hitters were shut down by Newman, a burglar slipped into the seventh-floor room of reliever Johnny Klippstein and backup catcher John Sevcik at the Continental Hotel, owned, incidentally, by Angels owner Gene Autry. While the players slept, the visitor lifted ninety dollars from Sevcik's wallet and plucked fifty dollars from the pocket of Klippstein's pants, hanging in a closet. For the Twins, losses seemed to have a way of multiplying.

FOUR

An All-Star Summer

While extreme spring weather was front and center to upper-Midwest residents, those living in the Deep South were consumed by the budding civil rights movement. In the early days of 1965, Martin Luther King Jr. and his Atlanta-based Southern Christian Leadership Conference (SCLC) turned their attention to guaranteeing voting rights for African American citizens. For years following the Civil War, southern states had amended their state constitutions, adopting a host of laws to suppress Black voting. They had excluded African American voters through literacy tests, poll taxes, property-ownership requirements, and arbitrary morality tests.

Despite passage of the Fifteenth Amendment in 1870, which guaranteed voting rights to all citizens, and the Civil Rights Act of 1957, which provided a mechanism to challenge voting rights violations, strict legal standards made it nearly impossible for the Justice Department to successfully litigate the South's discriminatory voting practices. Southern civil rights groups struggled as well to initiate change, and in time they called for help from the SCLC to work with them. King planned to draw national attention to the voting rights issue with a voter registration project and three marches in Selma, Alabama, where Sheriff Jim Clark and his deputies had refused to allow African Americans to register to vote that January.

When an Alabama state trooper shot and killed Jimmie Lee Jackson, an unarmed church deacon, during a violent attack on voting rights protestors on February 18 in Marion, Alabama, King dedicated the first Selma march, scheduled for March 7, to Jackson's memory. Roughly six hundred people—mostly older folks who had grown committed to the movement—planned to walk the fifty-four miles between Selma and Montgomery, the Alabama state capital. But on a day still remembered as "Bloody Sunday," the march didn't make it out of Selma.

As marchers approached the Edmund Pettus Bridge on the south side of Selma, looking to cross the Alabama River, awaiting them was a large contingent of Alabama state troopers, under orders from Governor George Wallace. Some were on horseback. Others stood with billy clubs, pounding them against their palms as the marchers took in the scene. Reverend Hosea Williams, an SCLC representative, asked to speak to Major John Cloud, the officer in charge, who replied there was nothing to talk about. A minute later he barked: "Troopers advance!" The front column of troopers charged into the crowd swinging billy clubs. Others lobbed tear gas canisters into the crowd or aimed shotguns at frantic marchers, who were driven back across the bridge into Selma.

Covered heavily by the press with news cameras rolling, the footage of "Bloody Sunday" shown on national news broadcasts fueled an immense wave of support for the civil rights movement. More than two thousand turned out for the second attempt to march to Montgomery, but again they were met at the bridge by Wallace's show of force. King had the crowd turn around to avoid another violent confrontation. Days later, several locals attacked three white ministers from the North, and one, John Reeb, died from his injuries. Solidarity protests broke out across the country, and President Lyndon Johnson called Wallace to Washington for a two-hour meeting. Before the week was out, the president spoke to a joint session of Congress, urging its members to pass a voting rights bill.

On March 15, a week after the violent attack of African American marchers in Selma, King stood before the full Congress and eloquently declared "We shall overcome." He spoke of "the dignity of man and the destiny of democracy" while advocating for a voting rights bill. King had the ear of those in power and spoke forcefully: "There is no Negro problem. There is no Southern problem. There is no Northern problem. There is only an American problem." It was an electric moment.

Nearly fifty thousand participated in the third Selma march on March 21, with protection from federalized National Guard troops. Participants reached Montgomery in four days, with Harry Belafonte and Aretha Franklin among the celebrities in the crowd when it celebrated a successful march at the Capitol. The events in Selma spurred quick action, and President Johnson signed the Voting Rights Act of 1965 into law in August. Nearly 250,000 African American citizens registered to vote in 1965.

By then, baseball had been integrated for nearly two decades, but well into the 1960s, African American players still faced Florida's institutionalized segregation during spring training. They couldn't stay in the same hotels as their white teammates, which was an affront to early-1960s Twins Lenny Green, Vic Power, Earl Battey, and Mudcat Grant. Battey—intelligent, articulate, with a razor-sharp wit, and quick with a quip—was born and raised in the Watts neighborhood of Los Angeles. Watts was a mix of races and less segregated than many urban areas, so Battey encountered the hardline institutional variety for the first time at Minor League stops and in Florida.

Always outgoing, Battey spoke up in the early '60s about segregated conditions in Orlando, where the Twins trained in the spring and he and Green were forced to live separately from the rest of their teammates. Orlando fiercely resisted change. Although city officials agreed in 1962 to end segregated seating at Tinker Field (the Twins' spring training park), the Cherry Plaza Hotel, where the team stayed, refused to revoke its segregation policy. Owner Calvin Griffith insisted that there were only two first-class hotels in Orlando, and both were segregated. As a result, the Twins were the last Major League club to spend spring training in an integrated Florida hotel. By spring 1964, with the Cherry Plaza Hotel still refusing to integrate, Minnesota attorney general Walter Mondale had spoken out against the Twins' lack of progress in moving their spring training base. When the NAACP began organizing a protest for the club's home opener, Griffith moved the team to the newly built Downtowner Motel that spring.

Grant was offended by the conditions in Florida as well, though he was familiar with southern-style segregation growing up in Lacoochee, a small Florida town fifty miles north of Tampa. Cleveland, his original team, trained in Arizona, and therefore 1965 was his first spring training in his home state. Like Battey, Grant wasn't afraid to express his opinion about segregation, though it wasn't something he could do as a youth. Like any hamlet in the Deep South, Lacoochee was a town divided—literally split down the middle by train tracks, with Blacks living on one side and whites on the other. White kids could throw rocks and direct hateful, vulgar comments at Blacks without fear of retaliation. Grant was one of eight children raised by his mother, Viola, a pillar of strength and a single mom, after his father died when he was an infant. He now says, "You couldn't afford not to be strong. My mother used to say, 'Strength is being able to take the blow.' That's what she taught us."

Signed by Cleveland in 1954, Grant joined the Indians four years later and was mentored by Indians star Larry Doby, who had broken the color barrier in the American League roughly three months after Jackie Robinson's Brooklyn debut in April 1947. Doby introduced Grant to a world that a young man from Lacoochee could never have anticipated. They went to music clubs in Cleveland and other AL cities, where Grant met many of the prominent African American musicians of the day, from Ella Fitzgerald, Duke Ellington, Sarah Vaughn, Billie Holliday, and Count Basie to Lionel Hampton, B. B. King, Bobby "Blue" Bland, and O. C. Smith.

In 1958, Grant and fellow rookie Gary Bell, a rough-and-tumble white Texan, became close friends. Bell had a sharp sense of humor and spoke his mind, which perpetrated a reputation as a redneck, but he was anything but when it came to race. The two outspoken friends kept things loose in the Cleveland clubhouse by hurling slurs and racially charged comments at each other, using the same language and stereotypes that separated people to defuse racial tension among teammates. They were among the first interracial roommates on the road and remain close to this day.

Grant and Battey grew close immediately after the June 1964 trade that brought the veteran pitcher to Minnesota. Grant moved into Battey's St. Paul apartment and the two drove together to Metropolitan Stadium on game days. On their route, they repeatedly drove by a Black jockey statue—a two-foot-high lawn ornament with exaggerated facial features. Such statues were widely considered a hallmark of more openly racist times. For days they joked about it, until Grant decided it was time to take action.

"One day I said, 'Earl, we've got to do something about that statue.'" Grant recalls. "He said, 'What are we going to do about it?' I said, 'We're going to take it and maybe put it somewhere where nobody will ever see it again.' He said, 'Okay, I'm with you.'" A middle-of-the-night visit revealed that their kidnapping target was cemented into the ground. The pair returned with shovels, but digging made too much noise and they gave up when a dog began to bark. The Twins soon went on a road trip, but Grant and Battey plotted again after returning to the Twin Cities.

"Earl had a Volkswagen," Grant says. "We got a rope from the hardware store and I tied the rope to the door of the car. I said, 'Earl, go slowly. I'm going to rope it like Gene Autry.' So I roped it, and he took off. And the thing was such a deep little project that it took the door off of the Volkswagen." The pair grabbed the door and vacated the premises. The Black jockey heist was abandoned, though the story has an epilogue.

"So now we're going to an old-timers' game," adds Grant. "We're both retired. And after the old-timers' game, we're sitting there having some suds, and I says, 'Earl?' He says, 'I know what you're thinking. Let's go.' So we left the ballpark. We went by this home and sure enough, there was that little man sitting right out there still."

The Twins had struggled mightily in June, but in the midst of their swoon, they learned that Earl Battey had been selected as the American League's starting catcher for the first All-Star game in Minnesota. On a Minnesota club featuring a plethora of power and speed, he may have been the least appreciated of the everyday players. He was overshadowed by the bigger bats in the lineup but was among the best hitting catchers of his era.

In the first five years of Twins baseball—through the 1965 championship season—Battey ranked among the game's top catchers in doubles, homers, runs, RBIS, and the three hitting percentages—with a .287 average, .363 on-base percentage, and .432 slugging percentage. No everyday catcher had posted a higher OBP. He hit despite a chronically bad knee and twice having cheekbones broken by pitched balls. After a pitch from Cleveland's Bobby Locke fractured Battey's left cheekbone in July 1961, Griffith had a special batting helmet designed to protect his catcher's jaw and temple—the prototype for what all hitters wear today. The two beanings never made Battey gun-shy at the plate. In 1963, his best season, he hit .285 with 26 home runs and 84 RBIS.

Battey also excelled *behind* the plate, winning three Gold Gloves. He had an uncanny knack for knowing how to work American League hitters, called a good game, and tutored the passel of young pitchers Minnesota employed in the early '60s. Fans didn't recognize those skills, but Battey's rifle-like arm stood out for all to see. He released the ball so quickly and with such zip, according to Tony Oliva, that Sam Mele rarely called pitchouts. When it came to throwing out base runners, Battey didn't need the extra help. Both Oliva and Harmon Killebrew have called Battey the best catcher they saw during their playing days.

Despite battling a host of first-half injuries in 1965, Battey would make his third All-Star start after batting .313 and posting a .398 OBP prior to the break. The thirty-year-old veteran endured physical setbacks on nearly a weekly basis, including a bad back and two finger injuries early in the season. In early May he suffered a pulled right hamstring that forced him to miss only two games. Later in the month Battey played through a virus. Then on May 29, a pitch from Washington's Frank Kreutzer struck the right-handed-hitting catcher just above the right wrist, sidelining him for seven games with a deep bone bruise. Three weeks later on June 22, with the struggling Twins battling four other contenders for first place, Battey dislocated the middle finger on his left hand behind the plate. This time he was out ten games.

The injury bug bit again the last week of June. Two days after Battey went down, Camilo Pascual pulled himself from his June 24 start in Cleveland after four innings with what appeared to be a mild ribcage strain. The right-hander had missed a few weeks due to shoulder issues in both 1962 and 1963, his two twenty-win seasons, but the original prognosis was that Pascual would be throwing within a few days. The Twins thought his injury wouldn't linger enough to impact the pennant race, but when he returned to action on July 4, the injury persisted.

When Pascual departed his Cleveland start with an 8-2 record and 3.13 ERA, Twins owner Calvin Griffith was more concerned about another starter, Jim Kaat, who was battling a mild case of tendinitis in his throwing arm. With both Pascual and Kaat out, the Twins called on lefty relievers Mel Nelson and Bill Pleis to make emergency starts in the final days of June. Pleis was on the mound on June 30, when Angels right-hander Fred Newman tossed a two-hit shutout. It was only the second time all season the Twins were held scoreless, but in their last twenty-three games they were batting just .229 and averaging a full run less per game than what they generated through April and May. With the loss, the injury-riddled Twins began July trailing first-place Cleveland by a half game, with Chicago, Baltimore, and Detroit all within four games of the top.

July began with a brief tirade from Billy Martin. Somebody needed "to shake these guys up a little. And I'm just the guy to do that," the fiery Martin told Arno Goethel of the *St. Paul Pioneer Press*. "We have to win all of our next five games," Martin said on the eve of a three-game series at Municipal Stadium against the Athletics. "Certainly we need at least four of them." Whether or not anyone heeded Martin's outburst, the Twins opened July by reeling off nine straight victories against the A's, Red Sox, and Yankees.

Cleveland's lead atop the American League lasted all of two days into the new month. Cleveland lost six in a row while Minnesota took off on its longest winning streak of the season. Tony Oliva, who had found his stroke in June after a dreadful start, was critical to Minnesota's surge. The Twins right fielder kicked off July with a fourteen-game hitting streak in which he batted .424. He also drove in the game-winners in two of the first three victories of the winning streak. The onslaught went on for weeks, as Oliva batted .394 in July.

Minnesota's pitching staff allowed more than two runs in a game just once during the streak, and Mudcat Grant set the tone in the first game, a 3–1 victory on July 2. After allowing three hits and Kansas City's sole run in the opening frame, he rediscovered the pinpoint control so critical to his first-half success. The Twins made it two straight in Kansas City the following night when Don Mincher powered two home runs, including an eleventh-inning shot that gave the visitors a 3–2 win. With Cleveland losing that afternoon, Mincher's second blast moved the 45-28 Twins into a first-place tie. They took over the top spot on Independence Day when Oliva lit the fuse on the day's fireworks with a three-run homer in the sixth inning, erasing a 2–0 deficit, and Killebrew blasted a two-run bomb for a 5–2 victory and a sweep of the A's.

Equally effective but far less flashy was Johnny Klippstein. He provided four perfect innings in relief of Pascual, who made his first start since June 24 but left in the third because of a flare-up of his muscle injury. The game also featured third base coach Billy Martin and pitching coach Johnny Sain squabbling over Jerry Fosnow's botched pitchout, which was bunted for a run-scoring squeeze play, but the Twins overcame the miscue to win. And they kept winning.

After posting a third straight victory for the first time in a month, the Twins returned home and swept a four-game set from Boston. The ninth-place Red Sox scored just four runs in the series, as Jim Perry and Grant tossed shutouts. In the second game of a July 5 doubleheader, the twenty-nine-year-old Perry stepped into the rotation for Pascual and blanked the Red

Sox on seven hits in his first start of the season. The nearly forgotten Perry had gone unclaimed on waivers in the spring and didn't seem to have a role with the Twins, but he had pitching effectively in relief and was now 5-0 with a 2.59 ERA.

Grant continued the run of zeroes the following evening, scattering eight hits and four walks in a 9–0 rout that pushed the Twins two games in front of Cleveland. He also turned two nice fielding plays and stroked two singles, but the big blows were a pair of two-run homers from Jimmie Hall. The twenty-seven-year-old center fielder, nicknamed "Wedge" for his broad shoulders and thin waist, was on a tear. Since the start of June, Hall had averaged nearly an RBI a game and now led the Twins with 16 homers and 50 RBIS. He had moved into the league's top five in all three Triple Crown categories and emerged as an early MVP candidate with Boston's Carl Yastrzemski and Detroit sluggers Willie Horton and Al Kaline.

After seven years in the Minor Leagues with two seasons lost to injury, the left-handed-hitting Hall had exploded onto the scene in 1963, powering 33 homers and driving in 80 runs. He was nearly as productive in '64, even after hard-throwing Angels lefty Bo Belinsky beaned him on May 27. He missed only a week and turned in a strong second half to finish with 20 home runs and 86 RBIS. Hall demonstrated virtually no power against southpaws after the beaning, however, and some teammates thought that Hall was never the same hitter after being struck by Belinsky's fastball.

On the July night Hall stroked his two homers against the Red Sox, left fielder Bob Allison was struck by a pitch from Boston right-hander Jerry Stephenson. He would be out for nearly two weeks with a linear fracture and small bone chip in his right wrist. Yet, all these injuries hadn't kept the Twins from contending, and with a seven-game winning streak, the confident club welcomed the defending AL champion Yankees to the Met for four weekend games leading up to the All-Star break.

The Yankees were floundering near .500, but at the start of the 1965 season, few believed the New York dynasty that began in 1949 was in trouble. Perhaps Opening Day—when the Yankees committed five errors in an extra-inning loss to the Twins in Minnesota—was an omen. The Twins also ruined Opening Day at Yankee Stadium and took both ends of a two-game set. The Yankees had never lost a season series to Minnesota, but with the first half winding down, they arrived at the Met having dropped five of the first seven matchups of 1965.

Prior to the series opener, New York pitching ace Whitey Ford told *St. Paul Pioneer Press* writer Glenn Redmann that he believed his 40-43 Yankees still could overtake the five teams in front of them and win the AL pennant. "We still think we have the best team in the American League. Once we get over that .500 mark, I think we'll be OK and ready to move." That might have been nothing more than trying to put a good face on a bad situation, but AL clubs knew you could never count out the Yankees. Certainly Ford and the Yankees had history on their side. Three years earlier, they had arrived at the Met to close out the first half with the Angels in front and the Yankees, Indians, and Twins all within two games of first place. With nearly forty thousand excited Twins fans in attendance for each contest, New York swept the three-game set and moved into first place. The Twins never recovered and finished five games out.

"It seemed like the same old story every year," recalls Jim Kaat, the Twins lefty who won eighteen games in 1965. "No matter whether it was a game, a series or a season, the Yankees always figured out a way to finish on top." But the scenario was markedly different in '65. The Twins were in front with Cleveland, Baltimore, Chicago, and Detroit suddenly struggling to keep pace. The Yankees were in sixth place, 12½ games behind the Twins. Anticipating an outcome far different than the club's three losses before the All-Star break in 1962, more than 138,000 fans walked through the Metropolitan Stadium gates for the series against New York.

In the Friday night opener, with 30,373 on hand, Don Mincher homered twice and Harmon Killebrew added a three-run blast as rookie Dave Boswell went the distance for an 8–3 victory, the Twins' eighth in a row. The Yankees fell another game under .500 but could close the gap on Saturday when the two clubs squared off in a day-night doubleheader. More than thirty-six thousand showed up for each game. Those in attendance for the matinee matchup saw Jim Perry continue his fine turn as the newest Minnesota starter. After pitching a shutout in his first start, he limited the Yankees to an unearned run over eight innings of a 4–1 win, upping his record to 6-0. Perry also squeezed across the first run of the game when he managed to lay down a bunt on an inside offering from Ford during a three-run fifth inning. Grant looked to make it 10 straight wins in the nightcap, but departed in the seventh with a lead the bullpen couldn't hold. New York's 8–6 comeback victory ended the win streak.

Sunday's series finale marked the last game before the All-Star break. The two southpaw starters, Kaat and New York's Al Downing, didn't last long, but the bullpens soon quieted both lineups. With the score 4–4 in the ninth, Elston Howard's single and an error by Rich Rollins put New York runners on first and third with two outs. Roger Repoz chopped a high hopper down the first base line, which Twins reliever Jerry Fosnow moved into position to field. Just as the southpaw gloved the ball, Repoz ran into him and jarred it loose while Howard crossed the plate with New York's fifth run. Plate umpire Ed Hurley immediately called Repoz out on an interference call, but Yankees manager Johnny Keane suggested first base ump John Flaherty was in a better position to make the call, and Flaherty overturned his colleague's original decision.

The Twins were on the verge of closing out the first half with a pair of losses. The go-ahead run generated a formal protest from Mele, though the point was soon made moot. In Minnesota's half of the ninth, Rollins drew a one-out walk from reliever Pete Mikkelsen. After Oliva was retired for the second out, Killebrew induced a 3-2 count from the Yankees right-hander before drilling a belt-high fastball into the left-field bleachers for a stunning 6–5 victory.

As a few of the more than thirty-five thousand ecstatic fans at the Met leapt onto the field, Killebrew, in typically stoic fashion, trotted around the bases with his head down. His sixteenth homer of 1965 allowed the Twins to take three of four from New

York, and ten of their last eleven games heading into the break. They closed out the first half at 53-29, good for a five-game bulge over both Cleveland and Baltimore, while the Yankees, now in seventh place, had fallen a shocking 14½ games back.

Killebrew was the center of attention in the clubhouse after the game. Reporters wanted to know where his game-winner, the 288th home run of his career, ranked among the others. The modest slugger was more prone to blushing than bragging before calling the homer "one of the sweetest." The scene spurred *Minneapolis Tribune* sportswriter Tom Briere to conclude that Killebrew would "much rather hit them than talk about them."

The euphoria generated by Harmon Killebrew's walk-off home run carried over to the first All-Star Game in Minnesota two days later. By virtue of an injury to White Sox first baseman Bill Skowron, Killebrew joined Earl Battey in the American League's starting lineup. In all, six Twins had been selected to play the Midsummer Classic in front of the home fans. Mudcat Grant, Jimmie Hall, and Zoilo Versalles were AL reserves, and Tony Oliva was added to the roster when injuries sidelined both Mickey Mantle and American League batting leader Carl Yastrzemski.

On July 13, a sunny Tuesday afternoon, a sellout crowd of 46,706 packed the Met, the largest gathering yet to see a baseball game in Minnesota. Fans had paid eight dollars for box seats, six dollars to sit in the grandstands down the line, or two or four dollars for seats beyond the outfield. Standing-room tickets were a hot commodity and even the press box was filled to capacity.

Players mingled on the field before the game, gathering in different combinations for photographers. The talent was immense, as sixteen future Hall of Famers populated the two All-Star rosters. Thirteen were National Leaguers, including the starting outfield of Willie Stargell, Willie Mays, and Hank Aaron. Two other future Hall of Famers, outfielders Roberto Clemente and Frank Robinson, were on the bench.

The NL squad also had pop at the infield corners and behind the plate in Ernie Banks, Dick Allen, and Joe Torre, as well as table-setters Maury Wills and Pete Rose in the middle infield.

Throw in a stable of hard-throwing starters in Juan Marichal, Bob Gibson, Sandy Koufax, Don Drysdale, Bob Veale, and Jim Maloney, and arguably the NL featured as much talent as any team ever to grace a baseball diamond.

The American League, which had lost the last two All-Star games, was the underdog in a matchup that would break a 17-17 tie in Midsummer Classic victories. The AL roster wasn't as formidable, though it still featured plenty of power with Killebrew, Rocky Colavito, Willie Horton, Brooks Robinson, and Dick McAuliffe. More pop came off the bench from Hall, Oliva, Versalles, Al Kaline, Max Alvis, Bill Freehan, Elston Howard, and Joe Pepitone. Grant, a month shy of his thirtieth birthday, was the elder statesman of a young AL pitching staff that included Sam McDowell, Milt Pappas, Mel Stottlemyre, Pete Richert, and White Sox knuckleballer Eddie Fisher, one of the game's premier relievers.

In pregame introductions, Killebrew and Sam Mele, serving as an AL coach, received the biggest ovations. San Francisco star Willie Mays drew the loudest cheers among the National Leaguers, and on the game's second pitch, he greeted Pappas with a drive that carried three rows deep into the seats in left-center field. Pittsburgh's Willie Stargell touched the Orioles right-hander for a one-out single to center, and with two out, Milwaukee Braves catcher Joe Torre stroked a Pappas pitch more than four hundred feet down the left-field line to give the NL a 3–0 edge. Then, in the second inning, Stargell drilled a two-run shot off Grant into the bullpen in right-center to make it 5–0.

Five homers were hit that day. Killebrew hit arguably the most dramatic one, a 410-foot bomb to deep left-center that tied the game at 5–5 in the fifth. For a second Killebrew uncharacteristically watched the ball take flight before circling the bases to a standing ovation. The crowd had buzzed with anticipation when the slugger stepped in, and on cue he delivered the game-tying shot . . . aided by a touch of luck. One pitch earlier, Killebrew foul-tipped a 2-2 offering that struck Torre's glove but didn't stay in his mitt.

Despite all of the long ball that afternoon, a crazy-hop infield single in the seventh decided the game. After Mays drew a leadoff walk and moved to third base on a single by Milwaukee slugger Hank Aaron, Cubs third baseman Ron Santo chopped a ball into the dirt in front of home plate. The ball bounced and didn't touch down until it cleared Cleveland's Sam McDowell on the mound. By then, Mays had crossed the plate with the run that would give the NL the 6–5 victory and its first lead over the AL in All-Star Game victories.

Both Versalles and Yankees second baseman Bobby Richardson were thinking "double play" when Santo first hit McDowell's pitch into the ground. Richardson decided the double play was impossible if he fielded the ball and gave way to Versalles, who fielded it three feet behind second base. "It took a bigger hop than I thought it would," Versalles said after the game. "By the time I got to the ball, there was only one play—to first base. As it turned out, I couldn't even get the hitter." The game was decided by, according to *Minneapolis Tribune* writer Tom Briere, "Santo's 130-foot single."

FIVE

A Pennant Race in a Rocking New World

The British Invasion was in full swing in 1965. In the days leading up to the All-Star Game at Metropolitan Stadium, the Rolling Stones topped the *Billboard Hot 100* for the first time with "(I Can't Get No) Satisfaction." The Stones, who had arrived in the United States a year earlier to far less fanfare than the Beatles, released nine singles in the United States before finally hitting it big with a song that Keith Richards once said the band considered a throwaway. "Satisfaction" connected with rock fans worldwide, a song that transcends the era. "It's the riff heard 'round the world," E Street guitarist Steve Van Zandt once said of Richards's creation. Equally memorable is hearing Mick Jagger dismissively sing what he later called his "view of the world, my frustration with everything."

The British imports came in all shapes and sizes. At the same time "Satisfaction" ruled the roost nationally, the Herman's Hermits hit "I'm Henry VIII, I Am" was the top-rated tune on WDGY radio. The vaudeville-styled song, an old British music hall tune, dated from early in the century. The peppy Hermits' remake became the fastest-selling song in U.S. history and landed at number one on the *Billboard Hot 100* for a week in August. The Yardbirds rocked Twin Cities radio with "For Your Love" and "Heart Full of Soul" that year. The Kinks, who broke through with "You Really Got Me" and "All Day and All of the Night" in

'64, had a hit with "Tired of Waiting for You" in '65. The Animals climbed the charts with "It's My Life" and "We Gotta Get Out of This Place."

If you wanted to hear the Beatles, of course, all you had to do was turn on a radio. They topped the *Hot 100* for nearly a quarter of the year with a host of singles, including "Eight Days a Week," "Yesterday," "Daytripper," "We Can Work It Out," and "Help!" the title track of their second Richard Lester film, a madcap adventure that the Beatles later admitted was filmed in "the haze of marijuana." On August 14, McCartney's solo performance of "Yesterday" was a highlight of the Beatles' final appearance on *The Ed Sullivan Show*. Girls shrieked as the song closed and Lennon dashed to the microphone to thank "Ringo," proclaiming: "That was wonderful!"

The group embarked on a second North American tour the very next day, setting attendance records and paving the way for the stadium rock concerts of the future. The Beatles drew more than fifty-five thousand to New York's Shea Stadium on August 15. The lowly New York Mets, on their way to losing 112 games, needed more than a week of games to put that many butts in the seats. The crowd awaiting the Beatles was far more engaged than the baseball fans enduring another difficult Mets season. The concert at Shea required two thousand security personnel to handle crowd control. For their safety, the Beatles boarded a Wells Fargo armored truck for the ride to the stadium. Beatlemania was at a feverish pitch.

The music scene in 1965 wasn't strictly British Invasion. Motown, the label started by songwriter Berry Gordy Jr. six years earlier, emerged as an extremely successful all-Black enterprise. That year the Supremes scored four number one hits on the *Billboard Hot 100*, including "Come See about Me" and "Stop! In the Name of Love." The Temptations scored with "My Girl," and for two weeks that summer, the Four Tops topped the *Hot 100* with "I Can't Help Myself (Sugar Pie Honey Bunch)."

By then, James Brown and the Famous Flames, whose grittier R&B sound laid the groundwork for so much funk to follow, had climbed the R&B charts with a string of hits going back to

1957. In 1962, Brown wanted to record a live album to convey how his songs came to life in concert. His label, King Records in Cincinnati, refused to finance the idea, so Brown put down nearly $6,000 to make it happen. In the words of Kevin Phinney, author of *Souled American: How Black Music Transformed White Culture*, the "sonic boom of *James Brown Live at the Apollo* reverberated throughout the music world. . . . The atmosphere is electric, the Famous Flames turn on a rhythmic dime, and Brown set a standard for recorded frenzy that would stand for decades to come." With the live album, the world now knew the power and sizzle of James Brown, who scored the pop charts with "Papa's Got a Brand New Bag" and "I Got You (I Feel Good)" in 1965.

Sam Cooke was an extremely successful singer-songwriter by the 1960s, with a soulful voice that generated a host of hits, beginning with "You Send Me" in 1957. Reportedly moved by Bob Dylan's performance of "Blowin' in the Wind" at the March on Washington in August 1963, Cooke wrote "A Change is Gonna Come," interspersing the story of a runaway slave and his own personal experiences confronting racism, while optimistically anticipating better times to come. The song, arguably Cooke's best as a songwriter, didn't get much play when it was released in 1964, despite Cooke singing it on *The Tonight Show Starring Johnny Carson* that February. In December Cooke was fatally shot at a Los Angeles hotel, never knowing that his song would become an anthem of the civil rights movement in 1965.

Some of the music in rotation was homegrown. Late in 1964, the Gestures, a Mankato-based band, had a national hit with "Run, Run, Run," a melodic, psychedelic-tinged song featuring surf-style guitars and tight Beatle-esque harmonies. Although "Run, Run, Run" climbed to number forty-four on the *Hot 100* and the Gestures performed it on *Bandstand*, it should have fared better on the charts. Minneapolis-based Soma Records, at the forefront of the region's budding rock scene, lacked the means to distribute the record nationally, making it hard to find in stores even as it went top ten in numerous markets, including New York City. After the group's four teenagers had toured much of the country in an old van, packed to the ceiling with their equipment, frustrated singer-songwriter Dale Menten, despite having written enough songs to record an album, left the group in 1966.

The Chancellors, formed in St. Louis Park, took the Twin Cities music scene by storm in early 1965. The quartet had a hit with their surf-rock take of "Little Latin Lupe Lu," penned by the Righteous Brothers' Bill Medley. The Chancellors' cover stayed atop the WDGY survey for three weeks beginning in late January and topped out at number forty-nine on the *Billboard Hot 100*.

Later that year, the Castaways, based in Richfield, climbed to number twelve on the *Hot 100* with "Liar, Liar," penned by band members Jim Donna and Denny Craswell. The catchy tune with a psychedelic touch featured guitarist Robert Folschow singing in a distinctive falsetto: "Liar, liar, pants on fire. Your nose as long as a telephone wire." The song, which was later covered by both Debbie Harry and the Pretenders, peaked on the charts during the 1965 World Series. By then, the song had topped the singles chart at KRLA in Los Angeles, and the group had opened several shows for the Beach Boys and appeared on television shows, including Dick Clark's *Where the Action Is*, *The Lloyd Thaxton Show*, and *Hollywood A-Go-Go*. In 1967, the Castaways performed "Liar, Liar" in *It's a Bikini World*, a low-budget musical comedy also featuring the Animals doing "We Gotta Get Out of This Place." Two decades later, "Liar Liar" appeared on the soundtrack of the film *Good Morning Vietnam*, starring Robin Williams.

Young music fans took to the explosion of rock bands, each offering its individual take on the budding art form. Even folk icon and Minnesota native Bob Dylan plugged in the electric guitar in 1965. By then, Dylan had written "Blowin' in the Wind" and "The Times They Are a-Changin'," songs that had become anthems for the growing civil rights and anti-war movements. So, his artistic decision was not universally loved.

On July 25, the twenty-four-year-old Dylan took the stage at the Newport Folk Festival in Rhode Island. He had performed solo and with Joan Baez the previous two summers in the quaint seaside town, but this year he appeared with guitarist Al Kooper and other members of the Paul Butterfield Blues Band. The jeers began when Dylan and the band kicked into a bluesy, up-tempo "Maggie's Farm." An energized Dylan brought the song to life and Kooper delivered blistering guitar fills. A powerful performance, though it was greeted with a mix of cheers and boos at song's end. The crowd turned unruly, and by the time Dylan closed his brief rock set with "It Takes a Lot to Laugh, It Takes a Train to Cry," some in the crowd were chanting "sellout!" Many who had followed Dylan the folk artist had dubbed him the voice of his generation. Now he was selling out; "going commercial" was the common refrain. Muddy Waters could do an electric set at the Newport Folk Festival, but Dylan, how dare he?

That summer, President Lyndon Johnson announced that another fifty thousand troops would soon be deployed to Vietnam, boosting the total to 125,000 on the ground. War protests grew larger and more frequent. The president also signed the Voting Rights Act into law on August 6, a year after the passage of the Civil Rights Act of 1964. But real change would be slow to come. Just days after the signing, riots broke out in the Watts neighborhood of Los Angeles, fueled by anger over discrimination in housing and employment, low wages in the jobs that African Americans could hold, and police brutality targeting the city's nonwhites. Thirty-four people died in six days of violence and looting, and it took the California Army National Guard to restore order. The shocking event, a pivotal moment in the civil rights movement, was a wakeup call to white America.

Bob Dylan going electric and the rioting in Watts were signs that the times indeed were changing. Another was the surprising American League standings at the 1965 All-Star break, as the Minnesota Twins sat atop the standings with the five-time defending AL champion Yankees lodged in seventh place and out of the race. The first-place Twins hosted the Kansas City Athletics to start the season's second half, having won ten of eleven games to move five games up on both Cleveland and Baltimore.

Even with the Twins struggling with injuries prior to the break, the time off wasn't good to them. The momentum they seemingly had less than a week earlier suddenly evaporated. The Twins opened the second half by losing four of five games to the Athletics and California Angels at Metropolitan Stadium, including four straight to tie their longest losing streak of the season. Meanwhile Chicago and Cleveland had swept opponents and inched close to the Twins once again.

The slow second-half start quelled a potential outbreak of unbridled pennant fever in July, but manager Sam Mele was confident the Twins would perform better after the break. Other than Jimmie Hall and Earl Battey, most of the regulars hadn't hit as they had in 1964. Plus, the Twins had endured a trying run of first-half injuries. If the lineup picked up its performance and Camilo Pascual returned to health after an impressive start, Mele believed the Twins would be fine.

But maybe they wouldn't be. With the Twins in the midst of losing four straight, rookie starter Dave Boswell was hospitalized with mononucleosis, a viral strain that kept him in a hospital bed for nearly two weeks of a thirty-day stint on the disabled list. Calvin Griffith was more concerned about the sputtering offense and called up Frank Quilici for the first time. Defensive whiz Jerry Kindall was batting .190 in seventy-four games, inspiring the owner to look for help at second base.

With Quilici arriving at the Met on July 18, the Twins looked to stage a turnaround against the Angels in a Sunday doubleheader. Mele departed in the sixth inning of Game 1. When California shortstop Jim Fregosi was called safe at first on a close play, Mele strolled from the Twins dugout and engaged first base umpire Bill Valentine as the arbiter approached him. Before Mele even reached Valentine, the umpire was pointing a finger at the manager. The exchange quickly became heated as Jim Kaat and Rich Rollins attempted to stop Mele from reaching his intended target. Mele was ejected and made enough contact with Valentine to anticipate a fine and possibly a suspension.

In a 5–3 loss to the Angels, the Twins couldn't overcome Fregosi, who also homered and made stellar defensive plays in the first two innings with Twins in scoring position. The good news was that Don Mincher collected his tenth home run in just his 121st at-bat of the season, ending a drought of thirty-three homerless innings

for the suddenly punchless Twins. Then Mincher slugged number eleven in the second game, a game-tying shot leading off the
eighth, and some Billy Martin-style little ball—a delayed double-
steal that brought Bob Allison home when the Angels botched a
rundown play—delivered a come-from-behind 5–4 win.

The next day, before the Twins and Angels squared off again,
AL president Joe Cronin announced that Mele had been fined
$500 and suspended for five days for his altercation with Valen-
tine. The skipper's vacation started immediately, and he learned
of it from his St. Paul dentist while sitting in the chair. Suddenly
more than just Mele's teeth irritated him. He complained to beat
writers that the penalty was too severe, but for all practical pur-
poses, his sentence was written in stone.

During Mele's suspension, on July 20, Camilo Pascual made
his first start in more than two weeks and was roughed up by the
Angels for five runs in 2⅓ innings. Former Twins first baseman
Vic Power, who was in the Angels lineup, told *St. Paul Pioneer
Press* writer Glenn Redmann that he had "never seen Camilo this
slow in my eleven years in the league." Pascual's ailing shoulder still wasn't right. He wasn't experiencing pain, but said he
couldn't get loose enough to generate velocity or good stuff. Pascual made two more starts, pitching respectable though short
outings before undergoing surgery on August 2.

The Twins rebounded, however, closing July by winning six
of seven games. They won their fourth straight on July 31, a 2–1
decision in which they pushed across the winning run in the
eleventh inning without getting the ball out of the infield. Leading off against O's relief ace Stu Miller, Tony Oliva legged out a
grounder that shortstop Luis Aparicio couldn't convert into an
out. After Al Worthington bunted Oliva to second and Miller
walked Killebrew intentionally, Joe Nossek bounced a ball to Baltimore third baseman Brooks Robinson, who started the around-
the-horn relay to "get two" and end the inning. But Nossek beat
second baseman Jerry Adair's throw to first as Oliva wheeled
around third and kept running. Catching first baseman Boog
Powell by surprise, Oliva slid home in a cloud of dust, just under
catcher Dick Brown's late tag.

The Twins' lead leapt to six games over the Indians and Orioles, but three days later another key injury provided a new challenge for a Twins club that had the injury bug drawing blood all season long. In the series finale of a four-game set with the Orioles on August 2, the Twins were looking to take three of four. The score was tied in the sixth when Baltimore center fielder Russ Snyder dropped a bunt down the third base line. Third baseman Rich Rollins fielded the ball on the run and rushed a throw that tailed into Snyder running down the line. First baseman Harmon Killebrew reached across the baseline for the ball a split second before Snyder collided with him. The loud "crack" coming from Killebrew's elbow was audible to teammates in the dugout.

"It completely dislocated my elbow around the ulnar nerve area," Killebrew said in a 2010 interview. "It felt like I broke my arm off. I was afraid to look at my arm because it was so painful. It was one of the worst injuries I'd ever had in my life." Not long after he was carried off the field, the Hall of Fame slugger recognized another downside of the severe injury. "After all those years that our ball club had not played in the World Series, it finally looked like we were going play in the World Series. And it didn't look like I was going to get a chance to play."

Killebrew had been on a roll, batting .336 in July with nine homers and 30 RBIs in thirty-one games. His game-winning blast off the Yankees the Sunday before the All-Star break was the biggest of them all, but the homers had kept coming even with teams pitching around him. "It could turn out to be our most costly injury so far this season," Sam Mele said after the game. "Let's face it, he's the big man on our club and this is the time of season when he usually gets hot." The Twins had already survived a rash of ailments that would crush most clubs' pennant hopes, but maybe this was the one that would finally take them down.

After losing Killebrew, the Twins lost only once in their next nine games. Jimmie Hall drove a Jim Palmer fastball into the seats for a walk-off homer in the game that Killebrew went down. In place of the injured Pascual, who underwent surgery earlier in the day, left-hander Jim Merritt made his Major League debut and pitched into the ninth, though Johnny Klippstein picked up the win after snuffing out a Baltimore rally in the 6–5 victory. The following night Don Mincher put the Twins in front for good with a two-run homer in a 4–3 win over Washington. Hall, Mincher, and Tony Oliva—Minnesota's three left-handed power threats—were expected to face more lefty starting pitchers with the club's right-handed slugger on the shelf, but lefty or righty didn't matter. In the forty-eight games that Killebrew missed, the Twins went 30-18 and won eleven of sixteen games started by southpaws. Mincher stroked eight homers and knocked in a team-high 34 runs in those forty-eight games.

Zoilo Versalles and Oliva solidified their MVP credentials with Killebrew sidelined and made the Twins far less dependent on the long ball. Versalles batted .335, stole 13 bases without getting caught, and scored 45 runs in those forty-eight games. The twenty-five-year-old shortstop tallied nearly a run per game from the start of August through the end of the season, a season-closing stretch in which he batted .346 and slugged .575 in fifty-nine contests. Oliva hit at a .356 clip with Killebrew out. Neither southpaws nor a week on the bench with a swollen right ring finger, suffered on a headfirst slide against the Yankees on August 24, slowed him. He had batted .394 in July, and in August his ongoing assault on AL pitching moved him into the thick of the AL batting race.

Three months earlier, Oliva's slow start had all but derailed the second-year player's chance to repeat as American League batting champion. His average had bottomed out at .227 on May 22, when he trailed Boston's Carl Yastrzemski, his primary competition for the crown down the stretch, by 77 points. Oliva finally pushed his average above .300 the last week of July and closed the month at .307, though he still trailed Yaz, the league leader at .339, by a substantial margin. The gap closed to 15 points when the first-place Twins swept a three-game weekend set from Yaz's Red Sox in early August. While the Twins suddenly had breathing room with an eight-game bulge over the second-place Orioles, the AL batting race was tightening. Twins pitching limited

Yastrzemski to a single hit in 12 at-bats, and Oliva inched closer by going 4-for-5 with two RBIS in the series finale on August 8.

Oliva's hot hitting carried into a fourteen-game road trip that included stops in New York, Cleveland, Detroit, and California. The Twins played .500 ball on the trip, which started with a 7–3 victory at Yankee Stadium on August 10. They blatantly took advantage of the ailing legs of Mickey Mantle, the Yankees slugger who had shifted from center to left field that season. Twins third base coach Billy Martin, who considered Mantle his best friend, had runners wheeling around the bases on balls hit in his former teammate's direction. Both Versalles and Hall scored from first on doubles hit to left, though Martin wasn't bragging about Twins base running after the game. "It's nothing to be proud of," said the highly competitive, former Yankees second baseman. "But I'll do it every time."

The Twins got a scare in the road trip's finale on Sunday, August 22, a 4–1 loss to 1964 Cy Young winner Dean Chance and the Angels. A first-inning pickoff throw by Chance to second base struck Oliva on the head and cracked his batting helmet. The hot-hitting right fielder left the game for precautionary X-rays. No skull fracture was found, so Oliva was able to travel home with his teammates.

Tony O fared better than Los Angeles Dodgers catcher John Roseboro on that Sunday. In a game at San Francisco's Candlestick Park featuring Sandy Koufax and Juan Marichal, two of the National League's premier pitchers, Marichal clubbed Roseboro in the head with his bat, opening a gash above his left eye. Marichal was angered because he believed Roseboro deliberately threw too close to his head when returning a pitched ball to Koufax. Marichal believed it was deliberate and later said the throw grazed his ear; years later Roseboro admitted in his 1978 autobiography, *Glory Days with the Dodgers, and Other Days with Others*, that the throw was intentional. Two days prior in this critical Los Angeles-San Francisco series between the two National League contenders, Marichal had barked at Roseboro from the Giants dugout when the catcher questioned a call by the home plate umpire.

Neil Leifer's widely viewed photograph, showing Marichal holding his bat in both hands high over his head and Roseboro on his way to the ground, took a toll on the pitcher's reputation. Yet Roseboro provoked Marichal and was ready to back it up. When Roseboro's throw whizzed by Marichal's ear, the two were at each other immediately, with San Francisco's nineteen-game winner swinging at the catcher's head several times. Marichal struck Roseboro just as Koufax reached the scene, and a fourteen-minute free-for-all broke out. Marichal was ejected and Roseboro departed with blood running down his face from the cut above his eye. Soon after, Marichal was suspended for eight game dates, or two starts, in the heat of San Francisco's pennant chase with the rival Dodgers.

Perhaps the one event generating more pandemonium that weekend took place in the Twin Cities, where the Beatles had landed on Saturday afternoon. The screaming from more than four thousand fans began upon their plane's arrival at Minneapolis-St. Paul International Airport and carried over to a press conference and concert at Metropolitan Stadium that evening. Hundreds of fans followed the group from the airport to the Met for the press event. After the usual banter between reporters and the Beatles, Ron Butwin and Randy Resnick, owners of local store B-Sharp Music, surprised George Harrison by giving him a Rickenbacker twelve-string guitar. John Lennon, standing alongside his band mate, smiled and joked, "That's fab, that! Where's mine?"

Roughly thirty thousand were on hand when the Beatles took the stage, which was set up near second base and faced home plate. Guitars, harmonies, and screams filled the air, together loud enough, according to *St. Pioneer Press* writer Ralph Ingerson, that "a Boeing passenger jet flew rather low over Metropolitan Stadium Saturday night—and nobody noticed it." The Beatles opened with "She's a Woman," and for the next thirty-five minutes of an eleven-song set, a World Series atmosphere and countless shrieks rocked the stadium. After the Beatles closed with "I'm Down," they dashed for the first base dugout and headed into the clubhouse that the road-weary Twins would return to the very next day.

On Sunday, August 22, roughly two thousand fans were at the airport to greet the Twins on their return. The crowd that greeted the Beatles on their quick stop through town the previous day was twice the size, but Twins fans put on an impressive and unprecedented display of pennant fever. By then, local newspapers were tracking the team's magic number to clinch the pennant. Twins fans, who months earlier were consumed by the wrath and aftermath of spring floods, tornadoes, and violent storms, were now caught up in anticipation of a World Series in Minnesota.

SIX

The Stretch Run

The Beatles weren't the only out-of-town visitors to capture the attention of Minnesotans that August. And
more than just pennant fever was in the air, at least
near Duluth, Minnesota. Locals began reporting UFO sightings
over the city and Lake Superior, including an August 4 touchdown of a "flying saucer" that reportedly dove into the St. Louis
River near the Interstate Bridge that crosses the lake's harbor
and connects the Minnesota city with Superior, Wisconsin. That
same day, according to noted ufologist Richard H. Hall, U.S. Air
Force and Royal Canadian Air Force radar tracked formations
of seven to ten UFOS over Lake Superior and Duluth, traveling
nine thousand miles per hour at an altitude of one to three miles
above the Earth's surface.

An overwhelming number of reported UFO sightings can be
explained as earthly phenomena, and good luck getting government confirmation on hard-to-explain airborne anomalies passing through U.S. airspace. But the alleged St. Louis River landing
was only the beginning of a rash of August UFO sightings. An
eight-year-old Duluth boy awoke to a buzzing sound on August
3. "I went to the window and saw a red ball-like thing over the
neighbor's house," Dennis Johnson told the *Duluth News Tribune*. "On the back of the red ball was a flap-like tail that was
silver and glowed." The boy, who lived on Jefferson Street, said

the object whirred as it moved to the front of his house and up toward Superior Street.

Young Dennis wasn't alone. Between midnight and 3:30 a.m. that same evening, the Associated Press reported numerous UFO sightings across the Twin Cities by more than fifty Minneapolis police and sheriff officers from both Hennepin and Ramsey counties. Sightings also were common in Rochester, where a colorful display caught the attention of locals and Chief Deputy Judd Reifsnider of the Olmsted County sheriff's office. He spotted an object flying "very fast and high and moving northward toward the Twin Cities," telling Red Wing's *Daily Republican Eagle* that it flashed red, blue, green, and white lights. John Sloan, meteorologist for the Rochester Airport Weather Bureau, also saw an object flying northward at high speed and altitude. A Sloan colleague who had been watching the sky for years said he had never seen anything like it.

On August 14, the *Duluth News Tribune* reported a host of UFO activity the night before. Several locals told a reporter that they watched a bright object flying erratically during the same one-hour span. Mrs. Joanne Johnson said she watched a moving object over her home for roughly fifteen minutes. "It wasn't moving in a straight path" before it disappeared behind cloud cover, she said. Mrs. Carol McDougall said the object was moving northwest on a downward, erratic path before disappearing behind some trees. Clarence Noel, an Air Force technical sergeant, estimated that the object was flying east to west at roughly eight hundred miles per hour, but disappeared just a few seconds after his sighting.

The phenomenon known as the Beatles seemed to pass through the area at a similar pace. On Monday, August 23, two days after the group's lone appearance in the Twin Cities, the Twins were back at the Met for their last 1965 showdown with the New York Yankees. The five-time defending American League champions, in sixth place at 63-61, could only play spoiler in the 1965 race. The 79-46 Twins took three of four from New York. In the series finale, Jim Kaat, who had gone 1-9 against the Yankees over his first five big league seasons, recorded his third 1965 win over New York by going the distance and scattering 10 hits in a 9–2 romp. The six-foot-four southpaw was at his best down the stretch. Beginning with his third win over the Yankees, Kaat went 6-1 with a 2.92 ERA and a save over the final six weeks of the season.

Zoilo Versalles shined in the New York series, collecting seven hits, tallying five runs, and drilling a home run off longtime Yankees ace Whitey Ford. Versalles victimized New York pitching all season, batting .342 and scoring 24 runs in eighteen games. His inside-the-park homer with a dazzling slide across the plate in April was a season highlight, and one of four homers he stroked against the Yankees. He made quite an impression on his New York counterpart, shortstop Tony Kubek, who called Versalles "a shoo-in for Most Valuable. . . . I don't know if he's played as well against the other clubs as he has against us. But when we've seen him, he's been fantastic."

Harmon Killebrew and Tony Oliva also excelled against the Yankees in 1965. Killebrew powered four long balls off New York hurlers and batted .366 with 11 RBIS in eleven games. Oliva hit .357 with 11 RBIS in seventeen games. During that final Yankees series, Oliva jammed his ring finger on a headfirst slide at the plate. He stayed in the game and recorded another hit, but the knuckle swelled markedly overnight. Oliva, on a .387 tear in his last seventeen games, was sidelined for the final week of August.

The Twins, coming off a 7-7 road trip, returned home for a fourteen-game home stand that carried into September. They had an opportunity to put away the other contenders, but won only half of those fourteen games at the Met. The home stand closed with a three-game weekend series facing the second-place White Sox, who had used a mid-August, ten-game winning streak to rebound from an eleven-game deficit and were 6½ games back of Minnesota with twenty-seven games remaining. There were two final Twins-White Sox matchups at Comiskey Park the following week, so these five games were Chicago's last-ditch chance to stay in the pennant race. The White Sox needed to win—if not sweep—the series in Minnesota.

The Twins claimed the September 3 opener, 6–4, as Oliva, on an 8-for-11 surge since returning from his finger injury, went 3-for-3 and drove in four runs. Kaat worked into the sixth for the win, and Johnny Klippstein and Al Worthington held the White Sox scoreless for the final 3⅔ innings. The duo received an assist from third baseman Rich Rollins, who fielded a wicked, hard-hit grounder to end the game with the tying runs in scoring position. The win sucked some of the drama from the series, though Chicago rebounded to defeat the Twins on Saturday and Sunday to stay within 5½ games.

When the two clubs gathered again in Chicago on September 8 for their final two meetings, the gap was five games with twenty-one to play. For the Twins, the series was the biggest of the season, perhaps the most important in five summers of Twins baseball. The White Sox weren't going to give the Twins any breaks, including the use of the Comiskey Park field the day before the series started. Killebrew, inching closer to a return after dislocating and fracturing his left elbow on August 2, wanted to take batting practice to loosen up the healing joint. The White Sox denied the Twins' request, sparking a Twins spokesman to complain to reporters that the White Sox simply "made excuses."

In the Wednesday night opener, White Sox right-hander John Buzhardt squared off against Mudcat Grant, who had already posted three wins and blanked the White Sox twice in 1965. The Sox scratched for two first-inning runs against Grant, but couldn't advance a runner beyond second base the rest of the way. Chicago held a 2–1 edge heading into the seventh, but after Earl Battey singled with one out, Jimmie Hall jumped on a 2-0 pitch from Buzhardt for his nineteenth home run. Protecting a 3–2 lead, Grant allowed only a walk over the final three frames to earn his eighteenth victory.

The Twins rolled to a 10–4 rout the following afternoon, sweeping Chicago to push their lead atop the American League to seven games over the White Sox and 7½ over Baltimore. The victory put the Twins firmly in the driver's seat and officially eliminated the sixth-place Yankees, but perhaps it was an omen that the biggest baseball story that day, September 9, was Dodgers ace

Sandy Koufax, who pitched a perfect game in a 1–0 victory over the Chicago Cubs at Dodger Stadium. Hard-luck losing pitcher Bob Hendley went the distance and allowed only one hit and an unearned run, but Koufax fanned fourteen Cubs and the Dodgers scored a fifth-inning run without a hit to secure his twenty-second win. The no-hitter was the fourth of his career, making him the all-time leader, surpassing Bob Feller, Cy Young, and Larry Corcoran, though Nolan Ryan passed Koufax in 1990 and retired with seven no-nos.

The reinvigorated Twins departed for Boston and swept a three-game set, finishing the year with 17 wins in eighteen games with the Red Sox. Oliva tallied six hits and drove in five runs at Fenway Park, while Carl Yastrzemski collected three hits and saw his lead in the batting race slip to just five points, .323 to .318. But the bigger story was Grant, who worked a four-hitter in the series finale, a 2–0 victory that was the right-hander's league-leading fifth shutout and nineteenth victory.

In recent weeks, reporters had begun asking Grant about winning twenty games. In fact, Grant was in line to become the first African American twenty-game winner in the American League, though that distinction largely went unnoticed at the time. When the chatter began about winning twenty games, Grant had a ready answer: "I'm not thinking about 20. All I want is the next one." After blanking Boston, Grant told *St. Paul Pioneer Press* beat writer Arno Goethel: "*Now* I'm going for 20. That's the next one."

With five straight wins after sweeping the Red Sox, the 92-54 Twins were greeted by the largest throng they had ever seen at the Minneapolis-St. Paul airport. Minnesota was nine games up on Chicago and pennant fever ran rampant in the Twin Cities. Local media began focusing on the once-unthinkable notion: a World Series in Minnesota.

The Minnesota Twins, closing in on the American League championship, were given permission to sell World Series tickets in mid-September. The pricey box seats would run twelve dollars, but sitting in the outfield was a more reasonable four dollars.

When the mail-order process began, which National League contender would be Minnesota's World Series opponent was still undecided. On Monday, September 13, an off day for the Twins after sweeping Boston, the San Francisco Giants led the Los Angeles Dodgers by 2½ games in the NL race, and the Cincinnati Reds were just 3½ back. The NL chase would go down to the season's final days.

During their early-September surge that began with sweeps in Chicago and Boston, the Twins celebrated the return of Camilo Pascual, less than six weeks following surgery to repair the knot of muscles behind his throwing shoulder. Although he was nowhere near 100-percent healthy, he was sharp in the middle game of the Boston series, pitching into the eighth for his first win in more than three months. Pascual was 8-0 a week into June, but his troublesome shoulder had stalled his ninth victory until September 11.

The Twins returned home to damp, cold weather that canceled Grant's first crack at 20 wins. They had beaten the Kansas City Athletics twice under soggy conditions before the rainout, extending their winning streak to seven games and opening a ten-game lead over the Orioles, who had taken over second place. Washington halted the winning streak on September 17, though Pascual was even better in the 2–1 loss to the Senators than he had been in his previous outing against Boston. He allowed just five hits and fanned 13 over nine innings, but the Twins lost in the tenth.

Although Jim Merritt took the loss in relief—on a two-out RBI single by pinch hitter Don Lock—the rookie southpaw bolstered a battle-weary bullpen and had saved two games during the winning streak. Both Al Worthington and Johnny Klippstein had been phenomenal all season, collecting 18 wins and 23 saves between them to that point. But they had handled heavy loads, and Worthington was trying to tough out a sore elbow, making Merritt's presence that much more valuable. Remarkably, both Klippstein, age thirty-seven, and Worthington, thirty-six, had defied typical player development and come into their own after turning thirty.

Klippstein had been pitching professionally for twenty years when Calvin Griffith purchased his contract from Philadelphia in June 1964. A mediocre swingman for the Cubs and Reds throughout the 1950s, he became a full-time reliever for the Dodgers in 1958 and worked two scoreless innings in the 1959 World Series. The lanky right-hander was at his best for Philadelphia in 1963, posting a career-low 1.93 ERA over 112 innings. Less effective for the fast-starting Phillies in 1964, he joined Minnesota that June and posted a 1.97 ERA for the Twins. The following spring, Johnny Sain tweaked Klippstein's curveball, a critical pitch that the righty used masterfully during the championship run. Klippstein didn't allow a run after July 27—a span of 23⅔ innings—and finished 9-3 with a 2.24 ERA and five saves.

Worthington was equally critical to the 1965 club after Griffith picked up his contract from the Reds three days before acquiring Klippstein. Eleven years earlier, in 1953, Worthington had made his big league debut with the New York Giants by tossing consecutive shutouts over the Phillies and Dodgers, but never was consistently effective. The Alabama native credits a religious awakening in 1958 with getting his life and career on track.

As a thirty-one-year-old reliever for the Chicago White Sox in 1960, Worthington learned that the team had a man with binoculars stationed inside the Comiskey Park scoreboard, stealing the opposing catcher's signs and relaying the pitch selection to Chicago batters by blinking lights on the scoreboard. He was fine with teams trying to steal signs on the field, but what the White Sox were doing was an affront to his Christian faith. He confronted White Sox manager Al López about the practice, but his plea fell on deaf ears. He fared no better with general manager Hank Greenberg, a recent Hall of Fame inductee, and White Sox owner Bill Veeck. Worthington felt forced to make a difficult career decision. "I had to leave the White Sox because they cheated," recalls Worthington. "You don't lie, steal and cheat when you become a Christian. And here I am a Christian and I'm playing on a team that's cheating. I couldn't do that. I was told I would never get back to the big leagues for what I did."

Worthington languished in the Minors for a few years before the Reds acquired him after a strong Triple-A performance in 1962. He was effective in 1963, posting a 2.99 ERA as a reliever, but struggled the following spring and landed in Minnesota. Like Klippstein, Worthington was instantly successful in a Twins uniform, recording a 1.37 ERA in 1964. As the primary ninth-inning guy in 1965, he won ten games, saved twenty-one, and posted a 2.13 ERA. "Klippstein and Worthington did a beautiful job," says Oliva. "Sometimes they went two or three innings— not like today, when you only pitch an inning."

The Twins lineup took another hit on September 14, when Oliva felt something pull behind his right knee while running out a ground ball and stretching for the first base bag in a win over the Athletics. He already had a floating bone chip in the knee, which occasionally caused it to lock up. Add the strained tendon and his pursuit of a second straight batting title suddenly seemed on life support, yet Oliva was intent on playing with the pennant race approaching its climax. He singled to drive in a first-inning run against Kansas City the following evening, but then his knee forced him to the bench.

Oliva's RBI single bumped his average to .318, with Carl Yas-trzemski at .322, but Oliva wondered if his reign as the AL batting champ was coming to end. He would be playing hurt and might not play every day. He wasn't the only Twin getting a day off the following afternoon, however, as rain washed out Grant's first bid for 20 wins. Even with the rainout at the Met, Tony O pulled within a point of Yaz after the league leader went hitless against Cleveland's Luis Tiant. Oliva would manage only two plate appearances over the next six days.

On Sunday, September 19, the Twins dropped their magic number to clinch the pennant—the sum of Twins wins and losses by the second-place team—to just three, with an 8–1 cakewalk over Washington. Oliva, planted in the dugout, took over the AL batting lead from Yastrzemski. He had trailed Yaz by 65 points barely more than two months earlier on July 9, but when the Boston outfielder went hitless that afternoon, he was two points ahead of Yaz at .317.

Oliva never relinquished the lead. He found his stroke immediately when he returned against Baltimore on September 21,
going 3-for-4 in a 6–4 loss. Although he was unable to play every
day, he went 8-for-18 (.444) the rest of the way. Oliva, who batted .374 from July 1 through the end of the season, closed at .321.
Once the Twins clinched, however, he rested his ailing right
knee for the final five games. When Oliva went to the bench,
Yastrzemski trailed by six points and immediately went 0-for-
10 to finish at .312, nine points behind Oliva.

On September 20, the day after Oliva took over the AL batting lead, the Twins were beaten soundly by the last-place Athletics, 8–2, in a makeup of their recent rainout. Appropriately, the
Monday showdown between a Catfish and a Mudcat took place
on a wet, drizzly afternoon that was more suitable to marine
life. Just 537 fans, the smallest crowd in Twins history, saw Catfish Hunter and Kansas City's bats deny Grant's second bid for
his twentieth win.

With the Twins hosting the Orioles for two games before
going on a weeklong road trip, they were still positioned to clinch
the pennant at the Met. But they dropped both games in cold,
damp weather that drew small crowds. The hearty but water-
logged locals weren't rewarded for braving the elements, so the
Twins were off to Washington, their original home, looking to
claim the franchise's first pennant in thirty-two years in front
of the fan base they had left behind.

Harmon Killebrew had returned to action during the Orioles
series. That meant both he and Pascual, the franchise player
and pitcher when the original Senators left town, would be on
the field in Washington if the Twins were to clinch. Owner Calvin Griffith, however, couldn't travel to Washington. Injunc-
tions filed against him when he moved the team to Minnesota
would have forced a lengthy stay in the nation's capital had he
even stepped foot into the District, so he stayed in Minnesota
and tracked his team's progress from his Metropolitan Stadium
office. Still, it was an exciting time for the Griffith family, which
had owned the franchise since former big league pitcher and
manager Clark Griffith bought it in 1920. The franchise's best

years had come in the 1920s and '30s, and the 1960s renaissance followed nearly three decades of futility in Washington.

The September rains that hovered over the Twins at home followed them across the country and washed out Friday night's game. A Saturday afternoon doubleheader starting at 12:15 p.m. was scheduled, and independent Twin Cities station WTCN-TV, Channel 11, picked up the twin bill with the pennant-clincher a mathematical possibility. ABC also carried the first game, with Grant facing twenty-six-year-old left-hander Frank Kreutzer, as its "Game of the Week."

When they arrived at Griffith Stadium on Friday, the Twins discovered that ABC had mounted cameras in the visitor's clubhouse in anticipation of a Friday night clinching. They had enjoyed a steady growth of national attention over the summer, but mounted cameras in the clubhouse were new to the soon-to-be AL champions. While the club waited out Friday night's monsoon, the cameras inspired some witty exchanges. "We weren't supposed to mention it," piped in one Twin, "but they're really getting ready to do *This is Your Life, Shorty Pleis*," spoofing the NBC television show of *nearly* the same name. Another teammate referenced a game show and Zoilo Versalles bidding up his spring training fine to $300 with manager Sam Mele. "I'll bet they're putting Zoilo on *What's My Fine?*"

The kidding ended when Grant took the hill for the first of two on Saturday. After Washington's Don Blasingame doubled in the third inning, Grant mowed down the Senators without allowing another hit. Only one base runner reached third base in one of his premier performances of the year, and Grant retired the last fourteen Senators in a 5–0 victory, securing his twentieth win and league-leading sixth shutout.

In the second game, the Senators scored three times in the second inning off Pascual, but Don Mincher's twenty-second homer closed the gap to 3–2 in the seventh. Then a quartet of Twins rookies took over. Sandy Valdespino ignited an eighth-inning rally with a one-out single and scored on pinch hitter Joe Nossek's game-tying double. With two outs, Frank Quilici delivered a bases-loaded single that scored two runs and put the

Twins in front, 5–3. And Jim Merritt held Washington scoreless over the final three frames to get the win.

The Twins still had a chance to clinch on Saturday if second-place Baltimore lost either game of its doubleheader with the Angels. The ABC cameras were poised and the champagne was chilled. Soon after the victorious Twins reached the clubhouse came news that the Orioles had won the first game, 2–1, on Jerry Adair's RBI single in the bottom of the ninth.

The anxious Twins faced a decision. Traveling secretary Howard Fox pulled the players aside, away from the waiting TV cameras and the press of reporters in the clubhouse. "It's up to you," he explained. "Do you want to wait here, so they can get the celebration on TV and radio, in case the Orioles lose the second game? Or do you want to move the party—if there is a party—to the hotel?"

"Bring on the champagne and we'll bluff it," retorted Earl Battey, always primed with a witty quip. "Guess we might just as well stay right here," offered Grant, not sounding altogether sold on the idea, but a low murmur of approval seemed to make it the team's first choice. "How's this?" chimed in Battey again. "Why don't we stay right here and I'm sure the club will pick up the tab for a carton of sandwiches or a couple of buckets of chicken."

"We'll do whatever you want," replied Fox. So, while a few Twins left and promised to return if Baltimore lost, most of the team hung out in the clubhouse. Card games broke out and players sipped on beer, awaiting word on the second Orioles-Angels contest. "I guess you drink beer on a title tie, then switch to champagne when you win it," noted Killebrew. The move to bubbly would have to wait until Sunday, as Orioles right-hander Milt Pappas took a no-hitter into the seventh inning and limited the Angels to three hits in a 2–0 win.

The 98-58 Twins were one win from a trip to the World Series heading into the September 26 series finale in Washington. The starters, lefties Jim Kaat and Pete Richert, went the distance in a classic pitchers' duel. Oliva's first-inning single was the only hit allowed by Richert through the first five innings. By then the Senators had scratched for an unearned run and a

1–0 lead. Leading off the sixth, Versalles drove a liner into the left-center-field gap and motored around the bases with a triple. With Nossek at the plate, Richert fired a low pitch that escaped Don Zimmer, a lifelong infielder filling in at catcher at the end of his career. The ball trickled no more than ten feet from the plate, but without hesitation Versalles tore down the line and slid under Zimmer's underhanded flip to Richert.

The game was still 1–1 when Quilici slashed a double past Senators third baseman Ken McMullen leading off the eighth. Richert retired Kaat, but not before Quilici advanced to third on a wild pitch that sailed past Zimmer. Versalles, on a 2-2 pitch, lifted a fly to strong-armed Don Lock in center field. Lock played the ball well, moving toward the plate and rifling a good throw, but Quilici was off and running and beat the ball home. Versalles had scored the tying run and driven home the go-ahead run. Despite collecting just three hits, the Twins now led 2–1.

Richert put the Twins down in order in the ninth to wrap up a three-hitter. Kaat, who had scattered eight singles and fanned eight to that point, popped out of the dugout to pitch the final three outs. The workman-like lefty induced Lock to fly to right field for the first out. Then he fanned first baseman Dick Nen on three pitches, though the third strike eluded Battey, who made a snap throw to Mincher at first to record the second out.

Next up was the thirty-four-year-old Zimmer, in the final days of a twelve-year career highlighted by World Series titles with the 1955 and 1959 Dodgers. He swung at and missed Kaat's first pitch and took strike two before fouling off the Kaat's third offering. Down 0–2, Zimmer started to swing at the next pitch and then checked it. When home plate umpire John Flaherty called Zimmer out before the veteran could turn around to see the call, the Twins had clinched the American League pennant— the franchise's first in Minnesota.

The Twins headed for their clubhouse, where Oliva uncorked the first bottle of champagne and soon the beverage of choice for baseball celebrations was everywhere. The youthful Twins demonstrated their exuberance. Two rookies, Valdespino and Quilici, administered a champagne shampoo and shower to Twins skipper Sam Mele. When Grant poured freely over the head of third base coach Billy Martin, the former Yankee who had been part of six such clinchings with New York took notice. "This is one of the wildest celebrations I've seen," he said.

Ray Scott and Frank Buetel were in the clubhouse covering the celebration for WTCN-TV. By the time Scott had Killebrew on camera with a microphone, both men, light on hair atop their heads, had been drenched in bubbly. Killebrew's first act was to run his hand across Scott's wet dome as he asked, "Is this not good for your hair, Ray?" To which the longtime Twins broadcaster replied: "If it is, you and I are going to have a new crop." Seconds later, Oliva and Valdespino descended on Killebrew, each with a bottle of champagne turned upside down on the Twins slugger.

Several Twins regulars and starting pitchers followed Killebrew to the dais. While Pascual was chatting with Scott, Grant approached and awarded the broadcaster a turkey leg from the pennant-clinching feast for his "fine announcing," as Pascual and César Tovar stood by laughing. "Don't say I never give you nothing," Grant concluded, laughing as he strolled away.

Battey walked through the clubhouse with a towel wrapped around his head in the way a woman wore a scarf, though it hadn't kept him dry. Perhaps no Twin was wetter than Mincher, who looked as if he had just stepped out of a shower when he talked on camera with Buetel. Jerry Zimmerman followed Mincher. When Buetel asked the catcher about the clincher, Zimmerman, in his deadpan manner, asked, "Who won the game?"

A few minutes later, Grant appeared on camera with shaving cream piled high on his head. Versalles stepped up to Grant as if he were a woman, took his hands, and the two waltzed across the clubhouse floor to the delight of teammates. When Grant stepped on the dais with his shave-cream do, Buetel asked him, "How are you doing, madam?" Grant responded: "How are you doin', doll?" Staying in character, Grant cooed that he was "just messin' around with the fellas." As Buetel asked Grant about his dancing, several Twins dipped into Mudcat's do and lathered Buetel's head and face. Soon every Twin seemed to have shave

cream smeared on his face. After witnessing the wild celebration in the clubhouse, Martin had a final word as the team bus
pulled away from DC Stadium and headed for the Twins' hotel:
"Workout at 9:00 in the morning! And don't forget the curfew
tonight!" Martin, of course, was kidding.

The Twins took three of their final five games to finish with
a franchise-record 102 wins and a seven-game bulge over the
Chicago White Sox. The club had been transformed. After leading the league in home runs the two previous seasons, the 1965
Twins stroked 71 fewer homers than the year before. But they
also stole 92 bases, more than their 1963 and 1964 totals combined. During the first four years of Minnesota baseball, only
the Boston Red Sox stole fewer bases than the Twins in the AL,
but with Martin manning the third base coaching box, the 1965
club ranked fourth in the league in steals.

Versalles, who set a career high in 1965 with 27 stolen bases, is
often assailed as a poor choice for the MVP Award. But he led the
circuit in runs, doubles, triples, and total bases—and it's unlikely
the Twins could have won the pennant without him. Consistently
stretching singles into doubles and doubles into triples, Versalles
easily led the league in runs with 126. The only other AL player to
reach the century mark in runs was Oliva, with 107. Oliva's torrid second-half performance put him in the mix for MVP honors with his good friend Versalles. Despite a dreadful start, Oliva
closed the season with 185 hits, most among AL hitters, and finished third in the league with 98 RBIS. In the AL, only Cleveland's
Rocky Colavito (108) and Detroit's Willie Horton (104) had more.

Twin Cities newspapers speculated which Cuban would be
named the American League's Most Valuable Player. Oliva was
MVP-worthy for the last four months of the season, particularly
when Killebrew went down in August, but Versalles was on top
of his game nearly all year. At one point that summer Oliva was
quoted saying, "Let Zoilo have the Most Valuable Player Award.
I'll settle for the batting title and the pennant." Oliva's touch of
prescience was on the money, and now, as the days were growing shorter and turning cooler, the Twins turned their attention
to winning the World Series.

SEVEN

Beating the Best

As the Twins celebrated their first American League pennant on September 26, the Los Angeles Dodgers and San Francisco Giants were tied atop the National League. Heading into the final week, the Cincinnati Reds, in need of a miracle finish, were three games behind the coleaders. Ten days earlier the Giants seemed destined to face the Twins in the World Series. They had beaten the Houston Astros for their fourteenth straight win, generating a 4½-game bulge over both the Dodgers and Reds. On the same day, however, Los Angeles kicked off its own thirteen-game winning streak and closed with a 15-1 flourish to claim the pennant by two games.

The Dodgers pulled even with San Francisco on Sunday, September 26, when Dodgers right-hander Don Drysdale pitched a 1–0 shutout over the St. Louis Cardinals, just hours after the Twins defeated Washington to claim the AL crown. The Reds had whipped the Giants twice that weekend, sticking their rival with consecutive losses for the first time all month. Suddenly the tide turned, as the Giants dropped six of eight.

It didn't matter that Los Angeles had scored fewer runs in 1965 than every National League club except the Mets and Astros, the two fledgling franchises that had lost ninety-five-plus games in each of their first four seasons. Nor that the Dodgers batted just .245 as a team, the all-time lowest regular-season batting average by an NL champion in the modern era. This Los Angeles pitching staff could carry the team and sustain a lengthy winning streak. En route to a Major League-low 2.81 ERA in '65, it was at its best during the club's 15-1 finish, allowing just 17 runs and tossing eight shutouts. The stretch run was an impressive tune-up for the World Series.

Beginning with his perfect game against the Chicago Cubs on September 9, Dodgers ace Sandy Koufax tossed three shutouts in his final five regular-season starts. The only run he allowed in his final three outings came on the season's penultimate day, when the southpaw fanned thirteen Milwaukee Braves in a 3–1 victory to clinch the NL flag. The clincher was an appropriate finish to a remarkable season. Despite the onset of painful arthritis in his throwing elbow, Koufax went 26-8, posted a big league-low 2.04 ERA, and struck out a record 382 batters in 335⅔ innings. Koufax, whose strikeout mark has since been broken by Nolan Ryan (383 in 1973), won his second of three Cy Young awards.

Drysdale fired shutouts in his final two starts and finished 23-12 with a 2.77 ERA. He and Koufax combined for 49 victories and 15 shutouts. The duo made it easy to overlook third starter Claude Osteen, a lefty who was just 15-15 despite a 2.79 ERA that ranked tenth in the league. He gave up only five earned runs over his last five starts.

Going into the Fall Classic, history might have been on the side of the Dodgers, who had already appeared in eight post-war World Series. They had won their last two, including a four-game sweep of New York in 1963. With Koufax and Drysdale likely to start at least five of seven possible games, the Dodgers were favored in many circles.

In the days leading up to Game One at Metropolitan Stadium, Dodgers president Walter O'Malley noted that the Twins showed little resemblance to the dethroned New York Yankees. "We'll be facing the most unusual American League champion in our World Series history," O'Malley told *Minneapolis Tribune* writer Dwayne Netland. "The Twins aren't merely a power club. They're a running team, too, with good pitching and a strong defense. They are actually more like a National League team."

Not surprisingly, the 1965 World Series was widely viewed as a classic matchup of Twins hitting versus Dodgers pitching. Pushing across runs was a challenge for the Dodgers, who had stroked a Major League-low 78 homers and struggled all summer to make up for a substantial loss in run production. Prior to the season, general manager Buzzie Bavasi had dealt slugger Frank Howard to Washington to acquire Osteen. In 1964, Howard had led the Dodgers by a large margin with 24 homers. To make matters worse, the Dodgers lost a middle-of-the-order hitter on May 1, when left fielder Tommy Davis suffered a broken ankle and was lost for the season.

Second baseman Jim Lefebvre, an offensive catalyst who won NL Rookie of the Year honors, and outfielder Lou Johnson, Davis's fill-in in left, shared the team lead with 12 home runs. Right fielder Ron Fairly topped the Dodgers with 70 RBIs, while the Twins had five players with more: Tony Oliva (98), Jimmie Hall (86), Bob Allison (78), Zoilo Versalles (77), and Harmon Killebrew (75), who played in only 113 games.

Other than Koufax and Drysdale, the only Dodger with flashy numbers was leadoff man Maury Wills, who easily led the Majors with 94 stolen bases. The speedy, switch-hitting shortstop, who turned thirty-three four days prior to Game One, had set the modern-day record for steals with 104 in 1962. Although he was beginning to show the wear and tear of his base-running exploits, he remained a key cog in the Dodgers offense, tallying 92 runs in '65.

Catcher Earl Battey and Twins hurlers would have to contend with Wills when the World Series got underway on Wednesday, October 6, but Twins hitters wouldn't have to face Koufax, the anticipated Game One starter. The opener was scheduled on Yom Kippur, the holiest day of the Jewish calendar, and Koufax chose to observe the solemn holiday and pitch Thursday's Game Two. He wasn't known to be particularly observant, but his decision resonated with the Jewish community—and still does today.

"I believe he was thinking, 'I'm going to pitch the next day. What's the big deal? We have Don Drysdale starting,'" Jane Leavy, author of *Sandy Koufax: A Lefty's Legacy*, told *Sports Illustrated* in 2002. "And, in a way, that makes it even sweeter. Yom Kippur is a day of sacrifice. . . . And here's Koufax, who's doing this reflexively not out of his own great belief, but really more in deference to others. So it was a much greater sacrifice on his part. For a more religious man it might have been a no-brainer. For Koufax, it was the right thing to do."

Drysdale drew the Game One assignment against Mudcat Grant. Facing Drysdale was no picnic. Largely a two-pitch pitcher—an electric fastball and sharp-breaking curve—he made life miserable for hitters when he changed arm slots. Right-handed batters hated to see the six-foot-five Drysdale bring heat from a sidearm motion.

Manager Sam Mele surprised with a pair of lineup changes before the opener. Even with two of the game's best pitchers starting for the Dodgers, Mele chose to platoon a pair of rookies in his outfield. Bob Allison had struggled mightily after returning from his fractured wrist in mid-July, particularly against right-handed pitching, so the skipper had him share left field with left-handed-hitting Sandy Valdespino. The twenty-six-year-old rookie from Cuba, coming off a breakout Triple-A season a year earlier, was a solid defender who had contributed to the 1965 club as a pinch hitter and part-timer. Teammates were taken with Valdespino's ready smile. He was quick to laugh, and Joe Garagiola, who teamed with By Saam on NBC Radio's coverage of the World Series, commented how upbeat and loose Valdespino was before the start of Game One. The rookie was up to the assignment, going 3-for-11 in the World Series and delivering hits off both Drysdale and Koufax.

Jimmie Hall had had a stellar first half and a productive year as the primary center fielder, though he slumped over the final seven weeks and didn't hit lefties well all season. Mele turned to right-handed-hitting Joe Nossek in the five games that lefties Koufax and Osteen pitched. The twenty-four-year-old rookie, who hadn't done much to distinguish himself against southpaws during the season, went 4-for-20 in the Series. Facing an elite Dodgers pitching staff, the two rookies together were as productive as the veterans with whom they shared playing time.

The World Series opened on a windy, overcast day, though the sun came out two hours before the sellout crowd settled into their seats. With the sun shining on a full house, and red-white-and-blue bunting adorning the facades of each deck, Metropolitan Stadium never looked better. It had opened with a capacity of eighteen thousand for the Minor League Minneapolis Millers in 1956, and through various expansions, the park had taken on a mish-mash look. The bleachers in left and right field were mismatched, and then there were those folding chairs that made up the seating along the left-field line. For the 1965 season, the Minnesota Vikings replaced the old bleachers in left field with a double-decked grandstand, which increased the capacity to roughly forty-eight thousand. And with all decks filled for its first World Series game, the Met looked majestic.

Twins broadcaster Ray Scott and Dodgers legend Vin Scully covered the game for NBC television on a beautiful fall day. The wind was blowing out to left-center, making the power alley a dangerous place for pitchers. Los Angeles struck first—in atypical fashion. Fairly, playing with a painful bone bruise on his hand, opened the second inning by drilling a 3-2 pitch from Grant into the right-field seats.

Minnesota was quick to respond. After the first five batters had failed to hit the ball out of the infield off Drysdale, Don Mincher, in his first World Series at-bat, lofted a 1-1 breaking ball deep into the seats in right to tie the game. Like Valdespino, Mincher was in good humor before the first pitch. The slugging first baseman had approached a reporter and asked: "Who says you get nervous before a game like this?" The reporter looked up to see a burning cigarette sticking out of Mincher's left ear.

The Twins broke through in the third, roughing up Drysdale for six hits and six runs. Frank Quilici kicked off the rally by driving a two-strike pitch over third base for a leadoff double. Garagiola had talked to Quilici before the game. "My pop is in the stands and he's going to see me in the World Series. What more could I ask for?" Quilici had told him. The twenty-six-year-old rookie put his name in the record book that afternoon. Soon after his leadoff double, he tied a World Series record with his second hit of the *inning*: a run-scoring single to right to make it 7–1 and end Drysdale's outing.

The big blast of the Twins' third, though, was Zoilo Versalles's three-run homer. After Quilici doubled, the game turned for Drysdale. Grant, trying to bunt Quilici to third, reached when Drysdale slipped and fell while fielding the slow roller. Even planted on his backside, he made a good one-hop throw to Lefebvre at first base. Umpire Tony Venzon had already thrust his thumb skyward, but reversed his call when the second baseman juggled the ball. Seconds later, Versalles turned on an inside fastball and put the Twins up for good. Valdespino lined Drysdale's next pitch into the right-field corner to ignite another three-run surge. Battey delivered a two-run single before Quilici collected his second hit to score Mincher.

The Twins claimed a convincing 8–2 victory with Grant going the distance and scattering 10 hits. In the clubhouses after the game, sportswriters took up the question whether the two starting pitchers were throwing spitballs. Drysdale had a reputation for throwing wet ones, but the press asked both hurlers. Initially Grant downplayed the idea that he was using the pitch, but when questions persisted, he laughed and said, "I'm not going to say I don't throw a spitter. I wiped it off every time today."

A few Twins, including Mele, believed Drysdale threw a wet pitch to Tony Oliva. An unidentified retired Major Leaguer attending the game told reporters he thought the Dodgers right-hander had struck out Killebrew with a doctored pitch. If that was the case, Drysdale wouldn't admit to it. "All I can say," he told writers, "is if I was using a spitter, it wasn't getting by them any better than the other pitches I threw. They kicked the daylights out of me."

Soon after the Twins had secured the opener, the skies opened and rain deluged the Twin Cities. The rain persisted into the morning, so conditions were far from ideal for Thursday's Game Two. Excited Twins fans had endured a year of weather like no other in memory, so a little precipitation wasn't going to spoil their celebratory mood.

It wasn't a good day to pitch, as Jim Kaat explained to Bob Showers, author of *The Twins at the Met*: "I was warming up in the bullpen before Game Two, and it was a cold, misty, overcast day. Sandy Koufax was also warming up, and the bullpens were so close that I could hear Koufax say, 'Man, you guys play in this weather?' I had never seen Koufax pitch in person, and after seeing him throw in the bullpen I thought, 'This may be the best chance we've got, playing in bad weather.'"

Preparing the field required extreme measures. The outfield was a soggy mess, so Calvin Griffith had two helicopters on site before the game, hovering over the outfield grass to dry the wet spots. The weather was touch and go all day. Unlike the day before, the sky remained overcast and fans endured a steady wind and occasional drizzle, but the tarp was removed from the infield grass minutes before the start time and the game got underway.

The left-handers worked a scoreless duel through the early innings. No batter reached before Kaat issued a leadoff walk to Dodgers first baseman Wes Parker to open the third, and the first hit of the game was Nossek's one-out single off Koufax in the fourth. Nossek moved to third on Killebrew's two-out single, but Battey fouled out to Parker to end the Twins' first threat.

The Dodgers waged *their* first scoring threat in the fifth, when Fairly laced a leadoff single to right field for his team's first hit. Lefebvre drilled a liner down the left-field line that began to tail away from left fielder Allison. It was going to land in fair territory and had "extra-base hit" written all over it, but the hard-charging Allison robbed him with a diving catch, snagging the ball a foot off the ground with a backhanded stab before sliding into foul territory on his right hip. He came out of his long slide holding his glove high to show he had the ball.

"I knew it was drifting away from me," the former University of Kansas fullback said after the game. "Even so, I thought I had a good chance of getting to it." This wasn't readily apparent to the Met crowd, but the athletic, six-foot-four, 220-pound Allison came up with the ball in less-than-ideal field conditions. Fairly, who had rounded second base and was a good bet to score had the ball dropped, scampered back to first.

The importance of Allison's defensive gem was apparent moments later when Parker stroked a single that deflected off the outstretched glove of first baseman Mincher into right field. If not for the catch, the Dodgers might have had a lead with two runners aboard and no out, but instead had to settle for Parker on first and Fairly on second with one away in a still-scoreless game. That's where the base runners stayed. Kaat, successfully locating his pitches and flashing a lively curve, induced a pair of foul pops to kill the rally. The catch loomed large. Considering Koufax had allowed just a single run over his previous thirty-one innings—and had fanned six Twins through four frames—not falling behind the Dodgers was a boost to the home team. The Dodgers ace was capable of making a single run stand up through nine innings, which wouldn't happen in Game Two.

The Twins rallied in the sixth when Versalles, leading off the inning, drilled a hard-hit two-hopper that caromed off third baseman Jim Gilliam's body into short left field. The speedy shortstop, off and running on contact, never broke stride as he rounded first and slid safely into second. After Nossek bunted Versalles to third, Oliva had an ideal opportunity to push across a run against Koufax. Oliva had gone hitless in his first six World Series at-bats and quickly fell behind after he swung at two explosive fastballs and came up empty.

With a 2-2 count, Tony O hit a Koufax fastball off the end of his bat into the left-field corner. He had noticed left fielder Lou Johnson was playing him deep, so like Versalles, he had second base in mind when the ball cleared the infield. Oliva, still bothered by the strained tendon he suffered in September, sprinted hard and beat Johnson's throw for a run-scoring double. The Twins were up 1–0. Then Killebrew jumped on Koufax's next pitch and drove it into left field to score Oliva, making it 2–0. Battey followed with another first-pitch single to left, prompting a trip to the mound by Dodgers skipper Walt Alston. For once maybe Koufax's heavy workload and tender elbow were trumping his will to excel in big games. With relievers Ron Perranoski and Stan Williams warming up, Alston could have pulled his ace but returned to the dugout alone. Koufax quickly retired Allison and Mincher to end the threat.

The Dodgers cut the lead in half in the seventh on John Roseboro's RBI single, but Minnesota tacked on another run in their half of the inning and Kaat singled home the game's two final runs in the eighth to put the Twins up 5–1. After Kaat snuffed out a ninth-inning threat by snaring a hard liner hit back through the box by pinch hitter Dick Tracewski, he walked off with ball in hand and the Twins had a two-game lead in the Series.

Kaat, who seldom overpowered hitters and depended on his control and finesse, kept hitters off balance and executed big pitches. Several Dodgers concurred. "We've got left-handers in our league who are faster, like Koufax, Bob Veale and Chris Short," Willie Davis told writers as he and his teammates packed for their trip home to Los Angeles. "But you can't ask a man to pitch much better in a World Series game than Kaat did."

Koufax admitted he struggled with location at times. He credited Oliva with hitting a good fastball, but said he intended to throw high in the strike zone on the pitches Killebrew and Battey hit, but came in low in the zone and served up hittable offerings. Kaat topped Koufax on this day, though years later, Kaat downplayed the notion that his counterpart had an off day. "We barely did hit him," Kaat told *St. Paul Pioneer Press* columnist Charley Walters at the fiftieth anniversary celebration of the 1965 club at Target Field. "We scratched out two runs . . . one of them was earned. And that was the only (earned) run we got off him in three games."

EIGHT

Too Much Koufax, Not Enough Contact

The Twins were off to sunny California. After pulling off the unthinkable, beating Don Drysdale and Sandy Koufax in the first two games of the World Series, Twins hitters faced the challenge of generating offense against the pitching-rich Dodgers at pitcher-friendly Dodger Stadium. Runs were hard to come by and the ball didn't carry well in Chavez Ravine. The Twins were well aware of that, as Dodger Stadium had been home to the expansion Los Angeles Angels the previous four seasons. Plus, the mound was widely believed to be at least a few inches higher than the era's maximum height of fifteen inches. Tony Oliva said pitchers appeared to be throwing from a mountaintop. Pitching at home and on its game, the Los Angeles rotation picked apart the Twins lineup with a surgeon's precision.

For Game Three, comedian Milton Berle and actor David Jansen, who starred in the original television version of *The Fugitive*, were seated in premium seats alongside the Minnesota dugout. Berle, who got his start in the glory days of radio and became one of television's first personalities, posed for a photograph with skipper Sam Mele prior to the game. Singer-actress Doris Day—a rumored paramour of Maury Wills—sat in the next box over from Uncle Miltie, as Berle was known. Mudcat Grant took time out to meet her. Day, sporting sunglasses, posed with Grant along the railing for a photograph that appeared in the *New York Times.*

While the stars were out, the sun was in hiding; Game Three was played on an uncharacteristically hazy, smoggy day in Los Angeles. With the Twins up two games, Mele decided to pitch Camilo Pascual. The thirty-one-year-old righty, in his twelfth Major League season with the franchise, had pitched for some of its worst teams in Washington before the move to Minnesota. He had been the team's best pitcher for most of his career, which made Pascual the manager's sentimental favorite to work Game Three. The curveball specialist had made a remarkable recovery following August surgery, but wasn't at his best and often lacked his biting signature pitch. Jim Perry and rookie Jim Merritt were Game Three options, but Pascual got the nod—his only World Series appearance in eighteen big league seasons.

The Dodgers turned to Claude Osteen. The five-foot-eleven, 160-pound left-hander was far less imposing than the two flame-throwers, the six-foot-five Drysdale and the six-foot-two Koufax. Osteen needed to keep the ball down in the strike zone consistently to be effective, and the Twins knew how successful he could be doing that. Osteen had made six starts against them pitching for Washington, going 4-0 with a 2.74 ERA.

In Saturday's Game Three, Osteen was at his best. He moved the ball around low in the zone, causing Twins hitters to repeatedly chop pitches into the Dodger Stadium turf. They managed just five hits and only once collected two in the same inning of a 4–0 loss, but perhaps the game might have played out differently if not for a botched opportunity in the opening frame.

Game Three started well for the Twins when Zoilo Versalles lined Osteen's first pitch to deep left. The ball sailed over the head of left fielder Lou Johnson and bounced into the seats for a ground-rule double. After Versalles moved to third on a groundout, the Twins had two chances to score. Oliva hit a soft grounder for the second out before Harmon Killebrew drew a walk to put two runners aboard for Earl Battey.

When Battey started 2–0 against Osteen, Sam Mele gambled on a hit-and-run play. Battey missed the sign, however, and Killebrew, off and running, was a sitting duck. Dodgers catcher John Roseboro rifled a throw to Maury Wills at second base with Killebrew still off in the distance. The Twins slugger stopped dead in his tracks to induce a rundown that might bring home Versalles, who immediately dashed for the plate. But Versalles became trapped before he was tagged out by third baseman Jim Gilliam while sliding back into third.

The Dodgers struck for three runs in five innings off Pascual, who admitted later that he was too dependent on his fastball because he lacked his trademark curve. The Twins were down 4–0 when Oliva led off the ninth with a single to center. After Killebrew flew out, the game ended in appropriate fashion, as Osteen coaxed a double-play grounder from catcher Jerry Zimmerman. Eighteen of Minnesota's 27 outs were recorded on the ground. After the game, Osteen said his first pitch of the day, which Versalles drilled over Lou Johnson's head for a double, was his worst of the game. It was downhill from there for the Twins.

It had been a difficult day all around. Zimmerman was called into action when Battey suffered a frightening injury in the seventh inning. When Dodgers center fielder Willie Davis lofted a foul pop near the Twins dugout on the first base side, Battey and first baseman Don Mincher dashed toward the wall in pursuit. Only Battey was close enough to make a play on the ball. While tracking its flight, he slid to his knees as he approached the wall. His slide ended abruptly when his throat struck the metal rail atop the wall. With the help of teammates, Battey left the field with a severely bruised neck.

Battey was unable to speak the next day—and swallowing was difficult—but he was back on the field for Game Four. The discomfort was a constant throughout the Series, but Battey thwarted the Dodgers' attempt to capitalize on his injury by throwing out five of eleven base runners attempting to steal bases in the final four games. Battey, who later said the neck injury was difficult to recover from and hastened his retirement, checked into a hospital for treatment only after the World Series ended.

In Game Four, Drysdale was in top form in his second matchup with Mudcat Grant. After failing to last three innings in the opener, Drysdale allowed just four hits and struck out 11 in a 7–2 complete-game victory. The Dodgers' speed, which hadn't played a significant role in the first three games, was critical to tying the Series. On the Dodgers' first at-bat, Maury Wills chopped a pitch in the direction of Mincher at first. Grant hesitated on his way to covering the bag, thinking Mincher would win a foot race with the speedy shortstop; at the same time Mincher pivoted to make a throw to Grant. The pitcher resumed running, but Wills beat him to the bag, stole second, and scored on a force play.

The Dodgers had scored without the ball leaving the infield—and did it again in the second. Dodgers cleanup hitter Wes Parker beat out a leadoff bunt for a hit when Grant slipped fielding the ball. Parker stole second and advanced to third on a wild pitch before trotting home on a fielding error by second baseman Frank Quilici. Parker also powered a fourth-inning home run off Grant to put the Dodgers up 3–1, and the lead was 6–2 in the sixth after Lou Johnson bunted home Ron Fairly, pushing the ball past reliever Al Worthington to the first base side for a hit. Other than allowing home runs to Killebrew and Oliva, Drysdale was firmly in control. The two homers were the first runs scored by the Twins at Dodger Stadium—and they would be the last.

In Game Five, with the World Series now a best-of-three affair, Koufax was even more dominant than Drysdale. Despite his arthritic elbow, his fastball and changeup were exceptional and he located his pitches with ease. On a gorgeous, sunny afternoon in Los Angeles, the left-hander was perfect until Killebrew led off the fifth with a soft single that was nearly caught by Willie Davis in center field. Davis, slow to pick up the ball, charged hard and dove at the sinking liner. He gloved it a foot off the ground but couldn't hold onto it as he rolled. The crowd, already plugged into Koufax's flirtation with perfection, groaned when the ball dropped for a hit.

Killebrew's hit was one of only four for the Twins in a 7–0 loss that put the Dodgers one win from clinching the Series. While Koufax mowed down the Twins, scoring came uncharacteristically easy for the Dodgers in their final 1965 home game. They collected 14 hits against Jim Kaat, Dave Boswell, and Jim Perry, which equaled the total generated by the Twins in the three games at Dodger Stadium combined. Wills matched Minnesota's Game Five hit total himself, going 4-for-5 with two doubles and a stolen base, and scored two runs to lead the rout.

Meanwhile, Koufax struck out ten. Only five Minnesota hitters reached base, and three times a double play followed. In the ninth, the Twins finally advanced a runner beyond first base and put two runners on for the first time, but their only scoring threat ended predictably. After Quilici and Sandy Valdespino singled, Joe Nossek lined a pitch to Wills at short. With an easy flip to Dick Tracewski at second, Wills doubled up Quilici to end the game.

The Twins were happy to depart Dodger Stadium. As the club prepared to return home for Game Six, Billy Martin took a parting shot at the hardness of the Dodger Stadium infield, which caused grounders to travel faster to the outfield and played into the Dodgers' speed game. "The diamond at Chavez is more like concrete," Martin told writers. "Those so-called hits of theirs should have been what they were intended to be—one out apiece and a right turn at first base."

The Twins indulged in a little doctoring of their own when the two clubs returned to Minnesota. Before Game Six, Twins groundskeeper Dick Erickson added some loose dirt and extra water to the base paths, looking to slow down the Dodgers' speedsters. "I slowed it down a little," Erickson confessed later. "Manager Sam Mele likes a slow field." A pregame inspection of the first base line by Wills forced a few landscaping tweaks. "Instead of wetting it down just a little during batting practice and then coming back and watering it before the game, the dumb guy soaked the thing," Mele told the *Boston Globe*'s Ian Thomsen in 1987. "Wills ran down the base path once and he went straight to the umpires; they made us dig it up."

"The game didn't get underway until the grounds crew completed the biggest land reclamation deal west of the Everglades," wrote *Los Angeles Times* columnist Jim Murray. "The first base line was so marshy before the game started that Maury Wills went out and checked for alligators. . . . The groundskeepers removed what appeared to be two wheelbarrows full of quicksand."

A dreadful trip to Los Angeles ended with the Twins being greeted warmly by more than one thousand fans braving mid-thirties temperatures at the Minneapolis-St. Paul airport. The club worked out at the Met on the off day while Sam Mele agonized over who would start Game Six. His options were Jim Merritt, Camilo Pascual, and Mudcat Grant, who had pitched just two days earlier. Mele turned to his twenty-one-game winner. "I have told Grant to throw as hard as he can as long as he can" Mele said after the workout. "There will be almost everybody in the bullpen."

Although Mele was prepared to pull out all the stops to force a seventh game, drastic measures weren't required. On a sunny fall day with a standing-room-only crowd of 49,578 on hand, the largest ever at the Met, Grant was at his best. He held the Dodgers hitless until Ron Fairly led off the fifth inning with a single, giving the Los Angeles first baseman at least one hit in each of the six games. Nothing came of his leadoff single, though Fairly powered a seventh-inning home run that ruined Grant's shutout bid in a 5–1 Twins victory.

Minnesota's bats came to life, though the game remained scoreless until the fourth, when Bob Allison drilled a two-run homer deep into the left-field seats off Claude Osteen. The Twins, with their first lead in the Series since Game Two, added to it in the sixth when Howie Reed replaced Osteen. With one out, Allison drew a full-count walk and stole second on a checked-swing strike three to Don Mincher. Allison appeared to be out. Maury Wills argued with second base umpire Tony Venzon that he had applied the tag in time, which would have ended the inning, but the close play went Minnesota's way. With number eight hitter Frank Quilici due up and first base open, Reed intentionally walked the rookie to bring up Grant with two aboard.

Grant, a capable right-handed hitter who had collected three doubles and two triples during the regular season, drove Reed's first-pitch curveball nearly four hundred feet into the seats in left-center field. The sellout crowd rose and gave Grant a standing ovation as he rounded the bases. After the game, the thirty-year-old veteran was clearly moved. "That gave me a bigger thrill than the home run," Grant told reporters. "Imagine looking up and seeing more than forty-nine thousand standing up and cheering just for you. I'll never forget it."

Grant made quick work of the Dodgers, giving up only the long home run to Fairly. For the day, he threw 81 of his 107 pitches for strikes, didn't walk a batter, and limited Wills, the Dodgers' hottest hitter, to one hit. While Grant mostly threw fastballs, Earl Battey noted after the game that his batterymate's curveball was a key pitch: "His curve was probably the best it has been all season."

For Game Seven, it was Dodgers manager Walter Alston's turn to face a critical pitching decision. Game Four winner Don Drysdale was available and ready on normal rest. Or Alston could call on Koufax, who had blanked the Twins in Game Five, after only *two* days off. The two aces arrived in the Dodgers clubhouse before the finale not knowing who would start. Koufax got the call. Even on two days' rest, he was a better pitcher than nearly every mere mortal in the game—and Alston believed the Twins had more trouble with lefties. Drysdale, who said he could be ready to go after just fifteen warmup pitches, became the skipper's first option out of the bullpen.

Mele went with Kaat in Game Seven. Kaat and Koufax had squared off twice already in the Series, each had won once, and both would pitch the final game on short rest. Thunderstorms passed through the Twin Cities that morning, though by game time, another beautiful fall afternoon was the setting. With the weather improving, the Twins squeezed an extra thousand fans into the Met's crevices, once again setting a new single-game high with 50,596 on hand.

Koufax struggled to locate his curveball, which led to early trouble and forced Drysdale to warm up a few times. But somehow Koufax wiggled out of each jam. He flirted with trouble in the first inning, issuing two-out walks to Tony Oliva and Harmon Killebrew, but kept the Twins off the scoreboard by striking out Battey. In the third, Zoilo Versalles jumped on a high curveball and delivered his team's first hit of the game, a one-out single to center. He seemingly stole second with Joe Nossek at the plate, but home plate umpire Eddie Hurley ruled Nossek had interfered with John Roseboro's throw to second base. After Nossek was called out and Versalles was returned to first, Oliva struck out to end the inning.

With one out in the fifth, Frank Quilici lined a shot off the base of the fence in left-center for a double. A Drysdale entrance seemed imminent when Koufax walked pinch hitter Rich Rollins, but a terrific defensive play by third baseman Jim Gilliam kept Koufax in the game and the Twins scoreless. Versalles lined a wicked one-hopper down the line that Gilliam dove for and smothered. He got up and beat Quilici to the third base bag for the second out.

When another force play ended the threat, Gilliam had made what turned out to be the biggest play of a low-scoring Game Seven. Killebrew told him so when Gilliam singled and advanced to third base in the seventh. "I told Gilliam that his play saved it for them," Killebrew said after the game. "He didn't say anything back to me. But there is no doubt in my mind that the play he made on Zoilo's drive was the big one. It killed our chances of getting at least one run and maybe two. And you just don't get many chances against Koufax."

Early on Kaat looked steadier than Koufax in a game that remained scoreless until the Dodgers' fourth. Kaat had cruised to that point, but in a matter of minutes, three consecutive pitches spelled doom for the Twins. With a 1-1 count leading off the fourth, Lou Johnson hit a fly to left that barely cleared the left-field fence and struck the foul pole. The wind was blowing out to center, which may have been the difference in the ball leaving the yard. Johnson, a thirty-one-year-old journeyman, had spent most of the previous decade bouncing around Minor League locales and was playing his first full season in the Majors. He capped it with the biggest hit of his career.

Fairly, who hit safely in all seven games, powered the very next pitch into the right-field corner for a double. Then Wes Parker chopped *his* first pitch over Mincher's head near first base to score Fairly for the Dodgers' second run. Al Worthington came on to replace Kaat. Although Worthington, Johnny Klippstein,

Jim Merritt, and Jim Perry combined for six innings of score-less, two-hit ball the rest of the way, the Dodgers had scored all the runs they needed.

After Gilliam stalled Minnesota's fifth-inning rally with his defensive gem, Koufax took over. Throwing almost exclusively fastballs, he retired twelve Twins in a row before Killebrew stroked a one-out single to left in the ninth. With the Dodgers up 2–0 and two outs to go, the Twins still had life, but Koufax put a quick end to that fleeting bit of hope. He rifled three straight strikes by Battey, who took a called third for the second out, and then induced Allison to swing at and miss three of four pitches for the final out of the 1965 campaign.

With his second consecutive shutout of the Series—this one a three-hitter in which he again fanned ten Twins—Koufax was del-uged by teammates before a quiet Metropolitan Stadium crowd. Koufax, showing little emotion, strode passively toward the visi-tor's clubhouse as he was offered congratulations. Game Seven marked the twenty-second time he had recorded double-digit strikeouts in 1965, and he didn't appear any more excited about this performance as he headed down the third base dugout's steps.

"I started out with a bad curveball," Koufax explained to *St. Paul Pioneer Press* writer Jim Klobuchar in the winning club-house. "I never really did get it over. So, I laid off it after the fifth or sixth inning, and then I felt myself get stronger." Few pitchers could win a big game without a premier pitch. The left-hander did it in the biggest game a pitcher can work, and against one of the game's most dangerous lineups. "Koufax was so good," Oliva recalled nearly fifty years later. "He was in trouble the first few innings, but he was able to make the big pitches when he needed."

The potent Twins lineup, shut out only three times during the regular season, failed to score in three of seven games against the Dodgers. As a team, Minnesota batted .195 in the Series and often struggled to make contact. Los Angeles pitchers posted double-digit strikeouts in four games; Koufax alone fanned twenty-nine over twenty-four innings. "It was a hell of a Series," Sam Mele said in that 1987 *Boston Globe* interview, "but I lost to the calendar. If I'd had one more Jewish holiday, I could have beaten them."

In a World Series decided by inches—from Lou Johnson's home run that barely cleared the wall before hitting the foul pole to Zoilo Versalles's hard-hit ball that might have eluded Jim Gilliam at third base—the young Twins went home disappointed. Yet, their future was bright. The oldest everyday player, outfielder Bob Allison, turned thirty-one that summer. Catcher Earl Battey was the only other starter who had reached his thirtieth birthday. At twenty-nine, Harmon Killebrew was in his prime, and Versalles, Tony Oliva, Jimmie Hall, and others were just entering their prime years.

The Twins looked like the team to beat in the American League going forward. Although the Twins were in three pennant races in the next five years, another World Series eluded them. As careers played out, only five members of the 1965 Twins appeared in another Fall Classic. The first was reliever Mel Nelson, who pitched only one-third of an inning for the Twins after the 1965 season, but had his best year in 1968 for the St. Louis Cardinals. The left-hander worked a scoreless inning in the '68 World Series, won by Mickey Lolich and the Detroit Tigers in seven games.

Following the '68 season, the Twins traded left-hander Jim Merritt—a 1965 rookie who pitched remarkably well subbing for injured veterans down the stretch—to Cincinnati for shortstop Leo Cárdenas. Merritt was a twenty-game winner for the Reds in 1970. That fall he lost the Game Five finale to the talent-laden Baltimore Orioles, who also steamrolled the Twins in the ALCS that postseason.

Both Don Mincher and Ted Uhlaender retired following the 1972 season, but not before their teams squared off in the World Series that October. In the seven-game, back-and-forth affair between Cincinnati and Oakland, Uhlaender doubled in four pinch-hitting appearances for the Reds. Mincher batted only once for the Athletics—his last at-bat in the Majors—and delivered a game-tying RBI single in the bottom of the ninth of Oakland's Game Four victory. The A's went on to win Game Seven in Cincinnati.

Mincher wasn't the only 1965 Twin to eventually win a World Series ring. A decade later, at age forty-three in 1982, Jim Kaat pitched seventy-five innings, mostly in relief, for the Cardinals. He won his 283rd and final game that summer and made four relief appearances in the 1982 World Series for the eventual champions before retiring midway through the '83 campaign.

"Getting back there that last full year and finally winning it, that really stood out," Kaat said in a 2010 interview. "We went to the Series in '65 and we had a good team. I thought we'd be back. We never did get back. I'm sitting home in 1997, watching the Orioles and the Indians in the American League Championship Series. My friend Tim McCarver was calling the game. They said, 'If the Orioles win, Cal Ripken will be going back to the World Series. And he hasn't been back since 1983—fourteen years. Who holds the record for the longest period of time between World Series appearances?' I scratched my head and I looked at my late wife Marianne, who passed away a couple years ago—I looked at Marianne and I said, 'I think I'm the answer to that question.' And I was. It was seventeen years."

On October 16, two days after Sandy Koufax shut out the Twins in Game Seven of the 1965 World Series, more than one hundred thousand people participated in scores of anti-war demonstrations across the United States and abroad. By then, the U.S. ground war in Vietnam had escalated markedly and Americans had become accustomed to watching body bags arriving home from Asia on national news broadcasts. The dead were returning from an unfamiliar and difficult warzone not conducive to traditional war strategies. And the military's forecasts of the war's progress were always brighter than the reports in the field.

As the war escalated, so did the protest movement. After the United States began massive and sustained bombings of North Vietnam that spring, in April more than fifteen thousand protested the military campaign at the Capitol in Washington DC. Nearly seventeen thousand turned out for a June anti-war rally at Madison Square Garden in New York City. The opposition grew as more Americans were sent to Vietnam, and the October 16 demonstrations had been the largest yet.

One of the smallest anti-war protests of 1965, however, had a substantial legal impact on young Americans' right to dissent. That December in Des Moines, Iowa, sixteen-year-old high school student Christopher Eckhardt hosted a small gathering of students who supported Senator Robert Kennedy's call for a Christmas truce in Vietnam. To protest the deaths of both Americans and Vietnamese in the conflict, the group decided to wear black armbands to school during the last two weeks of December.

On December 16 and 17, Eckhardt, fifteen-year-old John Tinker, thirteen-year-old Mary Beth Tinker and two other students were suspended and sent home for refusing to remove their armbands while at school. Eckhardt admitted to being harassed and threatened by other students. After the suspension, the Tinkers received hate mail and a bomb threat. A window of the family's car was shattered by a brick.

After the local school board rejected an appeal to the suspensions, Eckhardt and the Tinkers took their case to court. In time the case advanced to the U.S. Supreme Court, which, in a 7–2 decision, ruled in 1969 that students are guaranteed the same right to free speech as all Americans, as long as their expression isn't disrupting the learning process. The case, *Tinker v. Des Moines Independent School District*, remains a frequently cited court precedent in deciding whether a school's disciplinary action violates a student's First Amendment rights.

In 2013, nearly fifty years after donning their armbands, John and Mary Beth Tinker returned to their Des Moines schools—North High and Harding Junior High, respectively—to discuss their decision to make an anti-war statement. Staying true to an unpopular opinion takes courage, John told students. Both Tinkers are still activists.

"The Tinker case is in history books . . . but it's not just history, it's the law today," said Mike Hiestand, an attorney with the Virginia-based Student Press Law Center, who accompanied the Tinkers that day. They "are from the Midwest," he added. "They're the politest rebels and radicals that you ever will meet, but their case really did change things."

NINE

Plymouth Avenue on Fire

Minnesotans were excited about the Twins' first spring training as defending American League champions. There was reason for optimism when the Twins gathered in Orlando in spring 1966. Young talent filled the roster and nearly everyone from the World Series club was returning. But the runs didn't come in bunches as they had in '65 and the lackluster Twins struggled to stay above .500 into August. Although they won twenty of their last thirty games to finish a respectable 89-73, they never contended. With Frank Robinson hitting for the Triple Crown in his first season in Baltimore after being acquired from Cincinnati, the Orioles won ninety-seven games. They ran away from the American League pack before sweeping the Los Angeles Dodgers in the World Series.

A better first half might have made the Twins a legitimate contender down the stretch. They were 40-45 at the All-Star break in another injury-plagued season. Zoilo Versalles, the American League's reigning Most Valuable Player, played through a host of ailments, including a blood clot in a damaged upper-back muscle, which sidelined him for roughly two weeks in June. Bob Allison suffered a broken bone in his left hand when he was struck by a pitch in July. Rich Rollins was terrific in June, hitting as well as he had at any time in his Twins tenure, but he wrenched his knee late in the month, an injury that affected his hitting for much of the season. When right-hander Camilo Pascual missed most of the second half with more arm trouble, Dave Boswell picked up the slack and won seven straight starts following the All-Star break, but he developed a sore shoulder in August after being struck by a batted ball. And relief ace Al Worthington was lost for three weeks just prior to the break when he caught the fingers on his pitching hand in his garage door at home.

While the 1965 Twins successfully overcame a rash of injuries, the 1966 club lacked the offensive firepower to compete with the Orioles. Harmon Killebrew and Tony Oliva had typically productive seasons, but the oft-injured Versalles and Jimmie Hall had down years, and Earl Battey, battered after a decade as an everyday, Major League catcher, was nearing the end. The Twins pitching staff was solid—posting a 3.13 ERA that was the lowest since the franchise move to Minnesota six years earlier—but the offense produced 111 fewer runs than in '65, tallying fewer than 700 in a season for the first time in Minnesota.

A rare highlight of a mediocre season was the home-run explosion from a quintet of Minnesota sluggers on June 9. The Twins were hosting the Kansas City Athletics in the finale of an eleven-game home stand in which they had lost seven of ten to fall to 22-26. They were on course to lose a second straight matchup to the A's, trailing 4–3 as they came to bat in the seventh inning. Battey drew a leadoff walk from twenty-year-old Catfish Hunter, but Kansas City's budding ace retired Bernie Allen for the first out. Rollins, pinch hitting for reliever Al Cimino, jumped on Hunter's first pitch and drove it into the left-field seats to put the Twins up 5–4. Versalles then drilled a Hunter fastball deep to left to make it 6–4.

Three left-handed hitters—Sandy Valdespino, Tony Oliva, and Don Mincher—were due up, so A's skipper Alvin Dark replaced Hunter with southpaw Paul Linblad. After Linblad induced a ground ball out from Valdespino, Oliva swatted a curveball into the right-field bullpen. Mincher, on the very next pitch, clubbed Minnesota's fourth home run of the inning. The Twins had matched an American League record they shared with Cleveland, but no AL club could match the five-homer innings pro-

duced by three National League clubs to that point in Major
League history.

Before Harmon Killebrew stepped into the batter's box with
the chance to hit the fifth homer, Dark replaced Linblad with
right-hander John Wyatt. The small Thursday night crowd of
9,621 buzzed with excitement, and Twins players were standing
on the steps of the dugout as Killebrew went 3-2 against Wyatt.
Killebrew pounded the 3-2 pitch into the Met's bleachers to set
the new AL mark.

If the Twins could hit five homers in an inning, why not six?
Jimmie Hall, the powerfully built center fielder who had averaged 26 homers per year over his first three big league seasons,
had everyone's attention as he strode to the plate. The left-handed
hitter turned on a Wyatt offering and drove it deep to right. It
had a chance to get out, but was hit so hard on a line that it
missed clearing the fence by less than three feet. Hall pulled
into second base with a double, but when Allen was retired for
a second time in the inning, the Twins had fallen inches short
of setting a new Major League record. They remained the only
AL club to hit five homers in an inning until the New York Yankees matched their record during the 2020 season.

With the Twins in the midst of a season-high six-game winning streak in mid-August, they turned their first triple play in
their sixth season in Minnesota. Closing out a more successful
home stand against the California Angels on August 18, Jim
"Mudcat" Grant found trouble in the second inning, allowing a
leadoff single to Angels first baseman Norm Siebern and walking Ed Kirkpatrick to put two runners aboard for Frank Malzone. The veteran third baseman, in his twelfth and final Major
League season, stroked a grounder that Rollins fielded at the
third base bag and stepped on it. He rifled the ball to second
baseman César Tovar, who pivoted and threw to Killebrew at
first. It wasn't a good day for Malzone, who also grounded into
a bases-loaded double play to end the seventh inning of a 6–2
Twins win. "I hit it tailor-made for a triple play," a glum Malzone
said after the game. "It was automatic. The ball was practically
on top of third base." Grant, on the other hand, was pleased to

see his infielders send Malzone's hard-hit grounder around the horn: "It saved me from a cool shower."

While the Twins stumbled along for most of 1966, Jim Kaat was a consistent performer and arguably the team's MVP. He won a career-high twenty-five games and his 2.75 ERA was his lowest as an ERA qualifier. The twenty-seven-year-old led the American League not only in wins, but innings (304 2/3), starts (41), and complete games (19). It was the second straight season he had led the league in starts, a two-year stretch in which Kaat posted 43 wins and a 2.78 ERA with Johnny Sain as Minnesota's pitching coach. The durable lefty believed he maximized his talent working with Sain, a sentiment shared by Grant, the ace of the 1965 Twins staff.

During Kaat's big 1966 season, however, Sain and skipper Sam Mele feuded, just as Sain and third base coach Billy Martin had the year before. Pitchers loved working with Sain, but the coach's push for complete control of the pitching staff irked Mele. So did Sain's motivational emphasis and the self-help books. Neither Mele nor Martin were on good terms with the pitching coach as the Twins closed out their disappointing 1966 season. Soon after, Mele asked Calvin Griffith to fire Sain and bullpen coach Hal Naragon, and the owner released both coaches.

Kaat heard the news on his car radio, following a speaking engagement in southern Minnesota, and his shock and anger forced him to pull off the road. He wrote an open letter to inform fans why he thought the firings were a terrible decision, though he couldn't get veterans Harmon Killebrew and Bob Allison to sign on with him. Kaat approached Sid Hartman about running his letter, but the *Minneapolis Star Tribune* writer did a radio show with Mele and declined to be part of it. Kaat persisted and the newspaper ran his statement. In it, Kaat criticized Griffith for firing the wrong men. "This is the worst thing that could happen to our club at this time," wrote Kaat. "We had the finest pitching coach money can buy, and now, suddenly, he is gone. I think the fans should know what a huge void we have to fill."

Festering anger wasn't limited to the Twins clubhouse in 1966. President Lyndon Johnson's War on Poverty had taken a backseat to the growing Vietnam conflict, and the extreme poverty and lack of opportunity that devastated urban Black communities continued to trigger frustration and resentment. Young African Americans increasingly believed that Dr. Martin Luther King Jr.'s pacifism was no longer enough to spur meaningful change.

Malcolm X, the former Nation of Islam leader who spoke more forcefully of the crimes long committed against African Americans, did not believe that nonviolent tactics could overturn centuries of inequality. Early on he saw integration as a surrender to white supremacy. After a life-altering pilgrimage in 1964 to Mecca, where he was strongly influenced by his exposure to a variety of cultures, Malcolm X developed a new outlook on integration that broadened his appeal. But Nation of Islam member Talmadge Hayer and four accomplices assassinated him at the Audubon Ballroom in Manhattan's Washington Heights neighborhood in February 1965, silencing a powerful voice of the movement.

Not long after longtime New York congressman Adam Clayton Powell Jr. told graduating Howard University students in May 1966 that "to demand these God-given rights is to seek black power," a movement promoting Black self-determination blossomed. The concept wasn't new, but civil rights activist Stokely Carmichael thrust the slogan "Black Power" into the national consciousness after fellow activist James Meredith was shot and wounded by a sniper on June 6, 1966, during his one-man, two-hundred-mile "March Against Fear" from Memphis, Tennessee, to Jackson, Mississippi.

Carmichael, who had long been active in the civil rights movement and recently directed a campaign to register African American voters in Mississippi, had lost faith in the notion of integration through nonviolence. In response to Meredith's shooting, Carmichael told a crowd in Greenwood, Mississippi: "The only way we're gonna stop them white men from whuppin' us is to take over. We've been saying 'freedom' for six years and we ain't got nothin'. What we're going to say now is '*Black Power!*'" With a clenched fist, Carmichael called to the crowd: "What do you want?" Those gathered roared back: "Black Power!"

For years civil rights campaigns had largely targeted conditions in the rural South, but the Black Power movement brought the focus to America's cities. "Black Power!" became a rallying cry for a wide spectrum of civil rights and community groups that promoted Black pride and self-sufficiency over desegregation. Most still took a nonviolent approach. Others—such as the Black Panthers, for which Carmichael became a leading voice—took the movement on a more militant path during the second half of the decade. Soon a torrent of anger over living conditions, the lack of adequate housing and jobs, and police brutality would be unleashed on city streets across the country.

Neighborhoods in Minneapolis and St. Paul endured abject living conditions. By the late 1950s, more than 90 percent of St. Paul's seven thousand African American residents lived in poverty in a community between Lexington Parkway and Western Avenue, bounded by Aurora Avenue on the north end and Dayton Avenue to the south. In Minneapolis, the Near North Side became a neighborhood of Jewish and African American families following a surge of Black flight from the South in the 1950s, spurred by the violent reaction to the budding civil rights movement. It was the city's poorest community, and by the 1960s the Jewish population had assimilated into mainstream culture and largely moved to other parts of the city and the suburbs.

An overwhelming majority of the Near North Side's African American population lacked adequate employment or housing— let alone the means to move out of the neighborhood. Roughly half of the businesses along Plymouth Avenue, the neighborhood's shopping district, were still owned by Jewish families, many of whom no longer lived in the neighborhood. Many young African Americans in the community who couldn't find employment came to resent the store owners. To some, in the words of longtime Minneapolis civil rights activist W. Harry Davis, "the shops became a near-at-hand symbol of what white people had and they did not."

Frustration boiled over on August 2, 1966, when roughly fifty young people began throwing rocks at moving cars, which escalated to breaking windows along Plymouth and stealing goods from local businesses. The kids entered Silver's Food Market at 1711 Plymouth, filled their pockets and overturned display shelves on their way out. Down the street, looters stole televisions from Koval's Furniture and Appliance. The crowds dispersed without an aggressive police intervention, an approach taken by Minneapolis mayor Arthur Naftalin, who believed that a brute show of force by the police had escalated violence in other cities. Mace and fire rigs with hoses were on hand but not used, and order was soon restored.

With the civil rights movement, 1960s youth culture, and the anti-war movement building to a feverish pitch, 1967 featured the anti-establishment Summer of Love, epitomized by San Francisco's Haight-Ashbury scene. The "long, hot summer" is what many in America's largest cities called it. In mid-July, racial violence erupted in a two-square-mile area of central Newark, leading to twenty-six deaths, twelve hundred injuries, and extensive damage to local businesses over five days of rioting. After the National Guard helped restore order, troops and tanks were required a week later in Detroit, where forty-three were killed and hundreds were injured in six days of urban warfare. Angry African American residents looted businesses and set fires that destroyed two hundred buildings.

Violence erupted across the country, not only in America's largest cities but in Cleveland and Cincinnati, Buffalo and Birmingham, Louisville, Nashville, and Wichita—and on Plymouth Avenue. With the Newark conflict still front-page news, trouble started in downtown Minneapolis at the annual Aquatennial Torchlight Parade on Wednesday, July 19, and moved up Plymouth Avenue later that evening. A large crowd began throwing rocks into stores and businesses on the street, then vandalizing and looting them. Ten shops in the eight blocks between Penn and Humboldt Avenues were set on fire during the night, and two—Silver's and Knox Food Market at Plymouth and Morgan Avenue—were burnt to the ground. "The scene that night on the street was nightmarish," W. Harry Davis told Iric Nathanson, author of *Minneapolis in the Twentieth Century: The Growth of an American City*. "The stench of the smoke was oppressive. The heat was intense enough to break display windows, exposing the stores to looting."

Roughly sixty police officers with helmets and shotguns were positioned along Plymouth. When firefighters arrived just before midnight to extinguish the Knox blaze, some in the angry crowd of roughly one-hundred-fifty people—gathered between Morgan and Oliver Avenues—pelted them with rocks and bricks. As fire crews retreated, police dispersed the gathering without going on the attack, forcing the crowd to move on by walking at them in lines, shoulder to shoulder. In most instances people gave way to firefighters. Most in the crowd, which included women and children, were simply milling around, taking in what had happened. Some were residents displaced by the risk of fire. As long as fire crews were allowed to work, the police avoided confrontation with people on the street.

A few Plymouth Avenue businesses, including the Peoples Baking Corporation and Hi-Hat Café, were firebombed the following day, igniting another wave of fires. Crowds also set cars afire, hurled rocks at police cars, and street violence led to two shootings. Minneapolis mayor Arthur Naftalin again chose not to escalate the violence or pursue massive arrests after Davis had convinced him that a police sweep might incite a full-scale riot and was unlikely to snare the people who had started fires along Plymouth Avenue. Naftalin did call Governor Harold LeVander, requesting a National Guard presence, and soon six hundred guardsmen patrolled Minneapolis streets. Tensions cooled considerably the next day, dampened by the National Guard's presence and heavy hailstorms.

Compared to the violence and destruction in Newark and Detroit, the Minneapolis disturbance never grew into a full-scale riot. Naftalin had resisted city officials who wanted a police sweep that arrested everyone along Plymouth that first night, a decision that would later reflect well on the police department. The *Minneapolis Tribune* credited the police for minimizing the scale and damage of the two-day confrontation: "There was no shooting, no club-swinging to produce the usual pictures of bashed and bloody heads, no police rush upon the crowd."

That's not to say Plymouth Avenue and other damaged areas, such as along Marquette Avenue between Fourth and Seventh Streets South, returned to normal after a brief outburst. Prior to the 1967 violence, only a handful of buildings along Plymouth Avenue sat empty, but by the following spring, nearly three dozen buildings were vacant and boarded up. Plymouth became an avenue of empty lots. The Minneapolis disturbance, no matter how small, destroyed a large piece of the community's infrastructure.

It was during that long, hot Summer of Love that the Minnesota Twins engaged in one of the most dramatic pennant races in American League history. Surprisingly the Baltimore Orioles, who had swept the Los Angeles Dodgers in the 1966 World Series, were never a factor in the 1967 chase. After averaging 96 wins over the three previous seasons, the Orioles won just seventy-six games and finished in a sixth-place tie with the Washington Senators. The Twins faced stiff competition, however, from the Chicago White Sox, Detroit Tigers, and Boston Red Sox. The Red Sox were the biggest surprise of the summer, coming off a one-hundred-loss season in 1965 and losing ninety games in '66. They hadn't had a winning season since 1958, and their stunning second-half surge inspired long-suffering Red Sox fans to dub the 1967 campaign "The Impossible Dream."

Before the wild American League pennant race captured the attention of baseball fans, tragedy struck the space program in the early days of 1967. By then, the solo flights of Project Mercury had launched the first Americans into space and the two-man missions of Project Gemini had worked out many of the maneuvers necessary to execute a moon landing. The three-man flights of the Apollo Project, intended to meet President John F. Kennedy's dream of putting a man on the moon during the 1960s, was to begin that winter—with a first trip to the moon on course for late 1968 or early 1969.

That timeline took a hit at Cape Kennedy on January 27, 1967, when the three *Apollo 1* astronauts were killed by a flash fire that trapped them in the spacecraft during a prelaunch test. Dead

were Virgil "Gus" Grissom, one of NASA's original seven astronauts, who had flown Mercury and Gemini missions; Edward
White, the first American to walk in space on *Gemini 4*; and
Roger Chaffee, preparing to take his first NASA flight after five
years in the program.

The astronauts were involved in a full-scale simulation of the
launch when the fire broke out. They were in their launch seats
and wearing spacesuits, which were hooked into a pure-oxygen
breathing system that fed the fire. "Fire . . . I smell fire," one
of the astronauts announced casually at the start. Two seconds
later, White cried, "Fire in the cockpit!" Roughly fifteen seconds
later, Chaffee uttered the final words from the spacecraft: "We're
on fire . . . get us out of here!"

The flash fire quickly consumed the command module in an
oxygen-rich environment, killing the astronauts in less than thirty
seconds and reaching a temperature approaching 2,500 degrees
Fahrenheit. Grissom and White had released their restraint straps
and made their way to the hatch, which required a ratchet and
nearly ninety seconds to open. Would-be rescuers were only a
few feet from the spacecraft at the time of the accident, but the
intense heat and dense smoke kept them from entering the craft
for five minutes after the fire began.

The damage to the command module was extensive, but it
is widely believed that an electrical spark under Grissom's seat
ignited the fire. The tragedy reopened a long-running debate
within NASA: whether a pure-oxygen breathing system was the
best option. In a three-thousand-page report released that April,
the NASA-directed, seven-member board investigating the fire
blamed NASA for failures in the spacecraft's wiring and plumb-
ing, citing poor design, engineering, and quality control. The
board also called out the agency for inadequately addressing
escape and rescue options for the crew. By the time the board's
findings went public, NASA was working on a hatch that could
be opened in two seconds.

With the Soviet Union also building a dynamic space program,
the rush to win the race to the moon may have led NASA to cut
corners. The agency, however, did execute substantial changes

to future command modules and made the interior more fire-proof. Astronauts were given fireproof suits and the atmosphere changed to a less-flammable mixture of oxygen and nitrogen.

Getting the space program back on track took time. The first manned Apollo flight, *Apollo 7*, was delayed more than a year and a half after the accident. Yet, less than a year after the *Apollo 7* mission, in July 1969, Neil Armstrong, Buzz Aldrin, and Michael Collins took that historic flight to where no one had walked before.

TEN

Change in the Air

I n the weeks prior to the *Apollo 1* tragedy in January 1967, Twins owner Calvin Griffith was smarting from a mediocre 1966 performance by his club. He quickly dealt cornerstones of the 1965 World Series team in his quest to retool the pitching staff. The Twins needed a number one starter, and in December 1966, Griffith shipped center fielder Jimmie Hall, first baseman Don Mincher, and pitching prospect Pete Cimino to the California Angels for Dean Chance. The right-hander had gone 20-9 to capture Cy Young honors in 1964, but finished a disappointing 12-17 in 1966 for the Angels.

Hall had exploded onto the scene with 33 home runs as a rookie in 1963, but his production declined steadily in subsequent years. His last season as a regular was 1966, and he saw mostly platoon duty before retiring in 1970. Mincher, a remarkably successful part-time player for the Twins, was a key contributor during the 1965 championship season, especially after Harmon Killebrew was lost to injury. Mincher played more in Anaheim, where he became a more patient hitter who drew walks as well as drove in runs.

The day after picking up Chance, Griffith dealt Camilo Pascual, the staff ace when the franchise departed Washington in 1961. After Pascual had spent thirteen big league seasons with the organization, Griffith shipped him back to Washington, dealing him and second baseman Bernie Allen to the expansion Senators in exchange for thirty-four-year-old Ron Kline, coming off four superb seasons in Washington's bullpen. The Twins had released Johnny Klippstein following the 1966 campaign, and Kline was slated to team with Al Worthington to anchor the relief corps.

Pascual, long blessed with one of the best curveballs in the game, won 145 games pitching for the Griffith family. He had not been the same pitcher since undergoing shoulder surgery during the 1965 pennant race, and Griffith felt he could move the thirty-one-year-old veteran with Chance coming aboard. With less zip on his fastball, Pascual made the necessary adjustments and enjoyed two productive seasons in Washington. If not for the shoulder injury, he and the Twins might have generated more October memories in the 1960s.

The athletic Allen, a quarterback and All-American shortstop at Purdue, displaced Billy Martin at second base in 1962 after playing just eighty games in the low Minors. He arrived with much promise and pop for a middle infielder, stroking 12 homers as a twenty-three-year-old rookie, but never again reached those heights. A knee injury in 1964, suffered when Washington's Don Zimmer rolled into his legs breaking up a double play, compromised Allen's budding career.

Killebrew had manned third base in 1966, but Mincher's departure put an end to Killebrew's movement between first, third, and the outfield—at least for a couple of seasons. He now would play first, his position of choice. With Hall gone, Ted Uhlaender was in line to be the primary center fielder if he could hit enough, with utility man César Tovar an option if he struggled. Tovar turned in the better season in 1967, and proved valuable for his versatility, deftly playing every position except pitcher, catcher, and first base.

Rod Carew, the last great position player the Twins developed in the 1960s, arrived in 1967. The Panamanian-born prospect grew up in the Canal Zone before moving to the Washington Heights area of New York City as a teenager. He never played baseball in high school, but Twins scouts discovered him play-

ing semipro ball in the Bronx in 1964. Just as Griffith had lobbied to make room for the unproven Oliva in '64, three years
later the owner did the same in spring training with the twenty-
one-year-old Carew. Griffith told reporters in camp that Carew
"could be the American League All-Star second baseman if he
puts his mind to it." The highly regarded prospect had to win
the starting job in camp before worrying about an All-Star berth,
and manager Sam Mele wasn't ready to give the second base gig
to an untested rookie out of Class-A ball. But Carew hit his way
onto the roster in Florida.

Compared to the previous spring, when Minnesota had come
off its World Series appearance, expectations for the 1967 club
were tempered somewhat. Yet, in Chance, Jim Kaat, and Mudcat Grant, the Twins had a trio of starters who had each posted
twenty-win seasons in the last three years, and the power trio
of Killebrew, Oliva, and Bob Allison anchored the batting order.
Allison was looking to rebound from a string of hand injuries,
including a fractured wrist in 1965, which had compromised
his stroke for two summers. He, Rich Rollins, Zoilo Versalles,
and Earl Battey were coming off disappointing seasons, so the
Twins were looking for comeback performances and hoping
that second-year men Uhlaender and Tovar would produce in
center. Carew was the only rookie with a major role on the club.

Pitching depth was a concern, but the Twins were looking to
two promising young starters, Dave Boswell and Jim Merritt,
to fill out a solid rotation. Also in the mix was swingman Jim
Perry, who had stepped into the 1965 rotation and won some big
games during the championship run. He had pitched effectively
as both a starter and reliever, making him valuable to the club.

The competition would be stiff. As was their habit, the Chicago White Sox were a light-hitting bunch that contended with
strong pitching and defensive prowess behind it. Joe Horlen, a
nineteen-game winner and the league ERA champion in 1967,
led a strong rotation that included lefties Gary Peters, Tommy
John, and Jim O'Toole. Struggling reliever Wilbur Wood had
joined the White Sox in an off-season trade, an addition to a
deep bullpen anchored by Hall of Fame knuckleballer Hoyt Wil-

helm. The forty-four-year-old vet convinced Wood to throw the knuckler exclusively and helped him refine both the pitch and his delivery. In time Wood controlled the knuckleball better than nearly anyone who ever threw it. Wilhelm, the aged master who was less likely to know where the pitch was going, posted a 1.73 ERA over eighty-nine innings in 1967.

The Detroit Tigers had won eighty-nine and eighty-eight games the two seasons prior to 1967—good for distant fourth- and third-place finishes—but winning ninety-one games in '67 kept them in the pennant race to the final out. Starter Earl Wilson, acquired in a trade with Boston in June 1966, was a key contributor. In his first full season with the Tigers, the thirty-two-year-old right-hander won a career-high twenty-two games under the tutelage of pitching coach Johnny Sain, who jumped to the Tigers in 1967 after the Twins had fired him. Wilson teamed with Denny McLain, Mickey Lolich, and Joe Sparma in the rotation, and Sain worked his magic on the young, impressionable McLain, who went 31-6 with a 1.96 ERA in 1968 and won twenty-four games in '69.

Unlike the White Sox, the 1967 Tigers had plenty of pop. Four Tigers connected on at least 20 homers during that memorable season—future Hall of Famer Al Kaline, first baseman Norm Cash, second baseman Dick McAuliffe, and catcher Bill Freehan—and homegrown slugger Willie Horton drilled 19. That summer, at age thirty-two, Kaline had his last great season, popping 25 homers and posting a .952 OPS that was his highest since winning the AL batting title at age twenty in 1955. Arguably 1955 and 1967 were his two best seasons in a productive twenty-two-year career.

The Boston Red Sox, after losing ninety-plus games three years in a row, hired Dick Williams to manage the club in 1967. Williams, a no-nonsense, drill-sergeant type, was just thirty-seven and had never managed in the Majors. But Red Sox executive vice president Dick O'Connell thought he was the right guy for a franchise that hadn't posted a winning record since 1958. That didn't deter Williams from promising at his introduction: "We'll win more games than we lose." In the minds of most report-

ers present, that was setting the bar exceedingly high, bordering on nonsense.

The Red Sox were a .500 club deep into June, an impressive
improvement but not a reason to anticipate a second-half pennant push. The club's pitching seemed especially suspect, but
twenty-five-year-old Jim Lonborg, a Stanford grad who had fore-
gone medical school to work atop a pile of dirt, broke through
with a career year in which he led the American League with
22 wins and 246 strikeouts. Gary Bell, who arrived from Cleveland in an early-June trade, won twelve games as Boston surged
into contention.

Rookies Reggie Smith and Mike Andrews were productive
for the young Red Sox, and second-year infielders George Scott
and Joe Foy improved on solid 1966 debuts. Local boy and fan
favorite Tony Conigliaro was having a big year—with 20 homers and 67 RBIS in ninety-five games—when on August 18 he
was struck on the left cheekbone by a pitch from Angels right-
hander Jack Hamilton. His season was over. With the vision
in his left eye severely compromised, Conigliaro managed to
return in 1969, delivered stunning numbers for the 1970 Red
Sox with 36 homers and 116 RBIS, but a year later was forced to
retire at age twenty-six.

For the 1967 club, Carl Yastrzemski was the straw that stirred
New England's Cape Codder. The man who had replaced Ted
Williams in left field six years earlier was at his best, winning
the Triple Crown by batting .326 with 44 homers and 121 RBIS.
Over the final month, Yaz batted .417 with nine homers and 26
RBIS in twenty-seven games. He produced in key situations all
season—to the very end—and the Red Sox couldn't have gone
from ninth place to the top in 1967 without him.

A bounce-back year by the Twins seemed unlikely in the early
going. For the first time since the franchise move west to Minnesota in 1961, the Twins lost their first two games of a new
season. They rebounded for a come-from-behind win in their
home opener against Detroit on April 14, thanks to four innings
of scoreless relief from Merritt, but lost their next two and managed to post back-to-back wins only once in April.

The Twins spent April making poor defensive plays and base-running blunders, throwing to the wrong base and committing various mental mistakes. After closing April losing three of four to the lowly Senators in Washington, the Twins occupied the AL cellar at 5-10. In a stretch of sixteen games that carried into May, Sam Mele watched his players commit 21 errors. He grew increasingly frustrated, and with management unhappy with the club's start, several Twins—including Battey and Allison—were mentioned in trade rumors.

To make matters worse, Minnesota had barely averaged more than three runs per game in April. Among the slow starters were Allison, Rollins, Battey, and Oliva, who was still struggling with neck pain and headaches brought on by a 1966 car accident. Then, just two weeks before the start of the season, Oliva pulled a back muscle while throwing from the outfield, an injury that lingered deep into the spring and bothered him when he swung.

Mele took an unusual get-tough approach after two key mistakes spurred a 4–3 Twins loss to the White Sox in a mid-April Sunday matinee at the Met. Oliva misjudged a fly ball in right, leading to two runs, and Tovar became trapped between second base and third base when he recklessly tried to tag up on a short fly to center with the Twins down three runs. When it was over, the Twins stuck around for postgame batting practice. "Mistakes, mistakes," Mele moaned after the game. "It's a repetition of spring training. . . . If we can't do it right, we'll stay out until we correct some mistakes. Every game we've lost we've contributed to our downfall."

One of the few April highlights was Carew's ninth-inning RBI single on April 19, which gave the Twins a 3–2 victory over the Orioles. The rookie jumped on a first-pitch changeup from O's relief ace Stu Miller and drove it up the middle to bring home Uhlaender with the winning run. The thirty-nine-year-old Miller, a masterful right-hander with 23 wins and a 2.04 ERA in more than two hundred innings over the two previous seasons, succeeded with an arsenal best described as slow and slower. Carew, who had faced Miller in a spring training game, knew to wait on the veteran's pitches.

"The first pitch came up like a big grapefruit, and I wasn't taking any strikes with the bases loaded," Carew said in a post-game interview. His hit gave the Twins their second win of the season, Chance's first in a Twins uniform. In a dominating performance, the right-hander skillfully mixed his stuff, including a nasty curveball that was sharper than it had been all spring. Facing a dangerous lineup anchored by Boog Powell, Frank Robinson, and Brooks Robinson, Chance struck out ten and out-pitched Orioles right-hander Jim Palmer.

After Carew delivered the game-winning hit against the Orioles, the Twins kicked off a ten-day road trip at Tiger Stadium on April 21. Oliva's bat showed some life in the Friday night opener, but even his best day of the opening month was tarnished by a once-in-a-lifetime blunder that epitomized the team's early struggles. After Tovar singled to center off Denny McLain to lead off the third inning of a scoreless game, Oliva drove a towering fly to right-center. As Al Kaline backtracked to the right-field wall in pursuit, Tovar, instead of going half-way to second base, retreated toward first in anticipation of a catch at the wall.

Both Oliva and first base coach Jim Lemon watched the ball land in Tiger Stadium's upper deck, which hung over the playing field. As he rounded first base, Oliva suddenly heard Tovar shout in Spanish, "Don't pass me on the bases!" Oliva had already run past his teammate and Detroit first baseman Norm Cash quickly alerted first base umpire John Stevens, who had been watching the flight of the ball and had his back to the infield. Tovar was allowed to score, but Stevens called Oliva out. Mele, convinced that Kaline's arm made tagging up impossible, thought Tovar should have known to go halfway. Tired of his team's mental mistakes, Mele fined Tovar for the lost run.

The day was dreadful all around. The Tigers jumped on Twins pitching for seven runs in the fourth and cruised to a 12–4 victory. The frustrated manager, fed up with his team's play, held a brief team meeting during a seventh-inning rain delay and another after the game. Then the Twins lost five of their next eight.

During Minnesota's post-meeting skid, on April 28, heavyweight champion Muhammad Ali and twenty-five recruits were to be inducted into the army at the U.S. Armed Forces Examining and Entrance Station in Houston. They filled out paperwork and took physicals, but when the recruits lined up to take the symbolic step forward into the armed forces as their names were called, Ali—who might have been assigned a noncombat role, as former heavyweight champ Joe Louis had been during World War II—refused. He opposed joining the army even if he might never be sent to Vietnam. Despite pleas from family, advisors, and friends, including star athletes Bill Russell, Jim Brown, Bobby Mitchell, and Willie Davis, Ali insisted that he wasn't going to take the easy way out.

It was another noteworthy moment in Ali's gripping but polarizing reign as the champion. He was known as Cassius Clay when he knocked out Sonny Liston in February 1964 to claim boxing's world heavyweight title. No one could call the boisterous and immodest Clay an Uncle Tom, and most sportswriters and much of white America turned on him when he joined the Nation of Islam and changed his name to Muhammad Ali. His refusal to be inducted into the army at the height of the Vietnam War was equally polarizing. On June 20, 1967, in Houston, Ali was sentenced to a five-year jail term and fined $1,000 for draft evasion.

Ali's conviction culminated a series of events that began three years earlier—just a few weeks before he won the heavyweight title from Liston—when the young contender was declared unfit for military service. A poor reader and student, he had failed the army's fifty-minute aptitude test and was classified 1-Y, a status that inspired Ali to respond defensively: "I said I was the greatest, not the smartest." With the war rapidly escalating, however, the military lowered its mental-aptitude requirement in 1966 and deemed Ali smart enough to serve.

New York Times sportswriter Bob Lipsyte was at Ali's Miami home when the news broke that the heavyweight champ was now draft eligible. Ali's phone began ringing incessantly, with reporters repeatedly asking for his take on his pending induction and the war. Lipsyte told Thomas Hauser, author of *Muhammad Ali: His Life and Times*, that it was apparent Ali was scared to be drafted. He knew little about Vietnam, but suddenly a war being fought in remote jungles halfway around the world was something to fear.

"Finally, after the tenth call," Lipsyte told Hauser, "'What do you think about the Vietcong?'—Ali exploded. 'Man, I ain't got no quarrel with them Vietcong.' And bang. There it was. That was the headline." Ali's quote appeared in nearly every newspaper, inciting the wrath of the war's supporters, including numerous sportswriters, political commentators, and politicians.

"It was *the* moment for Ali," Lipsyte said to David Remnick, author of *King of the World*. "For the rest of his life he would be loved and hated for what seemed like a declarative statement, but what was, at the time, a moment of blurted improvisation." Ali, who quickly learned about the war and developed a political stance, became the first famous, draft-eligible American to stand up and say he wouldn't go to Vietnam. His decision inspired a generation of young men who didn't believe in the war—especially poor Black men, who felt they were second-class citizens with few opportunities except to fight the nation's wars.

"Why should they ask me to put on a uniform and go ten thousand miles from home and drop bombs and bullets on brown people in Vietnam while so-called Negro people in Louisville are treated like dogs?" Ali told a *Sports Illustrated* reporter in the days before he was to report for induction in April 1967. "If I thought going to war would bring freedom and equality to twenty-two million of my own people, they wouldn't have to draft me. I'd join tomorrow."

A string of appeals kept Ali out of prison until the U.S. Supreme Court overturned his conviction in 1971, ruling that the Justice Department had never provided a reason for denying Ali's conscientious objector exemption. Still, he had paid a substantial price for refusing induction. An hour after Ali declined to take that symbolic step into the army, before he had even been charged with a crime, the New York State Athletic Commission suspended his boxing license. Soon after he was stripped of his title. He was forced to surrender his passport, meaning that he couldn't generate income by fighting overseas, and was targeted for constant FBI surveillance as Malcolm X and Martin Luther King Jr. had been. He didn't box for nearly four years, losing his peak years as a boxer and millions of dollars in income.

During his exile from boxing, Ali took to the lecture circuit to earn a living, speaking at college campuses across the country. He proved to be a dynamic speaker, discussing Black pride, his opposition to the war, and numerous other subjects to receptive audiences. As the war became increasingly unpopular, Ali gained the respect of a much larger segment of the country than boxing had allowed. In the words of Jim Brown, the former pro football star and civil rights activist, Ali "became the darling of America, which was good for America because it brought black and white together."

"Some people thought I was a hero. Some people said that what I did was wrong. But everything I did was according to my conscience," Ali said of the attention he received for refusing to enlist. "And I made a stand all people, not just Black people, should have thought about making, because it wasn't just Black people being drafted. The government had a system where the rich man's son went to college, and the poor man's son went to war. . . . So what I did was for me, but it was the kind of decision everyone has to make."

The Vietnam War escalated markedly in 1967, the year Ali made his decision not to serve in the army. American troops on the ground approached five hundred thousand and American casualties continued to rise, topping ten thousand that spring. The anti-war movement began a summer campaign in which four thousand college-age students across the country went door to door to drum up middle-class opposition to a military effort that was failing to produce substantial results. With television news crews on hand, Martin Luther King Jr. and Dr. Benjamin Spock kicked off this new approach, stopping at homes in Cambridge, Massachusetts, but the divisive nature of the war became apparent when they were heckled on the streets by supporters of the war.

After covering the war's early years for the *New York Times*, David Halberstam returned to Vietnam for three months in late 1967 for *Harper's*. He discovered little had changed since he left his Saigon post three years earlier. Despite U.S. military superiority, the war continued to be a stalemate, but the top military leaders of the Saigon command were still perpetrating an upbeat take of the war effort.

"It was the same false optimism I had first witnessed there five years earlier as a young reporter for the *Times*, when the stakes were so much smaller," Halberstam wrote in *The Best and the Brightest*, his book about the Vietnam saga. "It reflected once again the immense difference between what people in the field thought was happening and what people in the Saigon command, responding to intense political pressure from Washington, wanted to think was happening." Halberstam recounts how this "self-deception" surfaced in the pending Christmas celebration in which high-ranking diplomats were inviting friends to their "light-at-the-end-of-the-tunnel Christmas party."

Halberstam had witnessed firsthand the widespread deception that began in the earliest days of the American-led war. Domestic support for U.S.-backed dictator Ngo Dinh Diem was all but nonexistent, and Halberstam reported in *The Best and the Brightest* that American officials initially failed to see that "the problem was not just Diem, that Diem was simply a symptom of a larger failure." The South Vietnamese military under Diem's control, ideally the leading force of the war effort, was seemingly more interested in raiding villages and stealing property than protecting the citizenry. American support wasn't winning hearts and minds, but the news back home didn't reflect reality.

"The American military had been turning to the handful of American journalists in Saigon, using them as an outlet for their complaints," wrote Halberstam. "It was not particularly deliberate; but it was also impossible to keep their skepticism hidden. The journalists kept showing up in the countryside, and it was only a matter of time before they saw how hollow the entire operation was, how many lies were being told, and how fraudulent the war was."

ELEVEN

The Summer of Love Heats Up

While the Twins stumbled during the opening weeks of the 1967 season, sports fans were jazzed because major league hockey and basketball were coming to Minnesota. The National Hockey League, playing its fiftieth season that spring, scheduled a June expansion draft to stock six new clubs, including the Minnesota North Stars. At the same time, the fledgling American Basketball Association was looking to compete with the National Basketball Association.

The ABA's rag-tag collection of owners, without a plan or adequate financing, faced a stiff challenge taking on a twelve-team NBA in which half of the clubs were losing money. Yet, the new league was born, with the Minnesota Muskies taking to the hardwood that fall with ten other franchises that included the Indiana Pacers, Kentucky Colonels, Denver Rockets, Dallas Chaparrals, and Anaheim Amigos.

The new league quickly set itself apart from the NBA after hiring the NBA's first superstar as its commissioner: the six-foot-ten George Mikan, who towered over opponents and led the Minneapolis Lakers to their first NBA championship in 1949. Mikan, widely considered the Babe Ruth of the upstart NBA, was a masterful shot blocker and rebounder with an ambidextrous hook shot. He played seven seasons for the Lakers and guided them to five NBA titles. Four years after Mikan retired as the league's all-time scoring leader in 1956, the financially struggling Lakers relocated to Los Angeles.

Mikan, who practiced law and operated a travel agency in Minneapolis following his playing days, made several unilateral decisions after taking over. The new owners wanted the ABA office in New York, but Mikan insisted he wasn't leaving home, so the new league was based in Minneapolis. The bespectacled former player, who struggled to see the brown ball when he watched basketball games, also decided the league would play with a red, white and blue ball. "The owners acted like I wanted to burn the flag when I said to forget the brown ball," he told Terry Pluto, author of *Loose Balls: The Short, Wild Life of the American Basketball Association*. Mikan also instituted the long-distance, three-point field goal, a wildly popular innovation that the NBA later adopted. The three-point shot and the dunk became cornerstones of the new league's open, improvisational style.

During the ABA's initial player draft on April 2, 1967, the Muskies used their first two picks to select two future Hall of Famers: Mel Daniels, a six-foot-nine All-American center from the University of New Mexico, and Phil Jackson, a Little All-American forward for his home state school, the University of North Dakota. Daniels inked with the Muskies instead of the NBA's Cincinnati Royals, becoming the NBA's first first-round pick to jump to the new league. He learned a hook shot from Mikan, and in that first season led the 50-28 Muskies in points and rebounds.

Although the opportunity to play close to home intrigued Jackson, the NBA's New York Knicks also drafted him in the second round and the team's coach, Red Holzman, traveled to North Dakota and signed him to a better offer than Muskies owner Larry Shields could afford. Jackson, who joined a talented club featuring Willis Reed, Walt Frazier, Bill Bradley, and Dave DeBusschere, was part of two championship clubs in ten seasons with the Knicks. He went on to win eleven more rings coaching the Chicago Bulls and Los Angeles Lakers.

In the first playoffs the following spring, the Muskies failed to reach the ABA Finals when they lost a five-game series to the eventual league champion, the Pittsburgh Pipers, led by the inaugural league MVP and scoring leader, Connie Hawkins. Soon after, the Muskies, who failed to draw fans to the Met Center in Bloomington, departed for Florida and became the Miami Floridians. But Bill Erickson, a Minneapolis attorney, bought a majority share of the Pipers and brought the flashy, entertaining Hawkins to Minnesota for the ABA's second season. The Brooklyn-born future Hall of Famer, arguably New York's greatest playground legend and the ABA's leading attraction, had been spurned by the NBA following a point-shaving scandal at the University of Iowa, which likely did not involve him.

Hawkins, who was blackballed from college ball and played for the Harlem Globetrotters, averaged 30.2 points a game for the Minnesota Pipers during an injury-plagued 1968–69 season. Daniels told Pluto that "the Connie Hawkins that led Pittsburgh to that first title could play in the NBA and be on the same level as Magic Johnson, Larry Bird, and Michael Jordan." But having this immense talent in town was lost on Minnesota fans, who were no more inclined to drive to the Met Center to watch him and the 36-42 Pipers. The team returned to Pittsburgh after one season, a crazy business decision typical of the ABA. From that point on, Mikan was Minnesota's lone connection to the ABA.

Meanwhile, the National Hockey League, long a six-team affair, doubled in size for the 1967–68 season. The league had been mostly an East Coast phenomenon, with only teams in Chicago and Detroit not based in the Eastern time zone. In adding six teams, however, the NHL crossed the continent. The Los Angeles Kings and Oakland Seals took up residence on the left coast; joining them in the newly created West Division were the Philadelphia Flyers, Pittsburgh Penguins, St. Louis Blues, and Minnesota North Stars.

Minneapolis native and longtime amateur and minor league hockey administrator Walter Bush fronted an ownership group running the new Minnesota franchise. Prior to an expansion draft to stock the six new clubs, held on June 7, 1967, the North Stars hired the flamboyant, entertaining, and freewheeling Wren Blair to oversee personnel decisions as the club's general manager and coach. A few years earlier Blair had discovered fourteen-year-old phenom Bobby Orr and later signed him for the Boston Bruins. Bush and Blair had worked together as co-owner and general manager of the minor league Minneapolis Bruins, and on joining the North Stars, Blair wasted little time in shaping the roster.

At the time the Montreal Canadiens were the league's elite team, deep in talent they had to make available to the new franchises. Blair and Canadiens general manager Sammy Pollock were old friends who had climbed corporate ladders together. Adding excitement to the expansion draft, they executed three trades that allowed the Canadiens to protect certain players and stocked the roster of the fledgling North Stars. When the dust had settled. Blair had added thirty-nine players. Thirteen had been acquired from Montreal, including defenseman Mike McMahon, winger Dave Balon, and centers Bill Masterton and André Boudrias. The plucky Masterton, who led the University of Denver to NCAA championships in 1960 and 1961, scored the franchise's first goal in a 2–2 tie with the Blues in St. Louis on October 11, 1967.

Blair used the expansion draft to acquire a few cornerstone players, including Rangers goalie prospect Cesare Maniago and young Bruins wingers Wayne Connelly and Bill Goldsworthy. In the North Stars' inaugural campaign, sharpshooter Connelly led the way with 35 goals and 56 points. The flashy, exciting Goldsworthy led the club in goals six times in ten seasons.

That first North Stars team beat five of the Original Six clubs and came within a goal of reaching the Stanley Cup Finals. While the Canadiens advanced from the East Division made up of the Original Six, the North Stars, loaded with former Canadiens, lost in double overtime to the Blues in Game Seven of the conference finals. Four of the seven games required overtime, and the Scotty Bowman-coached Blues won three of them.

In the first extra session of Game Seven, Connelly skated in alone on St. Louis goaltender Glenn Hall when he was pulled down from behind by the Blues' Jimmy Roberts, which didn't draw a penalty shot or even a two-minute minor penalty. Then, early in the second session, Ron Schock beat Maniago on a breakaway for the 2–1 win, setting up the expansion Blues for a four-game sweep at the hands of the mighty Canadiens. After limiting Montreal to one-goal victories in all four games, the thirty-six-year-old Hall, who was known to vomit before every game later in his career, won the Conn Smythe Trophy as the league's playoff MVP.

With the two expansion franchises getting off the ground as the weather turned warm in 1967, the Twins had already fallen flat during a dreadful April. They opened May by winning four straight at home against the Yankees and Red Sox, but their struggles were far from over. Still, a few bright spots emerged in the early going. Zoilo Versalles, coming off a disappointing sequel to his 1965 MVP season, batted .345 with 18 RBIS in his first twenty-two games. And Rod Carew was emerging as a dangerous hitter following a slow start. The left-handed-hitting rookie had struggled with the breaking ball in camp, but quickly learned to make adjustments. He had collected just nine hits in his first eleven games, but soon turned things around.

On May 8, in the midst of an eight-game hitting streak, Carew collected his first five-hit game in a 7–4 loss to the Senators. He enjoyed seven such games in nineteen seasons; the first seemingly jumpstarted his AL Rookie of the Year candidacy. Carew lashed three more hits against Washington pitching the next day, and in the next week delivered two more three-hit performances. After going 3-for-4 and driving in three runs in a 5–2 win over California on May 19, he was batting .340 in his first 100 at-bats.

All the while the Twins were chasing the .500 mark, alternately winning a few and losing a few. Dean Chance, the Twins' big off-season pickup, almost single-handedly kept the mistake-ridden Twins from a lengthy losing streak that could have proved disastrous. After the Orioles roughed up Chance in his first Twins start on April 13, the lanky right-hander reeled off seven straight wins. Four came after the Twins had lost at least two games in a row.

On May 11, in the only game of four the Twins won at home against lowly Kansas City, Chance tossed a one-hit shutout, winning 8–0 to post his fifth straight "W." He walked six on a night he said he didn't have good stuff or control, serving up only a fourth-inning single to Danny Cater. Chance made it six in a row when the Twins began a road trip in Chicago on May 16. The 18-7 White Sox had won ten straight games to take over first place in the American League, 7½ games in front of the Twins, but Chance pitched a second straight shutout, 1–0, the twelfth 1–0 victory of his young career. He allowed the leadoff man to reach in five of the first six innings, but had White Sox hitters chopping the ball into the dirt all night. Versalles and Carew turned three ground balls into double plays.

With Chance facing his old club for the first time, in Anaheim on May 20, his winning streak reached seven, though his scoreless-innings streak stalled at twenty-six in a 7–2 victory. The win came during a four-game Twins winning streak that evened their record at 16-16. They dropped three of four to close May, however, and headed into June at 20-22, trailing first-place Detroit by 6½ games. Chance kicked off the new month with his third shutout, scattering five hits and fanning ten in a 4–0 win over Boston.

Chance displayed the electric fastball-slider combo that fueled his 1964 Cy Young season. At a time when Major League Baseball gave one Cy Young Award for both leagues, Chance was the only man not named Sandy Koufax to be honored between 1963 and 1966. Hitters hated facing Chance, who, with a corkscrew motion, turned his back to the hitter before exploding toward the plate with a pitch. His stuff was terrific, his control less so, so turning his back to the plate could unnerve a hitter. His big 1964 season inspired Yankees star Mickey Mantle to tell New York sportswriter Phil Pepe: "Chance, not CBS, owns the New York Yankees. Lock, stock and barrel."

In his Cy Young campaign, Chance went 20-9 and led the Majors with a 1.65 ERA and 11 shutouts, including six 1–0 victories. He held opponents scoreless or to a single run in 20 of his 35 starts. The handsome, blue-eyed kid was all of twenty-three, and for him and his playboy sidekick, Angels left-hander Bo Belinsky, Los Angeles was for the taking. Together they caroused after games, partying in the same circles as Frank Sinatra and Hollywood types. Occasionally they found trouble, which spurred the question: who was a bad influence on whom? The Angels pointed the finger at Belinsky and traded him in 1964, but not before the pair had a memorable brush with federal authorities. They got the unexpected news from Angels manager Bill Rigney:

"We're in the clubhouse in Washington and Rigney calls us into his office," Chance explained to sportswriter Maury Allen, author of *Bo: Pitching and Wooing.* "'J. Edgar Hoover wants to see you two guys.' I'm wondering what we did now that the FBI would want us. We were escorted up to Hoover's office and he had a big grin on his face, wanted to shake our hands and just wanted to meet us. We hadn't done anything wrong. . . . It was pretty exciting. We went all through the FBI building and . . . had a great time. It was really a wonderful day. That's the way it always was when I was with Bo."

With the Twins, Chance connected with another free spirit, twenty-two-year-old Dave Boswell. The master of the head-scratching malaprop, with an ability to mimic various animal and insect sounds, he once had a team bus driver searching under the seats for a cricket. The confident, quirky right-hander with an offbeat take on nearly everything was one of the characters of the game.

Boswell and Chance were frequent targets of Twins reliever Al Worthington, a deeply religious man who encouraged both pitchers to attend his Sunday morning prayer meetings. Chance always politely declined, but when Worthington told him that Baltimore Colts football star Mike Curtis would be a guest speaker at the next meeting, he said he would attend if he woke up in time. Worthington made sure of that, wrote longtime sportswriter Jeff Miller in his account of the 1967 season, *Down to the Wire.* Worthington offered to provide a wakeup call, so Chance was there:

"Chance arrived and saw Boswell, each silently responding with looks that said, 'What are *you* doing here?' During the meeting, Worthington asked everyone to bow his head. He then noted that everyone in the group had sinned, and those who needed help should raise their hands. After the meeting ended, Boswell came straight over to Chance and shook his hand. Chance was puzzled, and Boswell explained: 'Those hypocrites. When the guy asked if anybody there needed help, I peeked. Dean, you were the only guy in the room that had his hand raised.'"

Flirting with piety did little for Boswell, who was looking to become a rotation fixture in his third big league season. He was roughed up early and often in April, leading to a run of May relief appearances, and his ERA was nearly 5.00 heading into June. To make matters worse, Jim Kaat, coming off his twenty-five-win campaign, had been extremely hittable. He was 1-6 with a 6.66 ERA in eleven outings, and opponents were batting a hefty .344 against the six-foot-four southpaw.

The starters' troubles meant too much time warming up and too many innings for relief aces Al Worthington and Ron Kline. Overworked early on, both relievers struggled in the middle months. Luckily for the Twins, young Jim Merritt stepped up when Mudcat Grant suffered a knee injury in May. The twenty-three-year-old lefty moved into the rotation to stay, tossing consecutive shutouts against the Athletics and Yankees and giving the bullpen some time off.

For Mele, the usually dependable middle of the batting order was another concern. Tony Oliva, fighting a recurring back ailment, missed half of Minnesota's first twenty-six games and barely hit when he was in the lineup. Harmon Killebrew also started slowly. In mid-May Mele decided to tweak his traditional batting order, which was to have Oliva bat third, just ahead of Killebrew, his cleanup hitter. Now Oliva would follow Killebrew in the fifth spot. Oliva didn't respond to the change, but Killebrew went on a homer binge, powering 10 and knocking in 22 runs in the first twenty-three games after the switch.

During a two-week stay at the Met in early June, Killebrew generated the most on-field excitement. The Angels were in town on June 3, a breezy Saturday afternoon that drew a small crowd of just 12,337. With Carew and Rich Rollins on base in the fourth inning, Killebrew drilled what is widely regarded as the longest home run ever hit at Metropolitan Stadium. He turned on a pitch from forty-year-old Lew Burdette and drove it several rows into the Met's upper deck in left field, a mighty blast that cleared the roughly thirty rows of lower-deck bleacher seats situated in front of the upper deck's façade.

The scoreboard's Twins-O-Gram quickly listed the homer as a 430-foot shot, measuring it to the point it landed. Considering the second deck stood more than seventy feet above ground level, a projection calculated by Twins executives Bill and Sherry Robertson estimated the ball would have traveled some 520 feet. The Twins acknowledged this first home run to reach the Met's upper deck by painting the seat red. While the Met is now gone, the red chair remains suspended at its original location, high on a wall at the Mall of America.

"It was a knuckleball of all things," Killebrew said of the pitch from Burdette, the longtime Milwaukee Braves righty who had won three games in the 1957 World Series, including Game Seven. "I don't know. Maybe it was a wet one, but it looked like a knuckler." Wet or not, the upper-deck shot wasn't the longest of his career. In August 1962, he powered a pitch from future Hall of Famer Jim Bunning over the left-field roof at Tiger Stadium. Whether Killebrew's homer off Burdette was the longest ever hit at Metropolitan Stadium became a point of contention the very next day.

When Killebrew stepped to the plate in the second inning against Angels righty Jack Sanford, Twins public address announcer Bob Casey informed the crowd that the previous day's home run was a 520-foot blast and the seat it struck would be retired. Before Casey had finished speaking, Killebrew stepped into Sanford's first pitch and drove it off the facing of the upper deck in left-center field, one section over toward center from the ball he'd hit the day before. The point of impact was measured at 434 feet and projections estimated the two homers would have traveled nearly the same distance.

Teammates debated which would have gone the greater distance. Mudcat Grant told the *Minneapolis Tribune*'s Tom Briere that Saturday's would have traveled the farthest. Earl Battey insisted that Sunday's, even without the benefit of Saturday's windy conditions, would have carried farther. What did Kille-brew think? "I think the second one would have gone farther," Killebrew said in a 2010 interview. "It was actually hit harder."

The second one provided some vindication for Burdette, who had coughed up the first blast. He confirmed Killebrew had teed off on a knuckleball during a conversation with Steve Aschburner, author of the 2012 biography, *Harmon Killebrew: Ultimate Slug-ger*. "I was practicing my knuckleball, trying to come up with a new pitch," Burdette told Aschburner. "I threw Harmon one. He swung and missed. So I threw him another one. The wind was blowing out, and he hit a towering fly ball. You should have heard Jack Sanford. He was cracking up in the dugout. He yelled, 'Nice going, Lew—you just gave up the longest homer in the history of the park.' The next day Harmon hit one off San-ford in the upper deck. I wish I could tell you what I told him."

Killebrew's two blasts were the last memorable moments of Sam Mele's managerial career. On June 9, with the 25-25 Twins lodged in sixth place, owner Calvin Griffith fired Mele, less than two years after the forty-five-year-old skipper had steered the team through a host of injuries to the franchise's first pennant in three decades. Griffith was itching to make a change after the Twins' slide in 1966, and their mediocre start in 1967 intensi-fied the itch. He relieved it after Cleveland had staged a four-run, ninth-inning rally to defeat the Twins. Griffith used the per-ceived managerial oversight of four straight left-handed pinch hitters igniting Cleveland's rally against right-handed reliever Al Worthington to shake up the team.

The firing caught most of the players by surprise, and cer-tainly Mele himself. The Massachusetts native still lived in the Boston area, and his family would stay behind and join him for the summer at the end of the school year. Mele's wife and five children had just arrived in Minnesota that day, and when Griffith summoned Mele, one of the manager's sons, thirteen-year-old Steve, was with him in his office. He returned to him without a job.

Mele had taken the reins from Cookie Lavagetto midway through the 1961 season, the team's first in Minnesota. Mele was 524-436 in parts of seven seasons, and his club won more than ninety games in three of his five full seasons at the helm. He was a player's manager, someone who didn't have a lot of rules and didn't criticize his players in the press. He reprimanded them and offered encouragement privately. Players responded to his approach, but Griffith thought Mele had been too soft on his underperforming club. That spring Jimmie Hall and Don Mincher, recently traded to the Angels for Dean Chance, told reporters that a relaxed attitude prevailed in a Twins clubhouse that lacked a work ethic.

The pressure was on Mele, who ran a tighter training camp that spring, but the Twins didn't respond on the field. After the club started poorly, a run of team meetings and postgame practices failed to spur a turnaround. The strife between Mele and pitching coach Johnny Sain in 1966 also took a toll, as players took sides and the manager may have lost the respect of some of the veterans. Jim Kaat questioned Mele's competence in his editorial regarding Sain's off-season firing, published by the *Minneapolis Star*. Kaat suggested that Sain, a coaching genius who challenged his managers for control of the pitching staff, should get a "name your own figure" contract and a manager who appreciates his talents.

Mele, despite his success with the Twins, never managed again. He received two job offers following his firing, including one from Oakland A's owner Charlie Finley, but Mele had no interest in working for the volatile owner, who in his day might have been the ideal host for a Donald Trump-style "You're Fired" reality show. Instead, Mele spent more than two decades scouting for the Boston Red Sox as a special assistant until his retirement.

1. For much of the 1960s, Bob Allison, Tony Oliva, and Harmon Killebrew anchored the middle of a power-laden Minnesota Twins lineup.

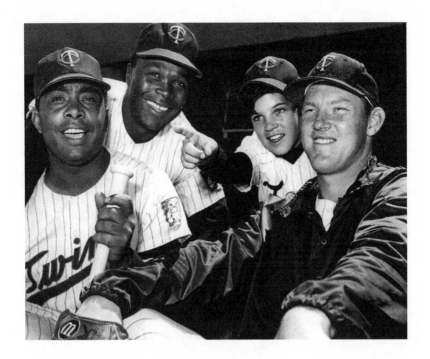

2. (*opposite top*) In 1965, Dave Boswell (left) was a promising rookie and Camilo Pascual was a two-time twenty-game winner who had fronted the Twins rotation for four seasons. Pascual was known for his devastating curveball. Boswell was best known as a character of the game.

3. (*opposite bottom*) Jim "Mudcat" Grant emerged as the staff ace during the 1965 American League pennant race. He won twenty-one games, led the AL with six shutouts, and posted two wins in the World Series.

4. (*above*) Earl Battey, Sandy Valdespino, and Jim Kaat share a light moment with a team batboy in the Twins' dugout before a game at Metropolitan Stadium.

5. Jimmie Hall broke out as a rookie in 1963, stroking 33 home runs. He was an early MVP candidate during a productive 1965 season.

6. (*opposite top*) Twins manager Sam Mele (14) went toe-to-toe with umpire Bill Valentine over a ruling at Metropolitan Stadium on July 18, 1965. Jim Kaat and Rich Rollins (in glasses) try to intercede.

7. (*opposite bottom*) Playing critical roles for the 1965 Twins were Al Worthington (left), an elder statesman of a young Twins team, and Zoilo Versalles, the youngest regular and the AL's 1965 MVP.

8. Johnny Klippstein was nearing the end of his career when, at age thirty-seven, he was at his best for the 1965 Twins.

9. (*opposite top*) The Twins celebrate clinching the AL pennant with a 2–1 win over the Washington Senators on September 26, 1965. César Tovar and Harmon Killebrew are about to join catcher Earl Battey and a leaping Sandy Valdespino in a collective hug of winning pitcher Jim Kaat.

10. (*opposite bottom*) Harmon Killebrew and Twins manager Sam Mele stand in the middle of the clubhouse celebration after the Twins clinched the AL pennant at Washington's DC Stadium on September 26, 1965. At far left, coach Jim Lemon fills two cups with champagne.

11. Zoilo Versalles, Mudcat Grant, and Don Mincher are all smiles after the Twins defeated the Los Angeles Dodgers, 8–2, in Game One of the 1965 World Series. Versalles and Mincher hit homers and Grant worked a complete game.

12. (*opposite top*) Manager Sam Mele (left) and rookie Frank Quilici celebrate after the Twins clinched the AL pennant in 1965. Seven years later Quilici would become the Twins' manager.

13. (*opposite bottom*) Rod Carew (left) stands with Vern Morgan, who as a Minor League manager served as a mentor and instructor for the promising prospect. Morgan joined the Twins coaching staff in 1969, the year Carew stole home seven times.

14. Dean Chance came to the Twins in a major trade and won twenty games in 1967, when the team fell a win short of making its second World Series appearance in three seasons.

15. César Tovar, who could handle multiple positions and played all nine in a game in September 1968, puts the tag on a base runner during a game at Metropolitan Stadium.

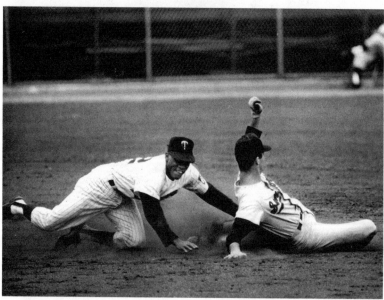

16. In 1968 the Twins acquired Leo Cárdenas, the elite shortstop they needed to compete in the late 1960s. Dubbed "Mr. Automatic" for his sure glove, Cárdenas garnered MVP votes in 1969.

17. A swingman for much of his Twins tenure, Jim Perry was a key contributor to the club's 1965 success. He emerged as the staff ace in 1969 and won Cy Young honors in 1970.

18. (*opposite top*) In his one season as Twins manager in 1969, Billy Martin brought an emphasis on fundamentals, an aggressive running game, and a heavy dose of intensity to the Twins.

19. (*opposite bottom*) A Dodgers pitcher for the 1965 World Series champs, Ron Perranoski later joined the Twins and led the AL in saves in 1969 and 1970—the first two years saves were an official statistic.

20. (*above*) Bert Blyleven began his Hall of Fame career as a nineteen-year-old rookie in 1970, when his impressive debut helped the Twins win their second straight AL West crown.

21. Even the Beatles' George Harrison
has donned the "TC" of the Twins, as
the group was housed in the home
team's clubhouse for its performance at
Metropolitan Stadium on August 21, 1965.
Courtesy of Beatles Book Photo Library.

TWELVE

Getting Better

A week before Calvin Griffith fired Twins manager Sam Mele—on June 1, 1967—the Beatles released *Sgt. Pepper's Lonely Hearts Club Band*, the kaleidoscopic collection of rock, Eastern musical influences, and turn-of-the-century British music hall that turned the pop-music world upside down. With *Sgt. Pepper's* release at the start of the "Summer of Love," the Beatles were at the psychedelic forefront with what was widely considered an early concept album, which inspired their peers to build their recordings around themes. As much as the *Hot 100* scene had been built around the single, *Sgt. Pepper's* spurred the album era, a decades-long span in which the full-length record was the dominant form of musical expression.

So much had changed for the Beatles. After continuously touring the world for nearly three full years, the nonstop travel and the mad passion of Beatlemania took their toll, particularly on George Harrison. Tested by the mindless screaming and inadequate crowd control at open-air performances, the Beatles decided in 1966 they were done with touring, an unprecedented move that was widely considered a risky career decision.

After their last live performance at San Francisco's Candlestick Park in August 1966, the four Beatles retreated to Abbey Road Studios in London. The recording studio, off limits to visitors when they were working, became their private workshop and sanctuary, a place where they increasingly experimented with new ideas and focused as much on production techniques as songwriting. Enjoying their artistic freedom, the Beatles wrote and recorded their most cerebral and complicated music once the endless touring stopped.

The transformation began with *Rubber Soul*, released in 1965. "Nowhere Man" was the first Lennon-McCartney composition not focused on romance. John Lennon's impressive writing and Harrison's use of the sitar on "Norwegian Wood (This Bird Has Flown)" epitomized the dramatic changes underway. Ringo Starr said this was the Beatles' "departure record," reflecting the group's influences and growing musical interests.

When the Beatles completed their final tour in San Francisco, they had just released *Revolver*, continuing the group's transformation with a substantial shift in instrumentation as well as lyrical content. The newest songs were intricate and melodic, and the group's innovative studio work, aided by longtime producer George Martin and sound engineer Geoff Emerick, gave interesting twists to classic compositions "Eleanor Rigby" and "Tomorrow Never Knows." A string octet of violins, violas, and cellos accompanied Paul McCartney's "Eleanor Rigby." Lennon sang parts of the *Tibetan Book of the Dead* in "Tomorrow Never Knows," the album's finale, highlighted by Emerick's treatment of Lennon's voice. Tape loops, multitracked guitars, Harrison's sitar, and the drone of a tamboura provided the psychedelic vibe.

The Beatles had been releasing several albums a year, but nearly a year passed between *Revolver* and *Sgt. Pepper's*, as the group went to extremes to generate certain sounds and textures. The process of recording *Sgt. Pepper's* became a piecemeal affair in which parts were often recorded separately from one another. The approach was another source of frustration for Harrison, who had grown increasingly tired of the trappings of being a Beatle and having his songs often dismissed by his mates. "Up to that time, we had recorded more like a band; we would learn the songs and play them," Harrison explained in *The Beatle Anthology* documentary. "It became an assembly process—just little parts and then overdubbing—and for me it became a bit tiring and a bit boring."

Harrison's frustration had a payoff on *Sgt. Pepper's*. Prior to the start of the album's recording sessions, Harrison ran off to India for six weeks without the others. The trip had a profound influence on his worldview, and intensive training on the sitar with Ravi Shankar inspired "Within You Without You." He recorded the track alone, integrating Indian influences and instruments— along with the Hindu tenant of removing the "space between us all" by diminishing one's ego—into a Western pop song.

The creative jag that generated *Sgt. Pepper's* began with long recording sessions that produced Lennon's "Strawberry Fields Forever" and McCartney's "Penny Lane," released together as a single in February 1967. Overdubbing layers of instrumentation and sounds was critical to the dreamy "Strawberry Fields." McCartney and George Martin went to great lengths with "Penny Lane," backing it with an arrangement for flutes, trumpets, piccolo, and flugelhorn. A highlight is the sensational piccolo trumpet solo by David Mason, once the principal trumpeter of the Royal Philharmonic Orchestra, who McCartney insisted on hiring after seeing him perform Johann Sebastian Bach's "Brandenburg Concerto No. 2" on television. "Penny Lane" and various *Sgt. Pepper's* recordings required a trip to Abbey Road Studio's sound effects cupboard, home to a wealth of paraphernalia: wind machines, thunder machines, bells, whistles, alarm clocks, all kinds of toys.

Other sonic textures were less easy to come by. "A Day in the Life," which closes *Sgt. Pepper's*, is a masterful Lennon-McCartney collaboration that stands as one of the Beatles' greatest works. Each songwriter contributed separate melodies and lyrics, and after the recording was completed, they added a sonic touch to bridge the song's two parts. Lennon had the abstract idea of "creating some kind of sound that would start out really tiny and then gradually expand to become huge and all-encompassing," wrote Emerick, who penned *Here, There and Everywhere* with Howard Massey. "Picking up on the theme, Paul excitedly suggested employing an entire symphony orchestra." Martin liked the idea until McCartney revealed that he simply wanted orchestra members to do a long, slow climb from the lowest note on their instruments to the highest note—in unison. Martin disliked asking classical musicians to engage in such an experiment, but the deed was done and what Lennon described as an "orgasm of sound" was also used after the final chorus to end the song.

Like the Beatles, many of the up-and-coming bands were moving beyond the two-minute pop song. Britain's Procol Harum had a Summer of Love hit with "A Whiter Shade of Pale." Further feeding the psychedelic frenzy were Strawberry Alarm Clock's "Incense and Peppermints," Small Faces' "Itchycoo Park," and Jefferson Airplane's "Somebody to Love" and "White Rabbit." Among other 1967 adventures in psychedelia were Pink Floyd's *The Piper at the Gates of Dawn* and the first two releases of the Jimi Hendrix Experience, *Are You Experienced?* and *Axis: Bold as Love*, which garnered radio play for "Purple Haze," "Foxy Lady," and "Hey Joe."

On March 23, 1967, the Who made their U.S. debut at "Murray the K's Easter Show," an annual rock event hosted by renowned New York radio disc jockey Murray Kaufman. The Who caught everyone's attention, wrote Nicholas Schaffner in *The British Invasion*, with "the blinding flash of the first smoke bombs ever to be detonated on a New York concert stage. Out of the wings with a flying leap comes a tall, lanky guitarist with a comically large nose, resplendent in a Union Jack jacket, slashing out the most ear-wracking Power Pop chords anyone in the crowd has ever been subjected to."

From Pete Townshend's opening leap, the Who never treaded lightly. The band's songwriter and lead guitarist, author of concept albums and rock operas, tossed guitars skyward and caught some of them; others were smashed into equipment or floors. The manic Keith Moon, wearing a bullseye t-shirt that night, wreaked havoc on drum kits and hotel rooms. The group had its first American hits in 1967 with "Happy Jack" and the psychedelic "I Can See for Miles."

Early in 1967, the Rolling Stones' "Ruby Tuesday" and the Turtles' "Happy Together" battled for supremacy on the *Billboard* chart and the local weekly surveys. Soon after, proving that the two-minute pop song wasn't dead, "I Think We're Alone Now" by Tommy James and the Shondells and "Something Stupid" by Frank Sinatra and Nancy Sinatra went head to head for the top spot on WDGY. When the weather warmed up, the Association topped the *Billboard Hot 100* for nearly all of July with "Windy," which had a five-week run as number one at KDWB. And arguably the year's biggest song from across the pond was Lulu's "To Sir with Love," the title track to the popular Sidney Poitier film that was all the rage that summer.

Aretha Franklin finally broke through in 1967. The beauty and power of her voice were apparent from her youth when she sang in her father's Detroit church, but success came slowly after she moved into mainstream pop and jazz as an eighteen-year-old in 1960. When she began working with producer Jerry Wexler and the Muscle Shoals Rhythm Section for Atlantic Records, her work became more soulful. She was electric on a handful of R&B hits in 1967: "I Never Loved a Man (The Way I Love You)," "Baby I Love You," "Chain of Fools," "(You Make Me Feel Like) A Natural Woman" and Otis Redding's "Respect."

Another stunning voice caught the world's attention that June at the three-day Monterey Pop Festival. The Who and Jimi Hendrix Experience made their first major American appearances at Monterey, as did Texas native Janis Joplin, who gave a raw, gripping interpretation of "Ball and Chain," the bluesy lament of singer-songwriter Big Mama Thornton. After the performance, Columbia Records quickly signed Joplin and her band, Big Brother and the Holding Company. And because the performance hadn't been filmed, festival organizers persuaded the group to take the stage and do the song again the following day.

While Beatles fans were contemplating the latent meaning of the newly released "Lucy in the Sky with Diamonds," the Twins were in need of a new field boss. Calvin Griffith hired Calvin Coolidge Ermer, a forty-three-year-old baseball lifer. After appearing in a single Major League game with Washington in 1947, the former second base prospect spent two decades playing, coaching, and managing in the Minor Leagues for the Griffith family. Ermer was managing Minnesota's Triple-A Denver affiliate when Sam Mele was fired, and Griffith promoted him to become the Twins' third manager. Nearly half of the 1967 roster had played for Ermer in the Minors; he had managed Harmon Killebrew and Bob Allison at Chattanooga a decade earlier and most of the young pitchers had worked for him at Denver.

Ermer had a reputation of being tough and "all business" on the field, but loose and easygoing with players when the workday was over. His fourteen-year wait to manage a big league team got off to a rough start, though, as the Orioles stuck Chance with only his third loss in 14 starts and came away with an 11–2 win in the opener of a four-game weekend series at the Met. Although Ermer's debut didn't go as planned, the Twins demonstrated an early sign of a turnaround in Ermer's second game.

Facing the Orioles on Saturday, June 10, Jim Kaat claimed his first "W" since April 22 by going the distance in an 8–1 victory. The big left-hander, who had been struggling with his control all season, didn't walk anyone. It was his one-hundredth career win—one that took seven weeks and ten starts to nail down. After working his first complete game of 1967, Kaat told *Sporting News*'s Max Nichols: "So many times I needed a big pitch and didn't come up with it." He was just 2-7 with a dismal 5.38 ERA, but soon began producing the big pitch consistently. Kaat was one of the league's best pitchers down the stretch.

Another positive from Saturday's win was seeing Tony Oliva drive in six of Minnesota's eight runs. Oliva, who was playing through an assortment of injuries and hitting .238 with just eight extra-base hits in thirty-four games, was batting fourth in the new skipper's lineup—with Harmon Killebrew moved up into the third spot and Zoilo Versalles dropped down into the fifth hole. The highlight of Oliva's debut as Ermer's cleanup hitter was a three-run shot into the bullpen in right-center off knuckleballer Eddie Fisher, just his second home run of the season.

The Twins won four of their next six games at home to move two games over .500 for the first time all season on June 15. At 30-28, the Twins had closed within four games of first-place

Chicago in what was shaping up to be a wild American League race. Suddenly showing some life, the Twins started a week-long trip in Cleveland, where their fate seemed tied to Municipal Stadium's outfield wall.

In the opener, Oliva, suddenly the Twins' hottest hitter, suffered a scary injury in a 2–1 defeat. When Cleveland catcher Joe Azcue lined a Jim Merritt offering deep into the right-field gap, Oliva sprinted toward the fence, leaped high, and crashed hard into it. His head struck a metal railing at the top of the wall and punched a hole in the cyclone fence behind the protective tarp. Briefly knocked unconscious, Oliva was carried off on a stretcher by several teammates, suffering from facial cuts and abrasions, plus two slipped vertebrae, which pinched nerves and caused neck pain. After Twins trainer George "Doc" Lentz worked the vertebrae back into place, Oliva was hospitalized for precautionary observation.

Oliva's newest ailment put a damper on the club's recent success, but less than forty-eight hours after running into the wall— and only a few hours after being released from the hospital—he was called on to pinch-hit by Ermer in the Sunday finale of the Cleveland series. He still had a stiff neck and vision issues, but in the eighth inning broke open a pitchers' duel between Kaat and Cleveland's Sam Mc Dowell. After Killebrew drew a bases-loaded walk to pull the Twins within a run, 2–1, Mc Dowell gave way to Steve Bailey. Oliva greeted Bailey with a bases-clearing double to put the Twins in front. The 4–2 victory required a game-saving catch from Sandy Valdespino, who climbed Municipal Stadium's left-field wall, reached over the top and robbed Larry Brown of a grand slam to end the eighth.

The following night in Baltimore, in the first of two games, Oliva broke up a scoreless affair in the sixth with a two-run homer off Orioles starter Tom Phoebus and local boy Dave Boswell tossed a three-hitter to claim a 4–0 victory over his hometown team. Two days later, however, after the Twins had flown from Baltimore to Detroit, Boswell and Oliva would be at the center of a team squabble. On the bus traveling from the Detroit airport to the team's hotel, the twenty-two-year-old Boswell, who often carried guns on road trips, took out one of his unloaded handguns and started pulling the trigger.

Mudcat Grant and Oliva asked him to put it away, and when Boswell continued his gun play, Oliva angrily told Boswell, "Don't be playing with that thing on this bus," noted Rod Carew in his 1979 autobiography, *Carew*, with Ira Berkow. To which Boswell replied: "Well, you guys play with guns in Cuba; why can't we play with guns here?" The argument quickly escalated into a confrontation between several white players, including Boswell and Ted Uhlaender, and African American and Latin American players. A *Sporting News* report had Oliva and Ted Uhlaender nearly coming to blows, and another source had Uhlaender and Sandy Valdespino ready to face off before teammates stepped in and Ermer made his way to the back of the bus.

The fray was Ermer's first touch of internal strife as manager. He threatened fines and the bus went silent. That wasn't the end of the incident. Ermer set up a meeting at the hotel to give players an opportunity to air grievances and make amends. And money exchanged hands, as the manager reportedly fined Boswell, Oliva, and Uhlaender $250 each for their roles in the dispute. Although the Twins were one of the most integrated Major League teams, clubhouse camaraderie took a hit. A few Latino and Black players were upset that Ermer failed to address the more egregious remarks of one of their white teammates.

Ermer and the Twins weathered the storm without the bus incident becoming a distraction. They closed June by taking two of three from Boston at the Met, and their 3–2 win in the series finale kicked off an eight-game winning streak that included doubleheader sweeps of Washington and New York in early July. Kaat won twice, giving him six victories in his last seven starts, and he, Boswell, Grant, Dean Chance, and Jim Merritt worked impressive complete-game victories to lead the surge. The offense also came alive and Oliva was at his best. The biggest blow was his game-winning, ninth-inning single off Yankees left-hander Steve Hamilton to give the Twins a 7–6 comeback win in the second game of a Fourth of July doubleheader. The walk-off single moved the Twins into second place, just three games back of Chicago.

Minnesota made it eight straight wins the following day, completing a four-game sweep of the Yankees before heading to Chicago to close the first half with four games against the White Sox. Chicago's lead had slipped to just 2½ games, but the White Sox stalled the Twins' surge with consecutive ninth-inning walk-off victories on Friday and Saturday. The Twins, after scoring just a single run off lefties Gary Peters and Tommy John in the two losses, gained some revenge when the first half wrapped with the Twins' third doubleheader sweep in a week. The bats produced a pair of convincing victories. Kaat hit a home run and evened his record at 8-8 in the opener, a 7–4 victory, and Boswell stroked two hits and pitched into the ninth of a 5–1 decision in the nightcap. The 45-36 Twins, with 12 wins in their final fifteen games before the break, stayed within 2½ games of Chicago.

Dean Chance made a triumphant return to Anaheim Stadium, home of his former team, the Los Angeles Angels, to start the 1967 All-Star Game. He allowed only a harmless single and a home run to the Philadelphia Phillies' Dick Allen in three innings. Having the 2–1 National League victory decided by a dramatic fifteenth-inning home run from Cincinnati Reds star Tony Pérez was an appropriate way to set up a second-half dogfight between four American League clubs—one that went down to the final minutes of the season. The White Sox led Detroit by two games when the season resumed. The Twins were in third, a half game behind the Tigers, followed by the California Angels. The Angels didn't stick around for long, but the fifth-place Boston Red Sox emerged as the fourth challenger.

After finishing ninth in 1966, the rejuvenated Red Sox were six games off the pace at the break, but an unlikely club to work its way into the race. Under the direction of rookie manager Dick Williams, they got off to the best post-break start and recorded a league-best 51-31 second-half mark in pursuit of the franchise's first pennant since 1946. Boston opened by splitting a twin bill with Baltimore before running off ten straight wins. The bats of

Tony Conigliaro, Carl Yastrzemski, and Joe Foy fueled the surge, and when the winning streak reached ten via a July 23 doubleheader sweep of Cleveland, the Red Sox were twelve games over .500 and within a half game of first-place Chicago.

On that Sunday afternoon, the Tigers and Yankees were playing two at Tiger Stadium. Tigers lefty Mickey Lolich recalls the smoke billowing beyond the left-field wall during the day, a sign of trouble on the streets. Anger and frustration in America's poorest urban communities had erupted in deadly, destructive riots in Newark ten days earlier and now Detroit was aflame. Detroit native and Tigers star Willie Horton drove to the area under siege after the doubleheader, stood on top of a car still in uniform, and made an impassioned but unsuccessful plea to stop the violence. Chicago teetered on the brink of a disastrous summer, but fared better than most U.S. cities, including Minneapolis, where storefronts burned along Plymouth Avenue for two days.

The Twins were in Kansas City at the time, starting a two-week road trip. They had opened the second half with four wins in five games at home. Meanwhile, the first-place White Sox dropped six of their first nine games after the break, so a Twins win at home against the Angels on July 17 would secure a first-place tie. But Angels lefty George Brunet, who led the American League with 19 losses in 1967, blanked the Twins on four hits, 2–0. The Twins wouldn't win again for another nine days. Mustering only a tie at Yankee Stadium on July 25 in a winless stretch of eight games, the Twins quickly plunged to fifth place.

The White Sox lacked run production—a shortcoming of the franchise throughout the 1960s—yet held first place for most of June and all of July. The starting trio of Joe Horlen, Gary Peters, and Tommy John claimed 28 of Chicago's 47 first-half wins and pitched quality innings all season long. The 1967 White Sox posted a 2.45 staff ERA that remains the Majors' lowest single-season team mark since 1919, the end of the dead-ball era. But even after acquiring aging veterans Rocky Colavito and Ken Boyer in late-July trades, the White Sox couldn't push across enough runs to take over the AL race.

The Twins made their move on first place with a 13-3 run in August. Lefty Jim Merritt started Minnesota's push on August 4, shutting out the Red Sox 3–0 on five hits. The twenty-three-year-old control specialist improved to 8-3 with a league-leading 2.06 ERA. He was in the midst of a month-long stretch in which he allowed just one walk in 59⅓ innings, and a week later, with the Twins in the midst of a seven-game winning streak, Merritt pitched the Twins to a 3–2 victory over Chicago. Minnesota would win seven of his eight August starts.

The pitching staff played a key role in the August upturn, recording four shutouts among the Twins' 13 wins. Jim Perry stepped into the rotation and worked consecutive shutouts against Washington and California. In a three-game sweep of Boston at the Met, Chance joined Merritt in blanking the Red Sox— and they and Dave Boswell limited Boston to a single run in the series. Chance also held the Red Sox hitless in the August 6 series finale. On a rainy Monday night, the twenty-six-year-old right-hander worked five perfect innings before the game was called with the Twins in front 2–0. The teams had sat through a twenty-five-minute rain delay in the fourth inning, but the weather won out an inning later. When the game was called with one out in the bottom of the fifth, Chance called his no-hit effort a "cheapie."

"I had good stuff, particularly my curveball," Chance said after the game, "but who can honestly tell whether you've got no-hit stuff or not? I doubt I could have thrown a no-hitter." If anyone was a good judge of whether he had the stuff, Chance was the guy. He had thrown 18 no-hitters in high school, four of them perfect games. On this night, he allowed only two hard-hit balls, both in the third inning. One was a liner off the bat of Boston catcher Elston Howard to Tony Oliva in right; the other was a long drive by losing pitcher Jim Lonborg, which backed Bob Allison to the warning track in left.

Chance's gem doesn't appear in the record books as a no-hitter. Major League Baseball ruled in 1991 that a hitless start must go at least nine innings to be recognized. Prior to his five no-hit frames, the closest Chance had come to a big league no-

no was a one-hitter he threw at the Met in September 1962 as an Angels rookie. He held the Twins hitless into the eighth inning before Zoilo Versalles ended his bid with an infield single. Official or not, Chance's five hitless innings completed a sweep of red-hot Boston, and for the Twins ace, the wait to work an *official* no-hitter was brief.

On August 25, less than three weeks later, Chance turned the trick in Cleveland, pitching fifty miles from his home in Wooster, Ohio. A historic performance seemed unlikely early on. Chance walked the first two batters he faced—Lee Maye and Vic Davalillo—and wild-pitched Maye home before the first inning was over. He walked five in the 2–1 victory. Cleveland starter Sonny Siebert balked home the eventual winning run in the sixth inning. Despite the walks he allowed, Chance was a little more certain about his stuff on that night.

"I thought I had no-hit stuff," Chance admitted in the clubhouse after the game. Jerry Zimmerman, his catcher for both no-hit games, said Chance was wild with both his fastball and curveball in the opening frame, but otherwise flashed the no-hit stuff that the catcher said he had seen nearly every time his battery mate took the mound. On that night, Zimmerman said the right-hander "was just wild enough to be effective. . . . The ball was really moving." Nearly fifty years later, Chance joked about the oddity of his outing: "I threw a no-hitter and gave up a run. And the damn run was earned, of all things. Hard to believe!"

THIRTEEN

Down to the Wire

The Chicago White Sox had topped the American League standings for two months when they arrived at the Met on August 11. Their visit for a three-game weekend set generated a wave of pennant fever in the Twin Cities. With the Twins within 2½ games of first place, nearly thirty-four thousand fans turned out for Friday night's opener. Twins ace Dean Chance went the distance for his fifteenth win, a 3–2 victory secured on Tony Oliva's two-out RBI single off Chicago knuckleballer Wilbur Wood in the seventh.

The Met crowd swelled to almost forty-eight thousand for the Saturday matinee, when Jim Kaat and Gary Peters squared off in a battle of southpaws. The White Sox scratched for two runs over the first four frames before the Twins tied the game in the sixth and tallied four more runs in the seventh when Bob Allison drilled a three-run shot off knuckleballer Hoyt Wilhelm. Kaat worked all nine innings in the 6–2 win, which moved Minnesota within a half game of Chicago.

With first place on the line in the Sunday finale, more than forty thousand fans saw Rich Rollins drive in all three runs and Jim Merritt toss a complete-game, 3–2 win to complete the sweep and bounce the White Sox from the top spot. Ted Uhlaender, a terrific defender who shared center field with César Tovar that summer, protected the one-run lead in the ninth with a strong throw. When White Sox center fielder Tommie Agee, leading off the inning, tried to stretch his drive into the left-center-field gap into a triple, Uhlaender fielded the ball off the wall and rifled a strike over the head of the cutoff man that retired Agee at third. Not only had the Twins taken over first place, they had improved to a season-high twelve games over .500 at 62-50.

Then they lost four in a row and the White Sox scrambled back to the top. When Chance induced three ground ball outs from the heart of the Cleveland batting order on August 25 to complete his no-hitter, the Twins were back in first place—momentarily. They fell to Cleveland the following day, and the Red Sox claimed the lead by getting to White Sox ace Joe Horlen early in an 8–2 win at White Sox Park. Boston's lead over the Twins was a mere half game, but it was the first time the Red Sox sat atop the AL standings at day's end since late in the 1949 season.

Sole possession of first place lasted a single day for the Red Sox, who split a Sunday doubleheader with Chicago on August 27. Meanwhile, Merritt improved to 10-4 with a complete-game effort in Cleveland, so the 72-56 Twins led the league by percentage points over Boston. But not for long. The four contenders continued to jockey for the top spot and on September 7, they were virtually tied for first place:

Table 1. American League Standings
(through games of Wednesday, September 6)

	Wins-Losses	Win Percentage
Chicago	78-61	.561
Minnesota	78-61	.561
Boston	79-62	.560
Detroit	79-62	.560

The Twins maintained a share of first place by winning four of their next five games in Baltimore against the defending World Series champions. A year earlier the Orioles were closing in on the American League pennant, but after falling victim to the Twins, dropped sixteen games under .500. Tony Oliva provided most of the drama, delivering 15 hits in 21 at-bats, including five doubles. He also drew three walks to reach base eighteen times in five games, and in one stretch collected a team-record nine consecutive hits. When the Twins completed their successful Baltimore stop with a 4–2 victory on Sunday, September 10, they were twenty games over .500 for the first time and held a half-game edge over Boston atop the AL.

The topsy-turvy nature of the AL race continued. The White Sox had lost five of seven to open September and were struggling to stay within three games of first place before surging back into the race by sweeping the red-hot Twins in a mid-September weekend series at White Sox Park. The Twins lost three straight for the first time in almost a month. After Ron Hansen's four hits and four RBIS sparked a 7–3 White Sox win on Friday night, the Twins shared the AL lead with the Red Sox and Tigers, all with 84-64 records. Hansen, who had collected seven hits in his two previous games, was heard telling a passer-by the next day, "Don't touch me . . . or you'll get burned!"

The Red Sox also had been given the broom treatment that weekend—at Fenway Park by the Orioles—sparking another change at the top. After only Minnesota and Boston had led the league the previous week, the Tigers, on a 9-3 tear led by hot-hitting Al Kaline, jumped a half game ahead of the revitalized second-place White Sox. With a dozen games to play, this would be the last day, however, that the Tigers held sole possession of first, as they hosted the struggling Red Sox twice to start the new week and lost a pair of close contests.

After the Red Sox claimed the second game on Tuesday, only they and the Twins held down the top spot the rest of the way. Although Detroit stuck around until the very end, the Red Sox and Twins suddenly turned it up a notch. Boston won four straight and the Twins secured five in a row. Dean Chance won for the nineteenth time during the surge, and Harmon Killebrew kicked off a season-ending ten-game stretch in which he batted .500, popped five home runs, and drove in 12 runs. Although Boston star Carl Yastrzemski led all three Triple Crown categories as the final days approached, Killebrew was closing in on Yaz in home runs and RBIS. Despite the challenge, Yastrzemski would hold off Killebrew by stroking four homers with 14 RBIS in the same ten-game span.

On Thursday, September 21, the Twins won their fourth straight over Kansas City, as Merritt pitched seven no-hit innings and finished with a two-hit shutout that kept Minnesota and Boston tied for first at 86-66. The deadlock ended when the Twins made it five in a row on September 22, opening a weekend set against the Yankees with a convincing 8–2 victory. Kaat won his fifteenth and ceded just two unearned runs while the Red Sox split a doubleheader with the Orioles in Baltimore. The Twins, now a half game in front of Boston, would stand alone in first place for seven of the remaining ten days of the season.

Both contenders lost the following day before rebounding to win series finales on Sunday, September 24. The Twins tallied seven runs in the first two innings against the Yankees and Chance went the distance to win his twentieth. Killebrew drilled his forty-first home run in the 9–4 victory, moving him within one of Yastrzemski in the AL race. The win was Minnesota's ninetieth after a 25-25 start. With a week remaining, the Twins were a half game up on the Red Sox. Three teams were just a game behind the Twins in the loss column.

Table 2. American League Standings
(through games of Sunday, September 24)

	Wins-Losses	GB
Minnesota	90-67	—
Boston	90-68	0.5
Detroit	89-68	1.0
Chicago	88-68	1.5

Boston started the final week with an off day on Monday, but still moved back into a first-place tie with the Twins, who were trounced by the Angels, 9–2, at the Met. After California pounded Merritt and the relief corps for nine runs and 15 hits, both Minnesota and Boston had four games remaining and their seasons would end with two games at Fenway Park.

The Twins regained the upper hand on Tuesday, September 26, as Kaat turned in another fine outing and struck out thirteen Angels on the two-year anniversary of his AL pennant-clinching victory over Washington. Killebrew hit two more homers in the 7–3 victory, tying Yastrzemski at 43. Yaz's team, playing at home, suffered a 6–3 defeat to the eighth-place Indians and fell a game back with just three games to play.

"We're running out of tomorrows," Red Sox skipper Dick Williams declared after the loss, his team's third in its last five games. This was one race, however, when there *always* was another tomorrow . . . until the season's final out. Adding fuel to the fire was a rebound by the White Sox, who had won eight of ten games to pull into a second-place tie with Boston. They had *five* games remaining—all against last-place Kansas City and Washington— and at that point seemed to many the favorite to cop the AL flag.

The White Sox were forced to play a Wednesday doubleheader in Kansas City after the two teams were rained out on Tuesday. Sweeping a twin bill never was easy, of course, and the light-hitting White Sox, limited to a pair of runs by young A's right-handers Chuck Dobson and Catfish Hunter, shockingly dropped both games. Hunter pushed the Sox to the brink of elimination with a three-hit shutout in the second matchup.

Chicago needed to sweep the Senators at home over the final weekend just to stay in the race. Having Boston and Minnesota playing each other offered Eddie Stanky's crew a glimmer of hope, but that was quickly snuffed. The White Sox couldn't score a run in the first two games against Washington's Phil Ortega and Frank Bertaina. They had been shut out three straight games, and when the Senators completed the sweep on Sunday, Chicago had closed the 1967 season with five consecutive losses.

The Tigers, on the other hand, stuck around to the end. On Tuesday, when the Twins took over first place behind Kaat and Killebrew, the Tigers ended a two-game skid, thanks to a season-saving outing from Mickey Lolich at Yankee Stadium. The stocky left-hander outdueled Yankees ace Mel Stottlemyre in a 1–0 victory that kept the Tigers within a game-and-a-half of the first-place Twins.

The race tightened on Wednesday when the Twins lost their final meeting with the Angels, 5–1. California rookie Rickey Clark shut down Minnesota's bats and former Twin Don Mincher sparked a four-run, fourth-inning rally with a homer off Chance, for whom he had been dealt the previous winter. With Chance facing his former team, the Twins lost an opportunity to head to Boston with a two-game edge with two to play. That inspired a Cardinals scout at the game to quip: "Nobody is good enough to win the pennant in the American League this season, but several clubs are going to lose it."

Even with the loss, the Twins stayed a game in front of the Red Sox, who fell to Cleveland for a second straight day. In a strange scheduling quirk, Minnesota and Boston had two days off before closing the season with Saturday and Sunday matinees at Fenway Park. Meanwhile, the Tigers were home against the Angels on Thursday and Friday, but consecutive rainouts forced the two clubs to play doubleheaders on Saturday and Sunday. Although the Tigers began the weekend tied with first-place Minnesota in the loss column, they likely needed to win at least three of four from the Angels to extend their season.

Table 3. American League Standings

(through games of Friday, September 29)

	Wins-Losses	GB
Minnesota	91-69	—
Boston	90-70	1.0
Detroit	89-69	1.0
Chicago	89-71	2.0

On September 29, the day before Minnesota and Boston began their season-ending, two-game set, the Twins held a clubhouse meeting to determine the team's split of World Series money if they were to secure the American League pennant with a win at Fenway Park. The talk turned contentious when a majority of players voted to not give a share to former manager Sam Mele, fired in June, less than two years after leading the club to the 1965 World Series. The bickering escalated when players supporting Mele suggested that manager Cal Ermer should be excluded from a World Series share as well.

Reliever Al Worthington, in his autobiography, *I Played and I Won*, penned with V. Ben Kendrick, wrote that he, Dean Chance, and Earl Battey were the most vocal in support of Mele. They couldn't persuade others to join the twelve Twins who were backing their former skipper. Worthington added that all twelve—a group that included nearly every core Twins veteran—were willing to contribute portions of their World Series shares to guarantee Mele one. In the end, Mele was denied and Ermer received a full share. It's unlikely that lingering anger factored into the team's Fenway Park performance, but the clubhouse quarrel wasn't a great start to the final weekend with the pennant on the line. It would begin with the Twins calling on their best pitcher down the stretch.

Jim Kaat got the Saturday start. The Red Sox hit southpaws at home all season, but Kaat, with seven straight wins and a 1.56 ERA in September, had pitched as well as anyone after the All-Star break. His fastball was breaking down and away to right-handed hitters, which countered hitters trying to launch pitches at the Green Monster. "You try to tell yourself it's just another ballgame, but you know it isn't," Kaat said in the hours leading up to his biggest start of 1967. One of the tightest AL races involving multiple teams had come down to the final weekend, and the Twins needed only one win to advance to their second World Series in three years.

After two mostly disappointing decades, Red Sox fans came out in droves, rooting their team to complete what had been tagged "The Impossible Dream" (after the hit song from the musical *Man of La Mancha*). A World Series atmosphere greeted the Twins. "I had never heard a crowd holler like that," Worthington said. "They hollered from the first inning through the whole night. I think that might have bothered us some. We always scored a lot of runs when we went into Boston, but we didn't score those two games. The noise was deafening."

Among the Saturday crowd of 32,909 were Massachusetts

Senator Edward Kennedy and Vice President (and Twins fan) Hubert Humphrey. Twins owner Calvin Griffith, who rarely traveled to watch the team, was at Fenway, too, hoping to celebrate another World Series bid after having to miss the 1965 clinching in Washington DC.

Zoilo Versalles opened the contest with a single to left off Red Sox starter José Santiago, a swingman who had made just 10 starts in 1967 but pitched brilliantly in August and September. With Boston needing a win to stay alive, Boston manager Dick Williams might have gone with staff ace Jim Lonborg on two days' rest, but it was Santiago flirting with trouble when he issued a one-out walk to Harmon Killebrew to move Versalles into scoring position. Tony Oliva singled up the middle to put the Twins in front, 1–0, and Bob Allison followed with another single to load the bases. The Twins were positioned to have a big inning, but Santiago recovered, retiring Rod Carew and Ted Uhlaender on a soft liner and easy ground ball to end the early threat.

Despite having worked more than sixty innings already in September, Kaat looked as though he would repeat his pennant-clinching success of two years earlier. Although he allowed three singles in the first two frames, he had the stuff that had made him so effective down the stretch and four of the first seven outs he recorded were strikeouts. When he threw a third strike past Santiago to open the third inning, however, he felt a pop in his throwing elbow. After bouncing a pitch ten feet short of the plate to Red Sox leadoff man Mike Andrews, Kaat was forced to leave the game.

Kaat had worked 568 innings since the start of the 1966 season and his eighth September start was the breaking point. For Kaat, who had won his last seven starts and was poised to pitch the Twins into the World Series, suffering an elbow injury in his most important outing was devastating. Yet, five decades later, Kaat fondly recalls that historic pennant race. "I think probably the most satisfying month of pitching I ever had was September of '67," said Kaat. "It was far and away my best month of pitching."

For several years after suffering the injury, the twenty-eight-year-old veteran would be nowhere near the same pitcher. His elbow didn't hurt, so he bypassed elbow surgery and continued to pitch. "They didn't have Tommy John surgery then, and I opted not to have them cut on it," Kaat explained. "In those days, you really didn't bounce back from ordinary surgery. So I let it heal on its own. It took me a few years to get back to full strength."

The Twins were still leading 1–0 when Kaat gave way to Jim Perry, who made quick work of the Red Sox in both the third and fourth frames. Boston's bats and the Fenway crowd came to life in the fifth when center fielder Reggie Smith led off with a double off the base of the Green Monster. Although the game was still young, Williams called on Dalton Jones to pinch-hit for starting catcher Russ Gibson. The light-hitting Jones hit a soft grounder that took a funny hop off the edge of the infield grass in front of Carew, who could only knock it down. The infield hit put runners on the corners with no out. Perry rebounded to fan both Santiago and Andrews before third baseman Jerry Adair tied the game by dumping a bloop single into shallow right, just beyond the reach of Carew.

Up stepped Carl Yastrzemski, who pulled Boston's wagon in the wild pennant race of 1967. On course for the Triple Crown and the favorite for MVP honors, he was the guy the Red Sox wanted at the plate with the pennant on the line. Yastrzemski delivered, slashing a hard hopper that eluded a diving Killebrew at first. Carew dashed to his left and came up with the ball deep in the hole, but Yaz was safe when Perry, expecting the ball to reach the outfield, failed to cover first base. Jones came home with the go-ahead run.

The Twins tied the game 2–2 in the sixth on a two-out RBI single by Rich Reese, pinch-hitting for catcher Jerry Zimmerman. Minutes later, leading off Boston's half of the inning, Red Sox slugger George Scott golfed Ron Kline's first pitch over the Green Monster. It wasn't a bad pitch; Kline had kept the ball down. After the game Scott admitted he had teed off on a ball out of the strike zone.

Up 3–2, the Red Sox all but put the game away in the seventh. With one out, Andrews beat out a check-swing dribbler down the third base line and Adair followed with a one-hopper back to Kline. The reliever spun toward second base and his throw was in plenty of time to retire Andrews, but Versalles started his relay to first before he had possession of the ball and dropped it. Both runners were safe. With Yastrzemski coming to the plate again, manager Cal Ermer opted for a lefty-lefty matchup and brought in Merritt, whose slider could neutralize left-handed hitters. Merritt fell behind, failing to get Yaz to chase the slider that he had used so effectively against him during the season. Then Yaz jumped on a 3-1 fastball and launched it into the right-field bullpen to put Boston up 6–2. The homer was his Major League-leading forty-fourth, and arguably his biggest of the year.

The lead stood up, although Killebrew hit his forty-fourth as well, a two-run shot into the netting above the left-field wall with two outs in the ninth. The late comeback ended abruptly when Oliva, facing Red Sox reliever Gary Bell, lined a hard shot that Adair speared at third base for the final out. The Red Sox had held on for a 6–4 victory. Perry's mental gaffe and Versalles's error loomed large, but also noteworthy were the Twins' failed scoring chances. They had the bases loaded in the first inning with one out and didn't tack on runs. They also failed to make something of a one-out double by Killebrew in the third frame and left the bases full in the sixth. That rally stalled when Carew lined a shot down the third base line, right into Adair's glove.

After the game, Ermer noted that he was bothered most by the lost opportunity in Minnesota's first at-bat. Santiago was a swingman, not a frontline starter, and his velocity in the opening inning had Williams on the verge of yanking him. Santiago had run the count to 3-1 to Uhlaender before the Twins outfielder grounded out to end the threat. Williams later said Santiago would have been replaced by Bell had he walked Uhlaender.

Minnesota and Boston were tied at 91-70. In Detroit, Mickey Lolich tossed a three-hit shutout in the first of two games with the Angels, his third straight shutout in a critical game. Now the Tigers were positioned to take first place by a half game if they could claim the nightcap. A six-run eighth inning by the Angels erased a 6–2 Detroit lead, however, and left the Tigers a half game behind entering the final day. Still, the Tigers controlled their own destiny. Sweeping Sunday's twin bill would force a playoff with the winner of the Minnesota-Boston finale to determine who would face the St. Louis Cardinals in the World Series.

The Fenway Park finale featured two of the league's three twenty-game winners. The Red Sox called on twenty-five-year-old Jim Lonborg, who, in his only twenty-win season, finished 22-9 with a 3.16 ERA. Manager Dick Williams had his ace taking the mound, but surprisingly, Lonborg had never beaten the Twins in twelve career appearances. The Twins had stuck him with three of his nine losses in their three 1967 matchups, and for his career, Lonborg was 0-6 with a 7.12 ERA in 36⅔ innings against Minnesota.

The Twins turned to Dean Chance, in pursuit of a career-high twenty-first victory. A two-time twenty-game winner by age twenty-six, the hard-throwing righty with the nasty, tailing sinker had won plenty of big games down the stretch for the Twins. And with a World Series berth on the line, there was no game bigger than this one. Chance had already defeated the Red Sox four times in five starts that season, allowing just seven runs total. He had tossed two shutouts, including his five perfect innings in a 2–0 win against Lonborg on August 6.

As they did on Saturday, the Twins scored in the first inning when Harmon Killebrew drew a two-out walk and Tony Oliva drilled his league-leading thirty-fourth double off the Green Monster. Third base coach Billy Martin waved Killebrew around third, though the runner was a sitting duck until first baseman George Scott made a wild relay throw home. The Twins added another unearned run in the third. Once again the rally started with a two-out walk, this time to César Tovar. Killebrew singled sharply into the hole on the left side for Minnesota's second hit, and Tovar scored from first base when the ball skittered past a hard-charging Carl Yastrzemski.

Although Chance was not hit hard in the early going, he did not have his best stuff. He allowed a pair of hits to Yaz and a leadoff single to Lonborg in the third, but with the aid of two double plays, the Twins still led 2–0 going into Boston's half of the sixth. With Lonborg leading off the inning, many managers might have turned to a pinch hitter. Even Lonborg thought his day might be over. He glanced at his manager as he approached the bat rack, but was greeted with encouragement. "Get on base some way," Williams said, "any way."

Acting on his own, Lonborg laid a bunt down the third base line. Tovar, playing deep at third, charged quickly but juggled the ball for a split second—allowing Lonborg to leg out a hit. Then the game quickly turned. Jerry Adair and Dalton Jones slapped balls beyond Twins infielders to load the bases for Yastrzemski. Chance's moving sinker gave most hitters trouble, but Yaz came to the plate looking for the pitch, breaking down and away from him. His approach was to make contact with an easy swing, not attack the ball. Yaz took Chance's first offering, an inside fastball, then got his pitch and lined it over the head of second baseman Rod Carew, scoring two runs to tie the game.

Chance did not survive the inning, during which the Red Sox tallied five runs, aided by two wild pitches from reliever Al Worthington and a Killebrew error. Yastrzemski was the only Boston hitter to hit the ball hard in that disastrous inning. "Biggest disappointment in my life was losing that last game of '67 to the Red Sox," Chance said in 2012 interview. "I beat them four times, shut them out twice, and then that inning they get five runs. It was like a nightmare."

Lonborg went the distance for the pennant-clinching victory. Trailing 5–2, the Twins took one last shot in the eighth inning, when Killebrew and Oliva singled with two outs to put runners on the corners. The season now hinged on Bob Allison, who pulled a pitch down the third base line that headed for the left-field corner. Had the ball gotten by Yastrzemski in the corner, Allison's hit would have scored two and pulled the Twins within one.

But Yaz, who had been manning left field for seven seasons at Fenway, instinctively dashed for the foul line to cut the ball off. He got a good jump and backhanded it just as he reached the grandstand along the line. In his 1968 autobiography *Yaz*, Yastrzemski noted that he often used the base of the grandstand wall to brace his foot before throwing. Normally he would throw home on a play like this, but as he planted his right foot firmly against the wall, he saw the speedy Oliva almost rounding third. Instead of throwing home, Yastrzemski pivoted and rifled a perfect throw on a line to second base, where Allison attempted a hook slide but Mike Andrews tagged him out. Only Killebrew had crossed the plate, making the score 5–3, and the rally was over. Soon the Twins' season was over, too.

In Detroit, the Tigers won the first game of their Sunday doubleheader with the Angels, but forcing a playoff with Boston went out the window when the Angels jumped on Denny McLain and three relievers for eight runs in the nightcap's first four frames. McLain didn't finish the third, and the six-month AL marathon finally came to an end when the Angels secured an 8–5 victory.

Boston's remarkable turnaround, still known throughout New England as "The Impossible Dream," erased the memory of consecutive ninth-place finishes in the ten-team American League. Winning the pennant revitalized a fan base that hadn't witnessed a pennant race in Boston since 1950. After the Braves had left Boston for Milwaukee and won a World Series title in the 1950s, many Bostonians wished that the Red Sox were the team that had relocated. Annual attendance dipped well below one million in the early 1960s, but the 1967 pennant was a turning point for the franchise. Red Sox Nation has consistently filled Fenway Park ever since.

The celebration began seconds after Boston's win in the season finale. Fans flooded onto the field with Twins and Red Sox players scattering to their respective clubhouses. A horde of fans reached Lonborg on the mound before Boston's infielders. Lonborg couldn't make it to the clubhouse and soon found himself hoisted on the shoulders of excitable strangers, who carried him into right field. In time he made it to safety with little more than a torn jersey and a frazzled psyche. "I was scared before the game," said Lonborg. "I was terrified afterward."

"The whole of New England was on fire," said Gary Bell, who joined the Red Sox that June, won twelve games as a starter, and saved Saturday's victory with two innings in relief. "I lived just down the street in Kenmore Square. I can remember after we clinched on the last day there, I walked over the bridge and down into Kenmore Square, and there was just nothing but people. Everything was stopped. There were people going berserk. It was crazy."

To this day Yastrzemski is most remembered by Red Sox fans for his 1967 performance. He claimed the Triple Crown, batting .326 with 44 home runs and 121 RBIS. Killebrew tied Yaz for the home run lead, but finished with eight fewer RBIS. More importantly, Yastrzemski almost single-handedly carried his club down the stretch, batting .417 from September 1 through the end of the season. Over the final two weeks, when the Red Sox won eight of their last twelve games to clinch the pennant, he went 23-for-44 (.523) and drove in 16 runs. If there was any doubt who would win AL MVP honors in 1967, Yaz put it to rest during the final month.

"I don't think I've ever seen any ballplayer have a better year," former Twins and Red Sox starter Lee Stange said of Yastrzemski. "If we needed to get a guy thrown out at second or thrown out at home, he did it. If we needed somebody to make a heck of a catch, he made it. Needed a base hit or needed a home run, and it seemed like he was always there. The right guy in the right spot." Yastrzemski was at his best in the final two games against Minnesota, going 7-for-8 with the three-run homer that nailed down Saturday's win. His success carried into the World Series, as the future Hall of Famer hit .400 and stroked three home runs, though his team lost a seven-game affair to Bob Gibson and the St. Louis Cardinals.

As for the Twins, they endured one of the quietest team flights in their history after losing to the Red Sox in the season finale. Going home for the winter after needing just one win in their final two games to reach the World Series was a tough pill to swallow. The sting of missing out on October baseball would diminish, and with the Twins returning to contender status, there was reason for optimism heading into 1968.

FOURTEEN

A Difficult Year to Forget

The year 1967, a remarkable one in popular music, closed on a sad note. On December 10, soul singer Otis Redding perished when his tour plane crashed into Lake Monona near Madison, Wisconsin. Redding was just twenty-six years old, but had been working professionally for a decade. The Georgia native recorded several albums for the legendary Stax label in Memphis, producing numerous top-twenty R&B hits that exemplified the Stax sound. Among the biggest was his 1966 treatment of "Try a Little Tenderness," backed by Booker T. and the M.G.'s.

By then, Redding was recognized as one of the great soul and R&B singers. In the months before his death, his popularity had expanded to an even larger audience. That June, Aretha Franklin had broken through with his song "Respect," which went to the top of the pop charts that summer. Also in June, Redding became a counterculture star with a dynamic performance for a largely white crowd at the Monterey Pop Festival. He won over enthusiastic festival goers with his soulful rendering of "Tenderness."

Redding died with his star on the rise. Three days before the fatal plane crash, which killed seven, Redding had recorded "(Sittin' on) The Dock of the Bay." Several weeks later, the song was released in its "unfinished" form, and Redding's whistled verse would become a trademark of this classic song. This post-humous release—the first to go to number one nationally—was Redding's biggest hit.

The new year began with another young man's untimely death, which shocked the hockey world just as Redding's passing had stunned music lovers. Bill Masterton, a twenty-nine-year-old forward for the Minnesota North Stars during the franchise's first season, died roughly thirty hours after landing hard on the back of his head during a game at the Met Center on January 13, 1968.

A year earlier, the notion that Masterton would be playing in the National Hockey League was highly unlikely, but a series of unusual circumstances dramatically changed his life, allowed him to realize a dream, and put him on the ice that night against the Oakland Seals. The Winnipeg native had starred at the University of Denver, leading the Pioneers to consecutive NCAA hockey titles in 1960 and '61. Two minor league seasons with the talent-rich Montreal Canadiens franchise didn't go as well, so Masterton began preparing for life without hockey.

He pursued a master's degree in business engineering from Denver and went to work for technology giant Honeywell. Still bitten by the bug to play hockey, Masterton, who had secured dual citizenship, played for the U.S. national team in 1966–67. That might have been the end of Masterton's competitive hockey career, but the NHL was doubling in size the following year and Wren Blair, the general manager of the new Minnesota North Stars franchise, had scouted the twenty-eight-year-old playing for the national team.

When Blair acquired his rights from the Canadiens, Masterton had to decide whether to abandon a promising career working on the financial end of the Apollo space program. Bob Masterton, in a 2011 interview with the *Toronto Star*'s Randy Starkman, recalled discussing the NHL option with his brother over dinner. "I looked at him and said, 'What are you going to do?' because he was just starting a young family. . . . But I knew what he was going to do. It was always in the back of his mind."

The decision came quickly. Masterton was the first player signed by the North Stars. Four months later, in the franchise's on-ice debut against the St. Louis Blues on October 11, 1967, Masterton tallied the franchise's first goal in a 2–2 tie. Three months later, the smart, soft-spoken father of two suffered the devastating injury that claimed his life. Masterton, helmetless like nearly all players of his era, was carrying the puck into the Seals' zone. As he slid a pass to a teammate, his skates became tangled in an opponent's stick, causing him to pitch forward. Then a clean check jarringly knocked him backwards to the ice.

"It sounded like a baseball bat hitting a ball," teammate André Boudrias told John Rosengren for a 2016 ESPN feature. "His eyes were gray at the time—it was like a horror picture. I knew he was done." Winger Dave Balon was among the first to reach Masterton, who soon lost consciousness. Before he did, he looked up at Balon and said, "Never again. Never again." The swelling in his brain was instantly so severe that it was impossible to operate. Masterton's parents flew in from Winnipeg, and they and his wife, Carol, made the decision to remove him from life support. He never regained consciousness, and soon after midnight on January 15, Bill Masterton died at age twenty-nine—the lone fatality from an injury suffered on NHL ice.

Since then, so much has been learned about the devastating effects of concussions. Masterton figures in that tragic story. Two weeks prior to his death, in a game against the Boston Bruins, Masterton had been checked hard into the Met Center boards, striking his head against the glass. He complained of migraines to Carol and a few teammates, but didn't inform coaches or management. Blair admitted decades later that Masterton sometimes seemed amiss during those two weeks—and said so to the team trainer—but their conversation went no further.

It's likely Masterton suffered a concussion that night. Two weeks later the Hennepin County medical examiner discovered evidence of a previous injury to the temporal region of the brain, caused by a blow to the left temple some days prior to the fatal injury. Two neuro-specialists—Dr. Charles Tator, a Toronto neurosurgeon, and Dr. Jesse Corry of the John Nasseff Neuroscience Specialty Clinic in St. Paul—maintain that Masterton died from second-impact syndrome. A person whose brain hasn't fully healed before suffering a second injury will experience the immediate and severe swelling that Masterton's brain suffered from his fatal fall.

As shocking as Masterton's death was, a league-wide change in attitude about helmets was slow to come. In the NHL, wearing a helmet was a sign of weakness. Hall of Famer Stan Mikita, the Chicago Black Hawks star and reigning league MVP, soon donned a helmet, though converts were slow in hockey's macho world. Longtime North Stars forward J. P. Parise told Starkman that helmets weren't allowed in Minnesota; wearing one would get you traded. Balon began wearing one, but Sandy Fitzpatrick, a defenseman who was added to the roster following Masterton's death, recalls Blair pestering Balon and Boudrias about wearing helmets. Balon was dealt to the New York Rangers at the end of the season. Boudrias, the lone North Star to wear headgear all season, finished second in points to Wayne Connelly during the franchise's debut. He was traded to Chicago the following season.

After chasing the American League pennant down to the final out of the 1967 season, the Minnesota Twins looked to make another run in '68. First, however, owner Calvin Griffith executed an off-season blockbuster. In November 1967, he shipped Mudcat Grant and Zoilo Versalles, two key contributors to the 1965 American League champions, to the 1965 World Series champion Dodgers for catcher John Roseboro and relief aces Bob Miller and Ron Perranoski.

Versalles, the club's shortstop since the franchise move to Minnesota, was coming off two disappointing seasons following his MVP campaign, and Grant had fallen out of favor with new skipper Cal Ermer, who had bumped the former twenty-one-game winner from the rotation soon after his midseason appointment in '67. The story goes that Grant asked for a trade soon after a 1967 road trip in which he was fined $250 by Ermer for missing a bed check. An angered Grant said he was in the lobby asking for a room with air conditioning.

Roseboro took over for Earl Battey, who had retired following the 1967 campaign. Roseboro was a frontline defensive catcher like Battey, though with less power at the plate. Perranoski and Miller added a talented lefty-righty duo to a bullpen that had lost Ron Kline in a winter trade with Pittsburgh. But in 1968, the Twins offense, among the game's most productive in recent seasons, finished in the middle of the American League pack in scoring—tallying 109 fewer runs than in '67—and the pitching couldn't pick up the slack as the Twins finished in seventh place at 79-83.

The Twins weren't the only club that struggled to score in a season dubbed the "Year of the Pitcher." Run production, on a steady decline throughout the 1960s, plummeted in '68 and eight of ten American League teams recorded fewer runs than in '67. Boston and Minnesota, after playing for the American League pennant on the final day of the 1967 campaign, experienced the league's biggest drop-off in runs per game. Pitching dominated in a summer that saw Detroit's Denny McLain win thirty-one games—the first thirty-win season since Dizzy Dean recorded thirty for the 1934 Cardinals—and Bob Gibson posted a 1.12 ERA that remains the lowest single-season mark in a century of the live-ball era.

The New York Mets and Houston Astros seemingly set the tone for 1968. A week into the season, the Astros defeated the Mets, 1–0, in a twenty-four-inning marathon spanning six hours, six minutes. When Houston's Bob Aspromonte drilled a bases-loaded ground ball through the legs of Mets shortstop Al Weis in the twenty-fourth, the lone run had scored on an error. The Astros-Mets tilt still tops all shutouts in Major League history for innings and longest time of game.

On May 8, the Twins were fed a steady dose of zeroes in Oakland, where twenty-two-year-old Catfish Hunter pitched the AL's first regular-season, perfect game since 1922. Hunter struck out eleven in a 4–0 win, but needed a little extra time to close the perfecto. Pinch hitter Rich Reese, the Twins' last hope in the ninth, fouled off four 3-2 pitches from Hunter before taking a called third strike. The 6,298 on hand—for the A's eleventh game in Oakland following a move from Kansas City—saw Hunter help his cause with three hits and three RBIs. In the Oakland clubhouse after the game, the young right-hander told representatives of the Hall of Fame they could have his uniform and cap, even the bat that had produced three runs, but he wouldn't relinquish the ball that retired Reese. "I'll keep it as long as I live," Hunter said, "because it sure took me a long time to get that final out."

Soon after, Dodgers right-hander Don Drysdale began chasing a seemingly unapproachable pitching milestone. He tossed six consecutive shutouts on his way to a modern-day-record 58⅔ scoreless innings, surpassing the 55⅔ scoreless frames pitched by Hall of Famer Walter Johnson in 1913. Gibson later flirted with Drysdale's record, pitching forty-seven scoreless innings and five straight shutouts. (Drysdale's mark has since been broken by Orel Hershiser.) At season's end, Gibson and McLain, who went 6-0 in six starts against the Twins that summer, were named the league MVPs—the only time pitchers have been named in both leagues in the same season since the Baseball Writers' Association of America began voting for award winners in 1931.

For the Twins, one of the more memorable moments of the season was Halsey Hall, the lovable, cigar-smoking sportswriter and Twins broadcaster who worked with the legendary Herb Carneal throughout the decade, setting a pile of ticker tape on fire with a hot ash while in the booth at Chicago's White Sox Park in June. While stamping out the blaze, Hall discovered his jacket was on fire. The third member of the broadcast team, Merle Harmon, watched Hall snuff out the flames and later retorted, "That's known as operating under fire." Twins catcher Jerry Zimmerman quipped, "Halsey's the only man I know who can turn a sports coat into a blazer."

Among the few on-the-field highlights of 1968 was César Tovar playing all nine positions in a late-September contest, during which he pitched a scoreless first inning and struck out Oakland slugger Reggie Jackson. For much of the first half, the mediocre Twins had stumbled along near the .500 mark. Whatever hopes the Twins still had to climb into the race were dashed in July, when Harmon Killebrew ruptured his hamstring stretching for a throw at first base during the All-Star Game at Houston's Astrodome.

While the Twins failed to compete in 1968, two Minnesotans engaged in a heated presidential race centered on the divisive Vietnam War and the civil rights movement. The year proved to be difficult as well for Vice President Hubert Humphrey, the one-time Minneapolis mayor, longtime U.S. senator, and Washington's most well-known Twins fan, who became the front-runner for the Democratic nomination when President Lyndon Johnson announced on March 31 that he would not seek reelection.

Humphrey had grown up enjoying baseball. As mayor of Minneapolis in the late 1940s, he often watched the Minor League Minneapolis Millers from the roof of old Nicollet Park. And he was a passionate Twins fan from the start. When the franchise shift from Washington to Minnesota was announced in October 1960, the Minnesota senator told the *Minneapolis Tribune* that it was "a great day for the Twin Cities and a great day for Minnesota." It sounded like typical on-the-stump rhetoric, but it rang true for thousands of baseball fans.

Humphrey soon struck up a close friendship with Halsey Hall, the veteran newspaperman and beloved broadcaster who covered the team during its first twelve years in Minnesota. When Humphrey was in Minnesota during the baseball season, he often joined Hall, along with Ray Scott and Herb Carneal, in the broadcast booth. When the Twins passed through Washington to play the expansion Senators, if Humphrey didn't stop by the Twins' clubhouse, he and Hall might meet away from the park. When the Twins faced the Los Angeles Dodgers in the 1965 World Series, Humphrey was on hand to throw out the ceremonial first pitch in Game One. In 1968, however, the vice president was preoccupied, consumed by the presidential race, though the Twins did little to coax him to the ballpark.

By the time Johnson had withdrawn from the race, Minnesota's senior senator, Eugene McCarthy, had run a close second to the president in the New Hampshire primary, a stunning result running against an incumbent president. McCarthy had entered the race in November 1967, committed to challenging Johnson's concept of endless, undeclared war, which he viewed as a threat to democratic principles. Although McCarthy voted for the Gulf of Tonkin Resolution in 1964, giving Johnson nearly unlimited powers to wage war, he broke with the president on Vietnam in 1966. In early 1968, a tidal wave of support from the anti-war movement on college campuses thrust McCarthy into the presidential spotlight.

McCarthy, known for his integrity and keen intellect, was a reluctant candidate. For months, he had encouraged New York Senator Robert Kennedy to run, but the former attorney general repeatedly resisted. In November 1967, McCarthy walked into the Senate Caucus Room and announced—without ever saying he was actually *running* for president—that he would challenge President Johnson in four 1968 primaries. McCarthy disliked campaigning, resisted it when he could, and took a casual approach to public speaking, rarely working from a prepared text or inspiring a crowd with his oratory. With his calm demeanor, he was the anti-candidate, the man with a cause more than a desire to occupy the White House.

With Johnson's March 31 announcement, the political landscape rapidly changed. Even though McCarthy swept the Wisconsin primary two days later, Humphrey jumped to the front of the line for the Democratic nomination upon declaring his candidacy in April. The vice president deliberately didn't announce in time to appear on the ballot of the remaining primaries—to avoid having to campaign for them—yet was in line to gather a hefty number of delegates controlled by city and state Democratic organizations. This was the last election before the party enacted reforms that changed the nominating system.

For Humphrey, the challenge to the Johnson administration wasn't limited to a fellow Minnesotan. Two weeks before the president's surprise announcement, Robert Kennedy entered the race. After resisting McCarthy's overtures, the New York senator reconsidered as more troops headed to Southeast Asia and the casualties began to mount. Perhaps McCarthy's success in New Hampshire finally convinced Kennedy to run. With Johnson out and Kennedy in as another anti-war candidate, McCarthy began to wage a more well-rounded and vigorous campaign; he no longer was simply running against Johnson on Vietnam. Although

McCarthy defeated Kennedy in May's Oregon primary, Kennedy's joining the race slowed McCarthy's momentum.

While the vice president still had the advantage of the nominating process in his favor, incumbency became a formidable obstacle to running a successful campaign. That January, with U.S. officials claiming "there was light at the end of the tunnel" and American troop totals in Vietnam reaching 500,000, the administration's Vietnam policy took a beating with the Tet offensive, a major assault on numerous provincial capitals and major cities by North Vietnamese and southern-based opposition forces. More than one thousand Americans died in the first two weeks of the military campaign, an offensive that illustrated the futility of the war effort and became widely viewed as a turning point in U.S. involvement. President Johnson's approval rating dipped sharply, as did overall support of his handling of Vietnam. With Americans becoming increasingly skeptical of the war, the offensive also had a detrimental effect on Humphrey's campaign.

The connection between Johnson and Humphrey dated to 1948, when they won Senate seats on the day that President Harry Truman scored an upset victory over Republican challenger Thomas Dewey. Once elected, the ambitious and politically savvy Johnson set his sights on a Senate leadership position, becoming the Senate minority leader just four years after winning his seat. Humphrey became a leader of the Senate's liberal bloc, a national voice advocating for civil rights and better race relations—at a time when such talk was not popular. He was thrust into the national spotlight at the 1948 Democratic convention, where the accomplished orator delivered a forceful speech encouraging the party to "get out of the shadow of states' rights and walk forthrightly into the sunshine of human rights."

What Johnson and Humphrey shared was a Cold War-driven anti-communist bent that was part of the era's liberal ideology. They also tag-teamed to pass revolutionary civil rights legislation soon after Johnson took office in November 1963, and together they rode to a landslide victory over Arizona Republican Barry Goldwater and his running mate, New York congressman William Miller, in the 1964 presidential election.

When Johnson offered Humphrey a place on the 1964 ticket at the Democratic convention, however, he made it clear that his vice president would not be part of his inner circle. As vice president, Johnson had not been an insider under President John Kennedy, and it would be the same for Humphrey. At the same time, Johnson demanded undying loyalty from his vice president. According to Humphrey's account of the interview, Johnson called the job "a marriage with no chance of divorce." Humphrey pledged his loyalty, surrendering the freedom to make a difference that he had enjoyed in the Senate. Johnson would say of Humphrey and others he similarly controlled: "I've got his pecker in my pocket."

The president excluded his vice president from policy meetings on Vietnam, a conflict about which Humphrey had misgivings. Soon after American ground troops entered the fray in 1965, Humphrey sent Johnson a detailed memo, expressing his reservations with more troops and bombing raids in a war that was politically hard to explain to the American people. The vice president's skepticism froze him out of all future Vietnam discussions. Yet, as difficult as the irrepressible and gregarious Humphrey found it to *not* speak his mind on the issues, he faithfully towed the president's line on the war. In fact, he eventually became the administration's biggest cheerleader on Vietnam. Humphrey underwent a political conversion, according to Carl Solberg, author of *Hubert Humphrey: A Biography*, becoming a hardliner on a war that he now deemed necessary to stem communism in Asia.

Humphrey's support for the war hung heavily over him in the 1968 presidential race. He had never been a target of the left, but amid charges that he was Johnson's puppet on Vietnam—and that LBJ's civil rights efforts had not gone far enough with the administration's focus now diverted to the war effort—the vice president was attacked for his "old-style liberal politics." Many of his liberal political allies abandoned him in his bid to win the presidency.

Despite his loyalty, the vice president also didn't have the full support of the president, who offered little in the way of an endorsement or financial backing, noted historian Walter LaFe-ber in *The Deadly Bet: LBJ, Vietnam, and the 1968 Election*. "Close aides believed Johnson saw Humphrey as weak, Nixon strong, and preferred the Republican—especially since Nixon would probably stay the course in Vietnam with more toughness than the Minnesotan," wrote LaFeber. "Humphrey found himself in a highly unusual place for a person who was the front-runner to his party's presidential nomination: neither his president nor many of his longtime political friends wanted much to do with him."

More than just a chaotic and unsettling year for the man known in political circles as "The Happy Warrior," 1968 was a year in which the entire nation faced extraordinary challenges and tragedy. With Americans divided over a war and the course of the civil rights movement, the country was shaken to its core that spring by the assassinations of Martin Luther King Jr. and Robert Kennedy in a span of nine weeks. After James Earl Ray murdered King in Memphis on April 4, violence erupted in more than one hundred U.S. cities, leading to forty-six deaths and millions of dollars of property damage. The assassination of the civil rights movement's leading advocate of peaceful resistance ignited the anger of Black Americans already frustrated by poor living conditions and lack of job opportunities in their neighborhoods. The urban violence spurred a call for law and order among conservatives, and when Nixon made "law and order" a key tenet of his campaign, many white voters embraced him.

Kennedy's assassination, just moments after he claimed victory in the California primary on June 5, shadowed the rest of the presidential campaign. McCarthy trumped Humphrey by winning a majority of New York's delegates from Kennedy's state, yet Humphrey was all but guaranteed the nomination at the Democratic National Convention that August in Chicago. Still, with delegates and thousands of protestors descending on the city, the gathering demonstrated the depth of emotion invested in a divisive war. Inside the International Amphitheater, squabbles between delegates and party leaders signaled a party divided, with McCarthy's and Kennedy's delegates relegated to being the opposition voice on party decision-making.

Outside, in oppressive summer heat, protesters took over parks, churches, and coffee shops after Chicago mayor Richard J. Daley denied permits for marches from the various political organizations in town. He set curfews for city parks to thwart organizers, but protesters opposed to Humphrey intended to be heard and looked to disrupt the nominating process. Grant Park, a large park across Michigan Avenue from the Conrad Hilton Hotel (which served as Democratic Party headquarters), became a primary gathering place.

Daley formally opened the 1968 convention at the amphitheater, welcoming delegates with both an assurance and a warning: "As long as I am mayor of this city, there's going to be law and order in Chicago." The center of the city looked like an armed camp. Chicago police were everywhere, nearly twelve thousand strong throughout the weeklong convention. Another fifty-seven hundred Illinois National Guard were called in to keep the peace by any means necessary. On three consecutive nights at the start of the convention, police swept through nearby Lincoln Park at curfew, using billy clubs on protesters, reporters, and a few local residents sitting on their porches. Some of the attacks were vicious, but unseen by television cameras.

The hot, humid weather continued and tensions ran higher each day. On August 28, the day before Humphrey accepted the Democratic Party's nomination, the Spring Mobilization Committee to End the War in Vietnam held an anti-war rally that drew more than ten thousand protesters to Grant Park. After the rally, roughly six thousand protesters were still on hand, planning to march to the convention site for a final opportunity to be heard on Humphrey's nomination. Because the crowd lacked a permit to march, the police blocked the sidewalks. With television cameras focused on the standoff along Michigan Avenue, large contingents of police began assaulting protestors. Hundreds of mostly college-aged young people were bludgeoned with billy clubs, teargassed, and arrested. The carnage appeared on national newscasts, and many political observers believe the Democrats lost the White House that evening in Grant Park.

"The 1968 Chicago convention became a lacerating event, a distillation of a year of heartbreak, assassinations, riots and a breakdown in law and order that made it seem as if the country were coming apart," wrote Haynes Johnson, covering the convention for *Smithsonian Magazine*. "In its psychic impact, and its long-term political consequences, it eclipsed any other such convention in American history, destroying faith in politicians, in the political system, in the country and in its institutions. No one who was there, or who watched it on television, could escape the memory of what took place before their eyes."

In the wake of the police attacks, Humphrey accepted his party's nomination. But trailing Republican candidate Richard Nixon by a substantial margin, Humphrey finally broke from the party line on Vietnam during a late-September speech in Salt Lake City. He came out in favor of halting the ongoing bombing of North Vietnam in the hope that it would advance the Paris peace talks already underway. McCarthy and Kennedy forces had lobbied unsuccessfully for this policy shift at the convention.

Humphrey's change of heart likely helped close the gap in the polls, though it came just six weeks shy of Election Day. Four years after Johnson and Humphrey won the largest popular-vote landslide in a presidential election, Humphrey fell a half-million votes short of Nixon, who, with Maryland governor Spiro T. Agnew as his running mate, carried thirty-two states. Alabama governor George Wallace and Air Force general Curtis LeMay of the American Independent Party, running largely on the issue of maintaining segregation, provided a strong third-party challenge that likely hurt Nixon more than Humphrey. The vice president had absorbed the most difficult political loss of his life.

During the 1968 presidential race, the Vietnam War may have been the biggest issue dividing the country. But when Tommie Smith won the gold medal and John Carlos the bronze in the two-hundred-meter sprint at the 1968 Olympics in Mexico City, they brought America's civil rights movement to the global stage. At the medal ceremony that followed the October 16 event, Smith ascended the podium's gold-medal platform, flanked by Carlos to his left and Australian sprinter Peter Norman, the silver-medal winner, to his right. Smith and Carlos stood barefoot, an acknowledgment of Black poverty. When "The Star-Spangled Banner" began to play, they bowed their heads and raised a black-gloved fist into the air to draw attention to the oppression and poor living conditions of African Americans.

The stadium went quiet, unnerving all three medal winners, though the speechless response was momentary. The U.S. Olympic Committee quickly sent Smith and Carlos home, where they were reviled by various news sources, including *Time*, the *Chicago Tribune*, and the *Los Angeles Times*. One vehement response came from *Chicago American* reporter Brent Musburger, who was not yet a national sports celebrity. Calling Smith and Carlos "a pair of black-skinned storm troopers," he wrote: "Protesting and working constructively against racism in the United States is one thing, but airing one's dirty clothing before the entire world during a fun-and-games tournament was no more than a juvenile gesture by a couple of athletes who should have known better."

Both men suffered repercussions for years. For a minority struggling to gain basic human rights and equal opportunity for a century following the Civil War, apparently no form of protest—symbolic, nonviolent, or otherwise—was acceptable. And the backlash against Smith and Carlos continued to grow. They were treated as pariahs in the Olympic community and banned from track-and-field competition, which at the highest level had been professional for years. What money they had earned from it dried up and the possibility of lucrative endorsements as medal winners never materialized. They needed jobs and struggled to land employment. Their families faced public ridicule and death threats.

After all these years, during which conducting peaceful protests of racism and apartheid in South Africa became commonplace among whites and Blacks, the overreaction to the silent gesture by Smith and Carlos seems absurd. As much as Smith and Carlos were chastised for executing a "Black Power" gesture at the Olympics, years later Smith noted it wasn't that, but instead a "human-rights salute." Smith, in a 1999 HBO documentary on the event, *Fists of Freedom*, said: "We were not Antichrists. We were just human beings who saw a need to bring attention to the inequality in our country."

Smith and Carlos weren't alone in being ostracized. Norman, the Australian who had won the silver medal, joined Smith and Carlos in wearing badges from the Olympic Project for Human Rights, a movement among athletes supporting the battle for equality. Australia's greatest sprinter lived in a highly segregated country and was blackballed from Olympic competition despite a strong showing in qualifiers for the 1972 Olympics. He and his family were outcasts and Norman struggled to find work. Norman, who wasn't invited to be part of the 2000 Olympics in Sydney, died in 2006. Smith and Carlos were pallbearers at his funeral.

FIFTEEN

Billy Ball Brings the Twins Back to Life

The Year of the Pitcher wouldn't have a sequel in '69. Major League owners looked to level the playing field by lowering the mound to ten inches. For decades, the maximum height had been fifteen inches—a limit that often went unchecked—and Dodger Stadium's mound was rumored to be closer to twenty.

A new round of expansion in 1969 also enhanced run production. Both leagues added two teams and split into two six-team divisions, which spawned a playoff round in October to determine the World Series clubs. Major League expansion had boosted run production in 1961, a trend that has continued whenever MLB has debuted new franchises. The American League expansion teams in 1969, the Kansas City Royals and Seattle Pilots, joined the Twins in the AL's West Division, which also housed the White Sox and the California clubs in Oakland and Anaheim. The best teams of the mid-1960s—the Orioles, Tigers, and Red Sox—would no longer be Minnesota's chief rivals, as the Twins would play fewer games against them and other East Division clubs. The game's landscape was forever changed.

The nation was undergoing dramatic change as well. In January 1969, Richard Nixon assumed the presidency after running a successful "law and order" campaign that portrayed the Johnson administration as soft on crime—on the rise in American cities—

and those who rioted in the aftermath of Martin Luther King Jr.'s assassination. Nixon's message resonated with voters across the country, and in Minneapolis, where police officer Charles Stenvig ran for mayor as an independent on a "law and order" platform and won convincingly to succeed the retiring Arthur Naftalin.

Nixon's election also meant a change in Vietnam policy. In fact, Nixon changed the course of the war before winning the 1968 election. In the weeks leading up to Election Day, with American leadership becoming increasingly convinced that the war couldn't be won, President Lyndon Johnson decided to halt all bombing of North Vietnam and negotiate a settlement. By then, more than thirty-five thousand Americans had died in Vietnam, and the president wasn't willing to up his commitment to a war effort that was going nowhere. Nixon, fearing that a breakthrough at the Paris peace talks would diminish his chances of winning the presidency, worked backchannels to get the South Vietnamese leadership to hold out for a better settlement.

Despite major concessions from the North Vietnamese, on the night prior to Johnson's planned announcement to halt the bombings, the South Vietnamese pulled out of planned negotiations, convinced they would get a better deal from Nixon. Johnson soon had evidence of the backchannels involved, but lacked absolute proof of Nixon's direct involvement. Nixon spent the final days of the campaign criticizing the Johnson administration for its inability to get America's Vietnamese ally to the negotiating table.

For decades, Nixon denied meddling, since doing so as a private citizen violated federal laws. Almost fifty years after the 1968 presidential race, however, journalist John A. Farrell, author of *Richard Nixon: The Life*, discovered a cache of notes from Nixon's closest aide, H. R. Haldeman, documenting that the president asked him to "monkey wrench" peace talks. Despite claiming he had a peace plan for Vietnam while on the campaign trail, once in office, Nixon had little intention of negotiating an end to the war. He quickly escalated it, and only after another twenty-two thousand American lives were lost did he negotiate a peace settlement that could have been reached five years earlier.

In March 1969, concerned by enemy war supplies moving along the Cambodian and Laotian borders, Nixon ordered the secret carpet-bombing of Cambodia—a violation of Cambodia's neutrality that contradicted the president's campaign promise that he had a peace plan for Vietnam. The bombing raids, which quickly escalated and soon targeted Laos, continued into 1973, dropping 2.5 million tons of weaponry and claiming hundreds of thousands of lives. The tonnage was roughly a million more than what U.S. warplanes dropped on Japan, including Nagasaki and Hiroshima, during World War II.

Another secret revealed to Americans in 1969 seemingly had a bigger impact on how they perceived the Vietnam quagmire. Late that year, investigative journalist Seymour Hersh broke the story of a brutal assault on a Vietnamese village by a U.S. Army battalion. The attack on My Lai, located in an enemy stronghold along the northern coast of South Vietnam, had taken place eighteen months earlier in March 1968. U.S. soldiers, led by Lieutenant William Calley, rounded up and massacred three hundred to five hundred unarmed villagers, including sobbing mothers clinging to their children. Homes were set afire. Soldiers tortured and raped villagers. Many were marched into a ditch and mowed down with machine gun fire. The massacre was stopped by a three-man helicopter crew, piloted by Chief Warrant Officer Hugh Thompson Jr., which had the assignment of hovering over the village in search of enemy positions. Thompson landed the copter between the soldiers and the surviving villagers before confronting the officers in charge.

"Mr. Thompson was just beside himself," recalled Larry Colburn, who was part of the crew, in a 2010 interview with PBS. "He got on the radio and just said, 'This isn't right, these are civilians, there's people killing civilians down here.' And that's when he decided to intervene. He said, 'We've got to do something about this, are you with me?' And we said, 'Yes.'"

Soon after Hersh broke the story on November 12, 1969, the *Cleveland Plain-Dealer* published graphic photos of the carnage. The outrage was immediate. The images turned more Americans against the war. More than a dozen army personnel were charged for their crimes, but the only one convicted was Calley, who served less than five years in prison. During Calley's trial, dozens of veterans testified that they witnessed similar war crimes, which inspired more Americans to oppose this polarizing war. The revelations caused many to see Calley as a scapegoat for a corrupt military operation.

Far from the battlefields of Vietnam, another dramatic change took place closer to home, as a new man took charge of the Minnesota Twins dugout. Stinging from the team's 79-83 finish in 1968, owner Calvin Griffith fired Cal Ermer and hired the combative Billy Martin. This was Martin's first big league managerial assignment, although he had been a Twins coach since 1965 before leaving the team midway through the 1968 season to manage the franchise's Triple-A Denver affiliate.

The match of a stubborn owner and excitable former player wasn't made in heaven, but Griffith had seen Martin motivate and nurture Zoilo Versalles to capitalize on his talent and win MVP honors in 1965. Two years later, Martin did much the same with Rod Carew, a moody, twenty-one-year-old rookie with immense talent. The athletic second baseman started the 1967 All-Star Game, batting second in front of teammates Tony Oliva and Harmon Killebrew, and went on to win Rookie of the Year honors.

Griffith also understood how Martin could change a team. As Minnesota's third base coach in '65, Martin made the Twins multidimensional by running more, forcing opponents to react. The Twins had mostly been sluggers when Martin arrived, but soon began executing the hit and run and running wild, stealing or taking the extra base. The owner hoped Martin could once again breathe life into his team.

Martin was a gambler in the dugout. Carew, Oliva, and César Tovar had the green light to run if they thought they could steal. Oliva said that if an attempt failed, Martin did not second-guess the decision to run as long as the player was hustling and playing hard. Trust ran both ways. Jim Kaat said a player could question or stand up to Martin, and he appreciated that the skipper would hear him out. Players respected that, and Martin's approach inspired them to give their best.

That spring, players found that Martin as a rookie skipper was just like Martin as a coach. Fundamentals were emphasized and practiced in camp, and Martin was on the field long before workouts or exhibition games began, giving instruction and working on the little details with young players. "The thing I think that he was best at was trying to keep the guys from making little mistakes," Killebrew said of Martin in 2010. "He was really big on fundamentals and the little things to win games. He knew as much about the game as anybody that you want to be around." Martin also urged veterans to make adjustments to gain an edge, encouraging Killebrew to occasionally hit the ball the other way, Carew to master bunting, and Oliva to abandon his spray approach and focus on pulling the ball to right field in RBI situations.

Despite Martin's reputation as an excitable boy—and he had to be excited by his first Major League managerial gig—spring training 1969 was orderly and quiet. Still, he was planning some excitement for once the meaningful games began. That spring he tutored Carew in the art of stealing home. Carew says Martin taught him to time a pitcher's delivery and start for home from a walking lead when he knew he could make it safely. The student mastered beating a pitch to the plate, stealing home seven times in 1969. At the time it was believed that Carew set the new American League record for stealing home, surpassing Ty Cobb's mark of six while matching the Major League record of seven, set by Pete Reiser of the Brooklyn Dodgers in 1946. Years later, however, a review of Cobb's career determined the Hall of Famer had stolen home on eight occasions in 1912, thus removing Carew from the record book.

Carew did tie a big league mark by stealing three bases in one inning against Detroit on May 18, and he wasn't the only Twin to steal home that afternoon. Tovar opened the third inning by beating out a slow roller to shortstop Mickey Stanley. After Tovar was balked to second base by Tigers ace Mickey Lolich, Carew drew a full-count walk to put two runners aboard. Then, with Killebrew swinging at a 2-1 pitch, Tovar and Carew executed a double steal to also move Carew into scoring position. Killebrew eventually struck out, but with newly acquired shortstop Leo Cárdenas at the plate, Tovar stole home for Minnesota's first run. Carew didn't advance, but swiped third one pitch later.

Then Carew dashed home—his third steal of the inning—bringing the Metropolitan Stadium crowd to its feet. With an infield single as their only hit, the Twins had stolen five bases in the inning, including home twice, to generate the only two runs allowed by Lolich that day in an 8–2 defeat. With Martin encouraging Carew to use his speed on the bases, the second baseman stole 19 bags in all in 1969, two more than he had swiped in his first two seasons combined. Calling on his speed and his ability to make contact, Carew also won his first batting title in 1969 with a convincing .332 average.

Nearly as dramatic as stealing home was the suicide squeeze, and Martin was equally inclined to send a runner home on a bunt attempt. In a ten-day stretch in late June, four Twins—Jim Perry, Cárdenas, Ron Perranoski, and Ted Uhlaender—executed bunts with runners dashing down the third base line. Perry's earned him and the Twins a "W" on June 22, when he dropped a perfect bunt to the third base side of A's reliever Rollie Fingers in the thirteenth inning to score Oliva for a 4–3 victory.

"Billy would try stuff only high school coaches would try. He loved to pull off the unexpected play," said Frank Quilici, who was a rookie infielder in 1965, played under Martin in 1969, and later became the Twins manager. Martin was a fanatic about forcing the opponent to execute. In what he dubbed one of those high-school maneuvers called by Martin, Quilici also stole home that spring. On May 4, two weeks before Carew's big day, a Bat Day crowd of more than forty-four thousand at the Met watched as Quilici led off third and Uhlaender first in the second inning. With the White Sox's Tommy John on the mound and rookie pitcher Dick Woodson at the plate, Uhlaender lingered off base long enough after a pitch to coax a throw to first from White Sox catcher Duane Josephson. As soon as the ball left Josephson's hand, Quilici headed home. He slid past Josephson and beat the belated tag to score the game's first run in a 4–3 come-from-behind victory.

Everybody ran with Martin calling the shots. On June 4 at the Met, Harmon Killebrew stole *two* bases in one inning. The Twins were nursing a late 3–2 lead over the Yankees with Carew on third base when Yankees reliever Lindy McDaniel issued an intentional walk to Killebrew. Aided by the threat of Carew coming home, the Twins slugger took off and stole second. In fact, he went in standing up as McDaniel intercepted catcher John Ellis's throw, hoping to decoy Carew into breaking toward the plate. After Twins catcher John Roseboro drew a two-out walk to load the bases, Carew did just that, swiping home on the front end of a *triple* steal.

The thirty-two-year-old Killebrew, who had never stolen more than three bags in a season, now had two in a single inning. He wasn't especially impressed with his feat. "I'd just like to steal one on my own, instead of riding on someone else's heels," Killebrew said, laughing, during a postgame interview with the *Minneapolis Star*'s Mike Lamey. He didn't wait long, stealing second base by his lonesome six days later in a 6–2 win over the Red Sox, during which he also legged out a triple. And twice more that season he stole bases on his own.

Not only did Killebrew finish the 1969 campaign with eight steals, his single-season high, he also led the Majors with 49 homers and a career-best 140 RBIS. At season's end, he claimed the American League's MVP Trophy. On top of that, he made himself valuable to the Twins in another key way. After two straight seasons at first base, Killebrew returned to third in midsummer. Martin had wanted to open first for Rich Reese, and Killebrew, always willing to do what was best for the team, reassumed the hot corner.

With Martin at the helm, the Twins improved by 18 wins and finished atop the AL West with a 97-65 record. They claimed the first AL West crown despite off years from both Dean Chance and Jim Kaat, who were expected to front the rotation but instead were compromised by injury. But Martin seemingly inspired players to produce beyond expectations. That certainly was true of Reese, an excellent defensive first baseman and left-handed hitter who moved into the starting lineup in June and batted .322 with 16 home runs and 69 RBIS—all career highs—in 132 games. If he had collected another 51 plate appearances, Reese would have finished second in the American League batting race—behind Carew.

Several of Reese's teammates also had career years. Cuban shortstop Leo Cárdenas, a defensive whiz who had come over from Cincinnati in an off-season trade that shipped lefty Jim Merritt to the Reds, gave the Twins a dependable option at short. The position was a key weakness the previous season, when a host of possible replacements for Zoilo Versalles—including the versatile Tovar and rookies Jackie Hernández, Rick Renick, and Ron Clark—auditioned for the job.

Cárdenas, dubbed "Mr. Automatic" for his sure-handed glove work, led all big league shortstops in putouts, assists, and double plays in 1969. After the Twins finished dead last with 117 double plays in '68, he contributed significantly to the team's 177 in '69, the third-most in the Majors and still one of the highest team totals since the franchise moved to Minnesota. Cárdenas, a superstitious player who would load his bats into his car's trunk and drive through a cemetery to chase away evil spirits, also had one of his best offensive seasons in '69. He batted .280 with 10 homers and career highs in walks (66), OBP (.353), and RBIS (70).

Tovar took over leadoff duties that summer. Martin initially platooned the right-handed hitter, starting him mostly against southpaws, but with a torrid second half in which he batted .331 and slugged .478, Tovar finished the season at .288 with 11 home runs, 99 runs, and 45 stolen bases—all career highs. He took over center field under Martin, who liked that Tovar played with a contagious enthusiasm. The manager called the 155-pound Tovar "my little leader" and considered him the catalyst to the Twins offense—on and off the field.

"He was the guy who got everything going," Martin wrote in his 1980 book *Number 1*, penned with Peter Golenbock. "When I wanted him to push Leo (Cárdenas) a little bit or if Rod (Carew) was getting down and I needed someone to give him a boost, I'd get César to do it." Tovar's defensive versatility was often considered his greatest asset—highlighted by playing all nine positions in a game the previous September—but in his fourth big league campaign in 1969, the twenty-nine-year-old Tovar enjoyed the first of three superb seasons as a table-setter and run scorer. Tovar drew MVP votes by tallying 313 runs in the three-year stretch 1969–71, most among AL players.

Pitchers Jim Perry and Dave Boswell joined the twenty-win club for the first time. Perry had a reputation as a hard worker, committed to succeeding, when he earned a starting assignment as a rookie with Cleveland in 1959. Inconsistency sparked a 1963 trade to Minnesota, however, and he barely survived spring cut-downs in 1965 before emerging as a key contributor when Camilo Pascual had midseason shoulder surgery. Despite Perry's success as a starter in '65 and '66, he was primarily a reliever in '67 and '68 before Martin returned him to the rotation. The thirty-three-year-old right-hander stepped up, going 20-6 with a 2.82 ERA in 36 starts and 10 relief appearances.

Perry won twenty-four games and Cy Young honors in 1970, which raises the question why he hadn't been in the rotation throughout the 1960s. Of course, the Twins gave their promising youngsters Merritt and Boswell every opportunity to succeed, and Perry—not blessed with overpowering velocity—had been effective in a swing role. Boswell had shown flashes of brilliance and Merritt had been terrific during the 1967 pennant race. Perry says it was simply his job to be ready regardless of his role, though he admits that he still believes he should have started the 1967 finale against Boston. Instead, twenty-game winner Dean Chance pitched the pennant-deciding contest on two days' rest and wasn't sharp.

Despite pitching with bone chips that caused swelling and severe pain in his right elbow, Boswell put it together in 1969, working a career-high 256⅓ innings and finishing 20-12 with a 3.23 ERA. Aggressive and competitive on the mound, he also was one of the game's true characters. The free-spirited right-hander's eccentricities amused teammates, although sometimes they overshadowed his on-field performance.

The malaprop was a Boswell specialty: often it was intentional, though one never knew for sure. After the Twins outbid Baltimore to sign him in 1963, he noted that "the Orioles disembarked from me." Once, when a catcher asked the young hurler if he was familiar with the opposing team's hitters, Boswell countered with, "I can't incogitate all I know."

He also could be the master of the absurd. Upon his first visit to Yankee Stadium with the Twins, he asked, "Is this the park where the Yankees play when we watch them on TV back home?" Author Jim Thielman, in his account of the 1965 season, *Cool of the Evening*, tells the story of Perry arriving in the clubhouse and announcing he had purchased a new stereo, to which Boswell replied: "Does it have a pinion gear on the seventh cycle?"

Boswell could regale teammates not only with language, but with antics as well. He often carried an assortment of guns on the road, which once came in handy when a snake invaded the Twins' training facilities in Florida. He mastered several animal and bird sounds, which he used to confuse unsuspecting team bus drivers. There are stories that Boswell slept wearing a motorcycle helmet and sunglasses, and roommate Frank Quilici recalled a hot, sticky night in Boston, where his roommate had his own answer to the uncomfortable weather. "I woke up in the middle of the night, and he had scared the daylights out of me," Quilici told *St. Paul Pioneer Press* columnist Charley Walters following Boswell's death in 2012. "He had put his mattress from the bed halfway out the window, and he was sleeping on it."

SIXTEEN

Killer, Carew, Two Twenty-Game Winners, and the Men on the Moon

Although most preseason buzz in 1969 favored the Twins to take the American League West, the starting rotation was a key question. Dean Chance and Jim Kaat had held out before settling contract disputes with Calvin Griffith, missing a considerable portion of spring training. Kaat then suffered a groin injury in camp. Although he missed little time and still won fourteen games, the ailment affected his performance. After posting 36 wins the two previous seasons, Chance developed arm trouble in the spring, sat out all of June and July, and barely was a factor in the pennant race.

Dave Boswell got off to a poor start as well, cutting two tendons in the little finger of his left hand while cleaning fish less than three weeks before the season opener. Despite the lost time in camp, he was ready by Opening Day, thanks to a specially made pad inserted into his glove to protect the eight-stitch cut. He was inconsistent in the early going, though, and had a losing record through May. Despite the bone chips in his troublesome elbow, Boswell came on strong to go 15-6 over the final four months.

Even with Minnesota's early pitching concerns, the 1969 schedule portended a fast start, beginning with road series against the newly hatched Kansas City Royals and the California Angels, who had lost ninety-five games in 1968. But Billy Martin's illustrious career as a big league manager began with four losses, including a pair of extra-inning defeats in Kansas City. Dropping four in a row never came easy to Martin, who admitted as much to *Minneapolis Tribune* writer Dave Mona after the Twins had clinched the division title in September. "Looking back," Martin said, "I think we were just trying too hard to win that first game. I threw up after the first loss. I don't recommend any rookie manager start with 12- and 17-inning losses." The skipper's digestive tract would remain unsettled for several days.

The Royals debuted with a 4–3 victory on April 8, 1969, on outfielder Joe Keough's twelfth-inning RBI single off Twins rookie Dick Woodson. The teams collected 26 hits and wasted multiple scoring opportunities. The lone Twins highlight was a two-run homer from rookie Graig Nettles, a promising third baseman who started the year platooning in left field with Bob Allison. Little changed the following day, except that this time it took seventeen innings and rookie Lou Piniella's game-winning single to stick the Twins with another 4–3 defeat. The twenty-five-year-old Piniella had collected his first Major League hit a day earlier, going 4-for-5 in the opener, and his third career RBI was the difference in Kansas City's second win.

The second game also featured Rod Carew's initial steal of home. He took advantage of Roger "Spider" Nelson, an "all arms and legs" right-hander with a big windup. With the Twins losing 3–2 and Carew perched at third base in the fifth inning, he timed Nelson's motion and signaled to Martin he was ready to run. Carew took his walking lead and dashed home under a high pitch to Nettles. The game stayed tied until Piniella came through twelve innings later.

The Twins moved on to California and lost twice more to the Angels, with forty-six-year-old knuckleballer Hoyt Wilhelm closing out a pair of close contests. After dropping a 4–3 decision to fall to 0-4 before a small Saturday night crowd in Anaheim, the struggling Twins retreated to their hotel. That included rookie Charley Walters, a hard-throwing right-hander who had been signed in 1965 after an open tryout at Metropolitan Stadium. The six-foot-four Minneapolis native, who had drawn little attention pitching for Edison High School, beat long odds again in spring 1969, when he traveled north with the Major League club. With the series finale scheduled the following afternoon, Walters turned in early. He didn't get the full night's sleep he anticipated, however, as he explained to Bob Showers, author of *The Twins at the Met*:

> I'm sound asleep in my hotel room when the phone rings at 3:30 a.m. It's Ted Uhlaender and he says: "We've got an unbelievable party going on. You've got to come down to room 203." I could hear women and music and laughter in the background. I was 22 years old and single at the time, but there was no way I was going down to that party. It was the middle of the night, we'd just lost our first four games and I wasn't going to do anything that might get me sent to the Minors. I told Ted I wasn't coming down and he tells me to hang on because someone wants to talk to me. Another guy gets on the phone and says, "Hey Big Shooter, this is Billy. You've got five minutes to get your ass down here." It was Billy Martin, our manager. I said, "I'll be right down."
>
> I get dressed and go down to the party. Half of our ballclub is there with a bunch of Hollywood types. Billy comes over and asks what I'm drinking and I say, "Billy, I just got up. I'll have what you're having." So he gives me a scotch and I have a seat. I remember thinking: "This is the big leagues." I left the room at 6 a.m. and the party was still going on. And, we won our next seven games.

In the finale against the Angels, Harmon Killebrew kicked off a ten-game hitting streak with an eighth-inning, go-ahead home run to secure Martin's first managerial victory. The Twins made it two in a row in Oakland against the Athletics, their chief rival in 1969, when Tony Oliva and Killebrew stroked back-to-back, eighth-inning home runs off A's ace Catfish Hunter to break a 2–2 tie.

Minnesota's winning streak stretched to four in the home opener, as twenty-one-year-old rookie Tom Hall tossed a two-hit shutout against the visiting Angels. The slight left-hander, all of

150 pounds and already nicknamed "The Blade," recorded his first complete game and shutout in the 6–0 win. Then Oliva and Killebrew homered the following afternoon, and the Twins again came from behind for their fifth straight win. Killebrew drove in the game-winner again, but not with the long ball. He secured the 6–5 walk-off victory by beating the "Killebrew shift" with a single through the right side of the infield. Teams sometimes moved their second baseman to the left side of the infield with the pull-hitting slugger at the plate. So, Angels second sacker Bobby Knoop was in no position to field Killebrew's grounder, which moved the Twins atop the AL West for the first time. "How about that Killebrew," Twins reliever and clubhouse humorist Bob Miller said after the game. "He's a regular Nellie Fox."

In the win, Carew tied the score in the late innings by stealing home for the second time in nine games. He victimized Wilhelm, the knuckleballer, whose floater danced slowly to the plate. With the Twins trailing 5–4 in the seventh and Killebrew at the plate, Carew signaled to Martin he wanted to go. Carew then relayed the sign to Killebrew—a touch of the belt with the right hand—and Carew believed Killebrew acknowledged the sign with a tap of his own belt. As Carew headed toward home, Killebrew began striding as if he were going to take a cut at Wilhelm's offering. Carew kept coming, well aware of the dangers of meeting his teammate at the plate. "If he swung," Carew recalled in his autobiography *Carew*, "I end up a double down the left-field line." At the last minute, Killebrew picked up Carew speeding down the line and held up. Carew slid across the plate safely, seemingly outrunning Wilhelm's knuckleball.

After the Twins won their seventh straight by defeating Oakland at Metropolitan Stadium, the streak stalled on April 22 when twenty-two-year-old rookie Rollie Fingers blanked them on five hits, 7–0, in his first Major League start. Two days later in the series finale, the budding rivalry between the AL West contenders heated up. Young A's slugger Reggie Jackson, in his breakout season, drilled home runs in his first two at-bats against Boswell. With the A's jumping out to a 5–0 lead, Boswell didn't survive the third inning and Woodson came on in relief. When Jackson came to bat in the fifth, the hard-throwing right-hander rocketed a first-pitch, belt-high fastball *behind* the left-handed hitter. Woodson sailed his second pitch four feet over the heads of Jackson, Twins catcher John Roseboro, and home plate umpire Cal Drummond, provoking Jackson to toss his bat aside and head for the mound. Jackson tackled Woodson and both dugouts emptied.

The melee centered on getting the enraged Jackson off Woodson, who soon sported a gash over his right eye and said Jackson had tried to claw his eyes out. The soft-spoken kid, who claimed the errant throws were caused by his cleats sticking on the mound, laughed off the incident as a "pretty stupid thing" and said the former Arizona State football player had "made a lousy tackle." Afterward, Oakland skipper Hank Bauer said, "It's the same old stuff. They say they didn't want to hit him. Sure." Martin admitted the pitches looked suspicious, though he countered that "if you intend to buzz somebody, you stick it right under his chin."

Such skirmishes weren't unfamiliar to Martin. Playing for Cincinnati in 1960, he had charged the mound and broken the cheekbone of Cubs relief pitcher Jim Brewer after a brushback pitch. It was one of several fights he was in as a player, but Martin showed remarkable restraint during the brawl. He grabbed Oakland catcher Dave Duncan by the throat when Duncan tried to join the scuffle before passing him off to Bob Allison for safekeeping.

After the game, Jackson blamed the incident on Martin, claiming the brushback orders came from the Twins dugout. Martin, who had suffered one of the worst beanings in the game's history in 1959 as a member of the Cleveland Indians, insisted he never asked a pitcher to intentionally throw at a hitter. Martin lambasted Jackson's trip to the mound as a stupid act that would encourage more pitchers to bust the young star inside. Word circulated that Jackson wanted to fight Martin that afternoon, but their showdown would have to wait until a much later date in the New York Yankees dugout.

April closed with Rod Carew racing home on the front end of a triple steal with Tony Oliva and Harmon Killebrew, highlighting a four-run fifth inning that produced a 6–4 win over the other new club, the Seattle Pilots. The Twins were in the midst of an eight-game winning streak, but when that ended, they struggled to play .500 ball for most of two months. If losing seven of eight mid-May contests wasn't enough to irk skipper Billy Martin, Dave Boswell did by running half-speed to first base twice during the skid. Boswell became a two-time offender in Baltimore on May 21, when he caught the Orioles infield asleep on a bunt but was still retired on a close play. Martin fined Boswell for both offenses.

After the stumbling Washington Senators defeated the Twins on May 27 to end a six-game losing streak, Martin took verbal swipes at several targets, including Washington manager and Hall of Famer Ted Williams: "He was one of the worst players I ever saw. He didn't worry about his team, only about Ted Williams. He wore the same uniform for fifteen years. It didn't even have to be laundered. He wouldn't slide to break up a double play. Never got his uniform dirty." The quote was twelve paragraphs into that game's coverage by *St. Paul Pioneer Press* writer Arno Goethel, but it was picked up by a wire service and drew national attention.

Goethel later wrote that "in the bombastic world of Billy Martin, there's no halfway. . . . Martin doesn't deal in halves. To Martin, a good play is the greatest of all time. A bad play is the worst he's ever seen." A rant about how to play the game, which questioned Williams's base running, was a typical Martin exaggeration that Goethel and his fellow scribes didn't take literally or too seriously. The uproar caught Martin by surprise. "Did I tell you Williams was the worst player I ever saw?" a forlorn Martin asked Goethel when the story broke the next day. "This could be the worst thing that's ever happened to me." As for Williams, he defended his base running, saying, "I must have passed second base along the way and must have done some sliding" in leading the league in runs six times. After talking with Goethel, Williams told reporters that Martin's statements were being misrepresented.

The dustup was one of many over the course of the season. Martin ripped other AL managers, criticizing Orioles skipper

Earl Weaver for resting regulars in a series against Cleveland and claiming Cleveland manager Al Dark was saving hard-throwing ace Sam McDowell for the Twins. Martin promised Dark that he would remember and get even if Dark ever managed a contending team. He barred a *Sports Illustrated* writer from the clubhouse and did the same to photographers on hand to cover a visit from former vice president and Twins fan Hubert Humphrey after a loss. There were the demonstrative tiffs with umpires, of course, and late in the season, Martin admitted to *Sporting News* writer Mike Lamey that "I'm afraid I would never make a good ambassador. I'd probably start a war or two."

Despite the team's early ups and downs, Carew quickly blossomed into a star under Martin's tutelage. All spring Martin had worked with the twenty-three-year-old second baseman on his bunting and on hitting the ball on the ground more consistently with his inside-out swing. On May 13, Carew erased a 2–1 Baltimore lead in the eighth inning with an inside-the-park home run in which he chased César Tovar around the bases and slid under the tag of Orioles catcher Elrod Hendricks. Days later, on May 18, Carew collected those three stolen bases in one inning against the Tigers, including his fourth steal of home. The three thefts in a single inning tied an American League mark held by fifteen modern-era players, including Joe Jackson, Buck Weaver, and Hall of Famers Red Faber, Eddie Collins, and Ty Cobb. Carew also was pursuing Cobb's single-season record for steals of home.

Late in May Carew sparked a 7–1 win in Washington with the first two-homer game of his career, impressing Senators manager and Hall of Famer Ted Williams with his power and speed. Carew was batting .403 heading into June, with a seventy-point lead in the American League batting race. The only obstacle to winning his first of seven batting titles was a military commitment. Carew had joined the Marine Corps Reserve in 1965, and his Marine duty kept him off the field for several weekends and two weeks in August. The time off not only messed with his timing at the plate, but also put him on course to fall short of the necessary plate appearances to qualify for the 1969 batting crown.

Early in June Carew pulled a thigh muscle running out a bunt, an injury that further cut into his playing time and slowed him on the bases. Teams were now paying him attention as well; many pitchers abandoned the windup for the set position once he reached third base. While stealing home became more challenging, the sore thigh muscle failed to slow Carew's bat. His .400 average spurred buzz in *Sporting News* that he could become the first player to bat .400 for a season since Williams hit .406 in 1941. Even Martin weighed in, saying he thought the rookie could do it the way he was beating out bunts that spring. Carew fell short in 1969, but legitimately flirted with .400 in 1977, when he batted .388 to claim his sixth batting title.

Despite injury and the additional scrutiny from pitchers, Carew stole home twice more in June to give him six for the season. In the eighth inning of a 4–2 win over the Yankees on June 4, the Twins held a one-run lead and had the bases loaded. Yankees reliever Lindy McDaniel was pitching to Twins shortstop Leo Cárdenas when Carew, his left thigh heavily wrapped, took his walking lead from third base and broke for home. Yankees catcher John Ellis partially blocked the plate, but Carew slid away from him and beat the tag. Killebrew and Twins catcher John Roseboro, neither known for blinding speed, also moved up on the back end of another triple steal.

On June 16, in an 8–2 win over the California Angels at the Met, the Twins were off and running in the opening frame. After Ted Uhlaender drew a leadoff walk from Angels starter Tom Murphy in the first, Carew reached on an error and Oliva delivered a run-scoring single that moved Carew to second. With Killebrew at the plate, Carew and Oliva executed a double steal to move into scoring position. They did it again with Killebrew still in the batter's box, as Carew dashed home and Oliva pulled into third. Killebrew singled home Oliva to give the Twins a 3–0 lead before Murphy had retired a single batter.

The early onslaught upset Angels manager Lefty Phillips, bothered that Carew took advantage of his young starting pitcher. Phillips told beat writers that "Minnesota better get some insurance with that showboat in there. Carew was successful, but stunts like that might cost this club the pennant." Billy Martin defended his prodigy and blew off his counterpart. "Mr. Phillips seems to forget the last time the Angels were here, Carew stole home on Hoyt Wilhelm," Martin told the *New York Times's* Ross Newhan. "You don't get any older than Wilhelm. You do and they bury you. . . . Apparently, they didn't do that sort of thing when Mr. Phillips was playing his five games in the Arizona-Texas League."

Carew settled nicely into the number two hole in the batting order, just ahead of Oliva with Killebrew in the cleanup spot. The trio powered Minnesota's offense. Carew and Killebrew went on to win the three Triple Crown categories while Oliva quietly turned in another strong season. He led the league in hits and doubles and recorded 100 RBIS for the first time. He batted .339 before the All-Star break, an average that might have led the league, but he and everyone else trailed Carew, Oliva's friend and road roommate, by a wide margin.

Tony O batted .556 during a ten-game hitting streak in late June and swatted two home runs in the second game of a June 29 doubleheader in Kansas City. In leading the Twins to a 12–2 victory, Oliva went 5-for-5, collecting each hit off a different Royals pitcher. The most memorable poke came off Royals starter Dave Wickersham, who had given Oliva trouble as a mid-1960s mainstay with the Tigers. Wickersham had "a little slider, a little sinker," remembers Oliva, who usually feasted on breaking balls. "I don't know how he got me out so easy. There's always someone who's got your number." On this day Oliva turned on a Wickersham slider for the longest ball he ever hit in the Major Leagues. One pitch after the right-hander had put the red-hot hitter on his backside, Oliva powered a towering 517-foot blast that sailed over the right-field upper deck and struck a house along Brooklyn Avenue outside old Municipal Stadium.

The 12–2 beating of the Royals ignited a 20-4 run by the Twins, who had trailed Oakland by 1½ games after Oliva's big day in Kansas City. Three weeks later at the All-Star break, the Twins were 59-37 and four games in front. The surge included a 14-1 home stand that began on the Fourth of July with the first of three straight wins over Oakland, allowing the Twins to overtake the A's. Oliva assembled a fifteen-game hitting streak during the surge and nearly every Twins regular hit during the home stand. No one, though, generated runs and wins like Killebrew.

Going into the Fourth of July weekend, Killebrew had 19 home runs and a league-leading 72 RBIS. His homer total ranked a distant second to that of A's slugger Reggie Jackson (33), but Killebrew closed the gap markedly by popping nine homers in those fifteen games at the Met. The binge began on the Fourth with Oakland in town and first place on the line. Uhlaender and Oliva greeted Catfish Hunter with first-inning doubles and Killebrew followed with a shot into the bleachers. He produced the early lead in a 10–4 win that moved the Twins within a few percentage points of the A's.

The Twins took sole possession of first place in the second game, pounding A's pitching in a 13–1 romp. Jackson stroked what is widely considered the longest right-field home run in the history of the Met, a drive that banged off a beer advertisement on the scoreboard more than fifty feet above ground level. But Killebrew countered with *two* homers and drove in six runs.

After the Twins clobbered Oakland pitching for 23 runs and 32 hits in the first two games, they claimed a more modest 7–6 decision on Sunday, erasing a 6–2 deficit with a five-run rally in the seventh inning. In the magical seventh, Oliva delivered a two-out RBI single off Rollie Fingers to move the Twins within a run. Then, despite a steady fifteen-mile-an-hour wind blowing in toward the plate, Killebrew drove a 360-foot game-winner into the left-field seats. He had slugged at least one homer in each game of the series—11 against the rival A's that season— and arguably none was bigger than his July 6 blast. It marked the sixteenth time he had driven in the deciding run for the Twins, who celebrated their forty-sixth victory after AL saves leader Ron Perranoski worked two quiet innings to seal the one-run victory. With 10 RBIS in the Oakland series, Killebrew pushed his total to a Major League-high 82 in eighty games.

To close out the home stand with nine straight wins, the Twins swept four from the reeling Chicago White Sox. In the finale on July 17, an 8–5 Twins win, Killebrew drove a Don Secrist pitch off the center-field backdrop at Metropolitan Stadium, 456 feet from home plate. Only Killebrew—in 1961—had done it, and with the blast, he had closed within seven of Jackson in the home run race. But it was Carew who electrified Twins fans when he stole home for a seventh time during the second inning of a 9–8 victory over the White Sox on July 16. Again the bases were loaded—with Killebrew on second and rookie Charlie Manuel on first—when Chicago hurler Jerry Nyman blundered on his first pitch to Twins catcher John Roseboro.

"Nyman went into a windup. He forgot I was in the game," Carew wrote in his autobiography. "His teammates were hollering, 'Hold him on, hold him on!' Too late. I slid home with No. 7." Exactly a month had passed since Carew last swiped home, an indication of how opponents had become more cautious with him at third base. Yet Carew had executed those seven steals without being caught once—and this was the steal that he and the baseball world believed had broken Cobb's single-season record. With Cobb credited with two additional steals of home in more recent years, Carew was in fact, one shy of Cobb's AL record of eight. He would still make two more attempts to steal home, both in September, including a last dash in the final week of the season.

Although Oliva pounded the ball all over Met Stadium during the home stand, he hadn't been feeling well and sat out the last three games of the White Sox series. The Twins were scheduled to fly to Seattle after completing the sweep of Chicago on July 17, but by then, Oliva had a fever of 104 and bumps had broken out over his entire body. He had come down with chicken pox, which knocked him out of action for ten days and stalled a 25-for-50 tear. The surge bumped his season average to a lofty .339, just 19 points shy of Carew's .358 at the top of the leader board. Oliva, who topped the AL in hits and doubles when he was sidelined, missed the All-Star Game ten days later at Washington's RFK Memorial Stadium. Oliva had appeared in all five Midsummer Classics since his 1964 arrival, and it took chicken pox to keep him from matching Hall of Famer Joe DiMaggio's all-time record for most consecutive All-Star Game appearances to start a career.

With Oliva resting at home, the Twins boarded a plane headed to Seattle for four games to close out the first half. A day earlier Neil Armstrong, Michael Collins, and Edwin "Buzz" Aldrin had taken flight on *Apollo 11*—the first manned mission to land on the moon—with roughly one million people watching the Cape Canaveral launch along Florida beaches. Once in the air, the staff in the Mission Operations Control Room at the Manned Space Center in Houston became the astronauts' lifeline. Such a mission required precise execution, and Mission Control's biggest task was to coach the astronauts through the intricate operations for landing the lunar module, nicknamed "Eagle" by the crew, on the moon's surface. For all the preparation required to complete a successful mission, however, a preflight press conference revealed that Armstrong had not given thought to what he might say to the world upon setting foot on the moon.

One critical aspect of the Apollo flight was that the spacecraft traveled in the constant sunlight between the Earth and the moon. The spacecraft's temperature was controlled by a slow rotation, which Collins compared to "a chicken on a barbecue pit. As we turned, the Earth and the moon alternately appeared in our windows. We had our choice. We could look toward the moon, toward Mars, toward our future in space . . . or we could look back toward the Earth, our home, with its problems spawned over more than a millennium of human occupancy. We looked both ways. We saw both, and I think that is what our nation must do."

With the *Apollo 11* crew nearing the halfway point of its 238,857-mile journey to the moon on Friday, July 18, the Pilots of Seattle quickly pulled the plug on Minnesota's winning streak with a pair of one-run victories. The Twins rebounded to win the final two contests of the weekend series, however, and assumed a four-game lead over the A's at the break. In a strange twist, Jim Perry matched Dave Boswell with 11 first-half wins by claiming the "W" in both victories. The Saturday night affair required extra innings when the Pilots rallied for three ninth-inning runs off Al Worthington and Perranoski. Scoring then dried up until the fifteenth, when both teams pushed across a run to keep the game tied at 7–7. After a quiet sixteenth, however, the league's curfew rule forced the game to be suspended until the following day.

By the time the two teams walked off the field at 1:00 a.m., *Apollo 11* had settled into an elliptical orbit of the moon, ranging 70 to 195 miles away. Roughly twelve hours later, while Collins piloted the command ship *Columbia* in lunar orbit, Armstrong and Aldrin flew the lunar module to the moon's surface. They executed a last-minute maneuver to avoid a rocky crater before safely landing on the moon's Sea of Tranquility. "Houston, Tranquility Base, here," announced Armstrong to Mission Control. "The Eagle has landed." In Minnesota, it was 3:17 p.m. on Sunday, about an hour before the Twins and Pilots began play. Pregame ceremonies in Seattle were interrupted by an announcement of the moon landing, spurring fans to stand and cheer. The small crowd sang "America the Beautiful" in celebration.

Sunday was Perry's scheduled day to start, so he took the mound when Saturday's game resumed. Perry himself scored the decisive run, as the switch hitter slashed a one-out double off Pilots right-hander John Gelnar in the top of the eighteenth. Perry advanced to third on Uhlaender's infield hit and trotted home on a bases-loaded balk by Gelnar. The Seattle hurler seemed to come unhinged by his mental mistake, surrendering three more runs in a wild 11–7 Twins win. Minnesota drew 18 walks off Pilots pitching, tying the Major League record for the most free passes drawn by a single team. The two clubs combined for a new big league mark by stranding forty-four runners. Even with such a dismal display of clutch hitting, the two squads still pushed across 18 runs.

After working two perfect innings to close the marathon, Perry went the distance and scattered nine hits for a 4–0 victory in the regularly scheduled game. Gelnar, who served up long balls to Tovar and rookie catcher George Mitterwald in seven innings of the second game, took both losses. During the game, a quarter-million miles away, Armstrong and Aldrin ate their first meal on the moon, lunching in the lunar module. They then rested for several hours before their big night.

When it was time to leave the module, the two astronauts depressurized the module's cabin and opened the hatch. As Armstrong began to descend the steps, he pulled a D-ring that opened a stowage area door and allowed a television camera to view the moon's surface. With a worldwide audience of nearly a half billion watching grainy satellite images on television—at 9:55 p.m. in Minneapolis and St. Paul—Armstrong stepped onto the moon's powdery landscape and described the historic moment with those immortal words: "One small step for man, one giant leap for mankind."

"The surface is fine and powdery . . . like powdery charcoal on my boots," Armstrong said moments later as he began to collect lunar material. "My feet only go in about an eighth of an inch and I can't see footprints here where I have walked." It was Armstrong's first observation on the moon's low gravity. When Aldrin joined him outside the module twenty minutes later, the two playfully indulged in the low gravity by bouncing along the moon's surface. Together they planted an American flag, set up devices for scientific experiments, and collected more than sixty pounds of moon rocks and dust for testing back on Earth. Before they climbed back into the lunar module, they took the longest long-distance phone call in history from President Richard Nixon. Armstrong spent more than two hours on the moon's surface, Aldrin a bit less than two hours. "It's different," Armstrong told the television audience, "but it's very pretty out here."

It's also a day Jim Perry will never forget: "I pitched 11 shutout innings. I won two ballgames. A man set foot on the moon. My brother (Gaylord) was pitching at San Francisco and (former Giants manager) Alvin Dark had said there will be a man on the moon before Gaylord hits a home run. He hit a home run that day, and a man set foot on the moon that day. How about that?" Indeed, the planets (and the moon) had aligned for the Perry brothers. Jim blanked the Pilots while Gaylord popped his first career home run in his eighth big league season, a solo shot off Dodgers lefty Claude Osteen in San Francisco's 7–3 win over Los Angeles. Gaylord also went the distance for his twelfth victory of the season, giving him one more than Jim at the All-Star break.

SEVENTEEN

Peace, Love, and a Division Title

The *Apollo 11* crew splashed down in the Pacific Ocean on July 24, the day the second half of the baseball season began. Despite losing eight pounds and not having swung a bat in ten days, Tony Oliva was in the Twins lineup in Cleveland that night. One of the league's hottest hitters when he went down, Oliva struggled to regain his timing as the Twins split a four-game set before returning home to host the American League East's two best clubs, Detroit and Baltimore.

The Twins were three games up on Oakland when the seven-game home stand kicked off with a July 29 doubleheader against the 1968 World Series champion Tigers. Nearly forty thousand fans passed through the turnstiles to see the Twins face World Series MVP Mickey Lolich and thirty-one-game winner Denny McLain. The opener featured southpaw Lolich, 14-2, and Jim Perry, who had gone 5-0 in July to improve to 11-4. Both worked two quiet innings before the Twins broke through in the third on Oliva's bases-loaded, two-run double. Later AL batting leader Rod Carew connected on a two-run, opposite-field homer off Lolich, and Perry worked eight innings for a 5–2 victory.

In the nightcap, the bats broke through against McLain, the league-leading fifteen-game winner who had won his last eight starts against the Twins since the start of the 1968 campaign. Twins hitters sent McLain to the showers with a seven-run outburst in the fifth. Oliva provided the big blast with a 453-foot bomb that rocketed off the batter's eye in center field. In the sixth, Harmon Killebrew hit his thirtieth of the season, drilling a pitch from reliever John Hiller roughly the same distance to left-center in an 11–5 victory.

After the Twins split the final two games of the Detroit series to close July at 64-40, August began with the AL East-leading Orioles coming to town for a weekend series. Baltimore, with the best record in the Majors at 72-31, featured a potent offense and two of the six AL pitchers who would win twenty games in 1969: lefties Mike Cuellar and Dave McNally, who were scheduled to face the Twins. In the opener, the Twins prevailed 4–3 in ten innings when Leo Cárdenas tripled off Orioles closer Pete Richert and Carew took a full swing that produced an elusive dribbler. The ball rolled past Richert on the first base side, scoring Cárdenas to secure the walk-off win.

The Saturday matinee looked to be a pitchers' duel, but neither Cuellar nor Perry finished seven innings in a 6–5 Orioles victory. Baltimore looked like the favorite in the rubber game between the two division leaders, as McNally—winner of seventeen straight decisions going back to 1968—started the Sunday finale with a 15-0 record and 2.85 ERA. The O's rarely lost when McNally started, while Jim Kaat had won just two of his last eleven outings.

With nearly forty-one thousand fans on hand, the southpaws kept the bats quiet through the first six innings. The only run had scored when Brooks Robinson hit into a double play in the fourth, but the Twins rallied in the seventh when Cárdenas and Frank Quilici singled with two outs. McNally intentionally walked reserve infielder Rick Renick to bring Kaat to the plate with the bases loaded. Billy Martin called on left-handed-hitting Rich Reese, who was successful against lefties all season. Reese teed off on a 3-2 waist-high fastball for a grand slam. With a 5–2 victory, the Twins stuck McNally with his first loss in nearly eleven months.

The Twins had won five of seven against the East's elite to stay three games up on Oakland, but the pennant race took a backseat when they moved on to Detroit and split four games with the Tigers. The biggest story of the Detroit stopover took place at the Lindell AC bar, a small hole in the wall not far from Tiger Stadium. Before the finale in Detroit, a 6–4 loss, Dave Boswell had failed to run his required laps, a fact reported to Martin by pitching coach Art Fowler. When Martin called out the pitcher at the bar following the game, Boswell fumed about being ratted on and threatened to get even with Fowler.

Boswell angrily stormed out of the bar with Bob Allison following him in an attempt to cool him down. Over the years, Allison had frequently stepped in when the high-strung right-hander needed a calming influence, but this time his effort put him in the line of fire. Allison had his hands in his pockets when he was trying to reason with Boswell. "If you're going to be tough about this, why don't you hit me," the pitcher said Allison had suggested. Without hesitation, Boswell obliged and knocked Allison to the ground with a sucker punch. Martin's account was that he dashed out of the bar to find Boswell and Allison tussling, and that the pitcher hurled insults at him when asked to go back to the hotel.

Both Martin and Boswell claim the other threw the first punch in their rumble, with Martin reportedly responding with several rapid punches to Boswell's stomach before connecting twice to the head and knocking him out. Boswell didn't recall much about the incident the following day, but insisted Allison didn't have his hands in his pockets. Whether the wiry five-foot-eleven Martin manhandled the six-foot-three Boswell without assistance is uncertain. Martin said he won a fair fight, while Clark Griffith, son of Calvin and a childhood friend of Boswell, has said that two bar patrons were holding the pitcher's arms when Martin's assault began. The pitcher said the last thing he remembers about the incident was being kicked in the face. The specifics of that alcohol-fueled altercation were hazy, and the protagonists are now gone, but the seven stitches Martin needed in the knuckles of his right hand and the nearly twenty stitches required to sew up Boswell's facial wounds were there for all to see.

The fray also put a sizable dent in Boswell's wallet, as Calvin Griffith fined him $500 for the incident. Martin didn't get off scot-free either. Although he wasn't asked to open his pocket-book, the skipper drew the owner's wrath and inched closer to cementing a one-and-done tenure in his first big league managerial assignment. Boswell went home for two weeks after the fight. Oliva says when the right-hander returned to the team, a few of the abrasions and black-and-blue marks were still visible. He credits Boswell with coming back ready to pitch. "He still won 20 games that year," Oliva says. "I think it made him better." The numbers support that notion. Boswell was 12-9 with a 3.45 ERA when he went home to recuperate; he posted an 8-3 record and 2.79 ERA in 12 starts following his melee with Martin. Most likely the time off gave Boswell's ailing elbow some much-needed rest for the season's stretch run.

By losing the final game of the Detroit series on August 8, the Twins' lead over Oakland had shrunk to two games. The A's inched closer when the Twins lost the first two matchups of a weekend set in Baltimore. In the Sunday finale, they couldn't manage a hit all afternoon as Cuellar took a no-hitter into the ninth. César Tovar, the first batter of the inning, ruined Cuellar's bid with a line-drive single just beyond the reach of Baltimore shortstop Mark Belanger. It was the second time that season that the five-foot-nine, 155-pound Tovar had broken up a no-no in the ninth. Tovar had victimized Cuellar's teammate, McNally, on May 15, telling teammates in the dugout beforehand that he would end McNally's bid. With one out, he laced a McNally fastball into left-center field for a single. Both McNally and Cuellar had to settle for one-hitters.

Cuellar sent the Twins to a 2–0 defeat, their fourth loss in a row and the first time they had been swept in a series since the season-opening losses to the fledgling Royals. The four straight losses matched the team's longest losing streak of 1969, and the skid reached five on August 12, when the Yankees roughed up Kaat and the Twins bullpen in a 10–3 decision at Yankee Stadium. The five-game skid wasn't as costly as it could have been; the Yankees had taken three of four games from the A's before the Twins arrived in the Bronx. With both AL West contenders struggling, Minnesota managed to stay a game and a half in front of Oakland.

While the Twins moved from New York to Washington for a mid-August weekend series with the Senators, hordes of young people flocked to a dairy farm in upstate New York for four days of peace, love, music, heavy rains, and mud. The crowd for the Woodstock Music and Art Fair swelled to nearly 500,000, far exceeding expectations and wreaking havoc on the local infrastructure. Traffic backed up for ten to twenty miles outside the grounds. Inside, the food supply and sanitation were inadequate. Musicians struggled to reach the grounds for performances, so personnel at the nearby Stewart Air Force Base airlifted many into the venue. Then the rain came, torrential at times. A Sunday thunderstorm forced the stoppage of musical performances for several hours, and they would carry over into Monday morning.

It's remarkable that the event came off at all. Artists were slow to sign for what the organizers hoped would be the East Coast's answer to 1967's Monterey Pop Festival, a gathering of 50,000–100,000 that featured the first major American appearances of the Who, Janis Joplin, the Jimi Hendrix Experience, and Otis Redding. Playing on a pig farm in upstate New York didn't hold the same allure, and no one signed to appear at Woodstock until April 1969, when Creedence Clearwater Revival became the first. The group had exploded onto the scene over the previous year, scoring hits with "Suzie Q," "Born on the Bayou," "Proud Mary," "Lodi," and "Bad Moon Rising." There was no slowing the group, which released three albums in 1969 and had "Green River" on the charts by the time Woodstock took place. Once Creedence committed, other bands followed suit.

The festival's location endured several forced changes in 1969, as nearby residents and ordinances stood in the way of the anticipated gathering of fifty thousand young people. Roughly three weeks before Woodstock kicked off on August 15, permits were acquired to hold the event at the six-hundred-acre dairy farm of Sam Yasgur, whose land formed a natural bowl that included Filippini Pond, where skinny-dipping would be a popular attraction.

The crowds far exceeded fifty thousand of course, and by the time Richie Havens took the stage to open the festival, the traffic heading to Yasgur's farm from all directions had come to a grinding halt. A large contingent of musicians was stuck at two hotels roughly seven miles away and hardly any musicians had arrived. Havens went out because he was virtually the sole option, even without a complete band. His bass player, Eric Oxendine, had left his car in traffic on the New York Thruway, twenty miles away, walked the rest of the way, and arrived as Havens finished.

By then, Havens had played nearly every song he knew, including "Freedom," a commanding improvisation that appears in the 1970 documentary movie, *Woodstock*. "I did about four or five encores, till I had nothing else to sing," Havens told Joel Makower, author of *Woodstock: The Oral History*. "And then 'Freedom' was created right there on the stage. . . . It was the last thing I could think of to sing. I made it up. It was what I thought of, what I felt—the vibration which was freedom—which I thought at that point we had already accomplished. And I thought, 'God, this is a miracle. Thank God I got to see it.'"

Despite difficult conditions, concertgoers who spent eighteen dollars for a weekend pass shared the grounds peaceably, admirably living the era's tenet of peace, love, and understanding. Even the rains couldn't destroy the vibe, as attendees danced and mud-surfed through the worst of it. All the while, the crowd was treated to performances from artists who had made their mark in various musical genres—from Havens, Joan Baez, Arlo Guthrie, John Sebastian, Ravi Shankar, Joe Cocker, and Janis Joplin to Jimi Hendrix, Jefferson Airplane, the Who, the Band, Sly and the Family Stone, Santana, Creedence Clearwater Revival, the Grateful Dead, Ten Years After, Blood, Sweat, and Tears, and Crosby, Stills, Nash, and Young.

The crowd dwindled to fewer than fifty thousand by the time Jimi Hendrix closed the festival on Monday morning. With most of the weekend crowd far from Woodstock, Hendrix, wearing a white leather jacket with fringe and a red scarf, provided a defining moment of the festival with his psychedelic rendition of "The Star-Spangled Banner." His take, awash in distortion and feedback to simulate bombs bursting in air, segued into "Purple Haze," an early hit that brought the guitar genius to the attention of rock fans. Hendrix's performance would have gone largely unnoticed if not for the 1970 documentary.

Joni Mitchell wasn't there, but the festival experience of then-boyfriend Graham Nash inspired her to write the song "Woodstock." Crosby, Stills, Nash, and Young recorded it as the lead single of their album *Déjà Vu*, and it quickly became a counterculture anthem. For many who attended the festival, the cooperative spirit of the Woodstock experience had a lasting effect. And for them and many more who were too young or too far away to travel to upstate New York, Woodstock became an indispensable cultural marker of a decade soon coming to an end.

After going 10-9 on an eighteen-day road trip, the Twins returned home on August 22, still leading Oakland by a game and a half. They finally put some distance between themselves and the pesky A's during an impressive 10-2 home stand at the Met. The Twins kicked it off with a sweep of the Yankees, aided by scoreless outings from twenty-one-year-old rookie Tom Hall and Dave Boswell, who returned from his run-in with Billy Martin to post his thirteenth victory. He was a long way from 20 wins with just 11 starts remaining, but the lambasted right-hander with the tender elbow turned in his best pitching in the heat of the 1969 pennant race.

After sweeping the Yankees, the Twins took two of three from both Washington and Boston before winning three games from Cleveland. Jim Perry earned his sixteenth and seventeenth wins during the surge, improving to 17-5 when he beat Boston, 6–2, on August 31. By then, the A's had struggled through a frustrating and costly road trip. When Boswell tossed a four-hitter on September 3, in a 7–1 victory over Cleveland, his fifteenth win gave the Twins a 6½-game bulge in the West with four weeks to play.

If the A's were going to stick around in the AL West race, they needed to capitalize on a four-game, Labor Day weekend set with the Twins in Oakland. The Thursday night opener appeared to be a mismatch. Perry, 11-1 with a 2.43 ERA since the start of July, was going for his fifth straight win. A's right-hander Jim Nash, a .500 pitcher, mostly worked out of the pen after the All-Star break. Perry struggled with his control, though, and didn't get out of the fourth inning. The A's carried a 4–1 lead into the eighth before the Twins erupted for four runs to gain a 5–4 edge. The big blast was Harmon Killebrew's fortieth homer, a two-run shot that continued his 1969 success against the A's. Reggie Jackson, who went hitless in five trips, still led with 45 home runs.

Oakland bounced back to tie the game in the bottom of the ninth, but in Minnesota's half of the tenth, the pint-sized César Tovar outdid both Killebrew and Jackson. After Tony Oliva led off with a double, and Killebrew and pinch hitter Charlie Manuel drew walks, the A's called on Lew Krausse to face Tovar. The 155-pound slugger, affectionately called Pepe, stroked the only grand slam of his career to give the Twins a four-run margin—and they tacked on another run for a 10–5 victory. Watching Tovar's slam leave the park surprised everyone in the Twins dugout, and perhaps Tovar, too, as he left the batter's box. "I don't watch it like Killebrew does," said Tovar. "I ran hard to first."

"You *know* I have power," Tovar joked with sportswriters and teammates, while rippling his muscles, after the game. Tovar deserved the attention; he was in the midst of a ten-game surge in which he batted .415, scored 14 runs and drove in 10—with some late home run dramatics to boot. Pepe wasn't done flashing his power. Two days later, he and his twenty-nine-ounce bat were at it again.

After the Twins had dropped the second game of the Oakland series, the third game went into extra innings, tied 5–5. In the sixteenth, Oliva pounded a shot off George Lauzerique—his second of the game—to give the Twins a 6–5 lead. The A's countered with a run in their half of the inning, but in the eighteenth, Tovar swatted another long ball to end the marathon, powering a two-run bomb off Lauzerique for an 8–6 win. "I like these hot games," said Tovar, who had been bothered that he didn't start a game during Minnesota's last trip to Oakland and cockily predicted on the team flight that he would make an impact this time. "These games make me hustle more and I play better. You watch me out there and we win." Tovar, with a career-high 11 home runs that summer, hit two of the biggest for the 1969 Twins.

Sunday's finale lacked the drama that had permeated the weekend series. The Twins scored eight runs in the first two innings en route to a 16–4 romp that pushed them 8½ games ahead of Oakland. Killebrew continued to destroy Oakland's pitching staff, driving in seven of the first eight runs with two home runs, one a grand slam off A's rookie Vida Blue. Killebrew, with 42 homers, was now within four of Jackson and two behind Washington's Frank Howard. After his productive afternoon, Killebrew's 128 RBIS were ten more than any other AL hitter.

Oliva drilled four home runs and went 8-for-19 in the Oakland series and now trailed only Rod Carew in the batting race. The difference was still substantial—.348 to .319—but with four weeks to play, Carew, having completed two weeks of Marine duty in August, was nearly 100 plate appearances short of qualifying for the batting title. His pursuit of the qualifying minimum went down to the season's final series in Seattle.

Also in Carew's sights was the Major League record for steals of home—at the time it was seven by Pete Reiser of the Brooklyn Dodgers. On September 10, nearly two months after stealing home for a seventh time, Carew attempted to set the new mark with White Sox left-hander Tommy John on the mound at White Sox Park. Leading off the third inning, Carew slashed a single to right field and stole second. After Killebrew walked, both runners advanced on Oliva's groundout. With a 1-1 count on Leo Cárdenas, Carew broke for the plate, but White Sox catcher Don Pavletich was able to put the tag on him. The All-Star second baseman had been caught for the first time on his eighth attempt.

Carew made one last mad dash for home on September 26 in Seattle. He recalls getting a great jump on rookie right-hander Skip Lockwood and sliding by the plate as the ball hit the mitt of Pilots catcher Jerry McNertney, yet he was called out by home plate umpire Jim Honochick. Carew was convinced he was safe and says McNertney concurred the next day. "I think the umpire's vision was blocked, so he automatically gave me the thumb," Carew wrote in his autobiography *Carew.* "That was my last good chance to steal home in 1969." And Cobb's record stands to this day.

Winning the dramatic Labor Day weekend series in Oakland seemed to take the edge off the front-running Twins—they lost five of their next seven contests—but the outcome all but drained the life from the A's. Oakland closed its home stand by losing twice to the expansion Royals and then struggled to play .500 ball on their next road trip. The trip included the final two meetings between the Twins and A's, decided by convincing performances from Minnesota's two best pitchers.

On September 15, Boswell, calling on a nasty curveball, defeated Oakland for the second time in eight days. He went the distance for a 6–3 victory, sparked by Killebrew's tenth homer in seventeen games against the A's. Boswell didn't allow a hit over the last four frames, and when he caught pinch hitter Ted Kubiak looking at a called third strike to end the game, the Twins were nine games in front. The win was Boswell's seventeenth, and at most, he would have four starts to get the three wins needed to reach twenty for the season.

The following afternoon, Perry pounded another spike into Oakland's dying playoff hopes. Killebrew hit a three-run shot in the opening frame, igniting an 11–3 thumping in the teams' final matchup. Perry posted his nineteenth win by beating the A's for the fourth time without a loss in 1969, and number 19 moved the Twins ten games ahead. In eighteen games against A's pitching, Killebrew batted .435, pounded 11 homers, scored 19 runs, and drove in 34.

Killebrew wasn't the only Twin to slap Oakland pitchers around that summer. Oliva hit .417 with 10 doubles, 21 runs, and 21 RBIS in eighteen contests. Tovar hit .408 and delivered two game-winning, extra-inning home runs in sixteen games. Carew batted a more modest .329, though with 15 runs and 15 RBIS in fifteen games. As a team, the Twins hit .310 and averaged more than seven runs per game against their main rival—and claimed thirteen of eighteen games.

On September 19 and 20, Boswell and Perry pitched the Twins to one-run victories over Seattle on consecutive days, cutting the team's magic number to two. Boswell kicked off a weekend series by striking out fourteen Pilots for a 2–1 victory and his eighteenth win. The following afternoon, Perry, at age thirty-three, pitched in pursuit of his twentieth win for the first time in his career. After Perry gave up a two-run homer to Seattle third baseman John Kennedy in the second inning, no Pilot reached third base. Carew and Rich Reese delivered RBI singles in the seventh to tie the game. With one out in the ninth, Carew singled off Seattle reliever Diego Seguí before Oliva made Perry a twenty-game winner by drilling a shot into the gap in left-center for a walk-off RBI double. The veteran right-hander went home with two souvenir baseballs—one for his one-thousandth career strikeout in the first inning and the other for win number 20.

Perry had mostly been used as a swingman by former Twins managers Sam Mele and Cal Ermer, but Billy Martin turned to Perry to anchor the Twins rotation. Beginning that spring, Martin had encouraged Perry to become a take-charge pitcher who challenged hitters. The manager thought Perry too often tried to pitch around left-handed hitters, "so I told him that with his good fastball and slider, he should be able to jam the lefties and get them out." Taking a more aggressive approach, Perry won his share of big games, going 9-2 with a 2.55 ERA after the All-Star break. As *St. Paul Pioneer Press* beat writer Arno Goethel noted in the heat of the pennant race: "Billy Martin dealt himself into the Jim Perry game and drew an ace."

Minnesota's magic number dropped to one later that evening, when the Angels whipped the A's in a blowout. That gave the Twins a chance to clinch at home in the final game of their ten-day home stand on September 21. The celebration was delayed, however, as the A's rebounded Sunday afternoon and the Pilots defeated the Twins with a ninth-inning run, 4–3. Twins fans might have been disappointed to not witness the clinching, but the game wasn't a total loss. Killebrew smashed two solo homers to give him 46 for the season. With his second blast, he moved into a three-way tie in the homer race with Reggie Jackson and Frank Howard. Killer had trailed both men by large margins, but drilled 31 home runs after July 1 in his MVP season.

The Twins headed to Kansas City, where Martin called on Bob Miller to pitch the potential clincher on September 22. The thirty-year-old right-hander, who had performed mop-up duties in 1968 and was left unprotected throughout the off-season expansion draft, was a key contributor all season as a reliever and spot starter with Dean Chance sidelined in June and July. Miller had not made a start in '68, but Martin gave him 11 in '69. Miller hadn't made one in six weeks, however, when he got the call in Kansas City.

The assignment demonstrated Martin's faith in Miller, who held the Royals to a single run on five hits through eight innings. Kansas City took the early lead, but Killebrew, leading off the fourth inning against left-hander Jim Rooker, stroked his forty-seventh homer, his third in two days, to tie the game and take the Major League lead. Bob Allison followed with a double and came around to score on a sacrifice fly by George Mitterwald. The Twins stretched the lead to 4–1 before entering the ninth just three outs from claiming the AL West crown.

Miller retired fifteen Royals in a row at one point, but in the ninth allowed a leadoff single to Ed Kirkpatrick and run-scoring double to eventual Rookie of the Year Lou Piniella. Martin brought in Al Worthington, who quickly induced Royals third baseman Joe Foy to hit a lazy fly to center for the first out. Worthington then walked light-hitting second baseman Jerry Adair, putting the tying run on, and Royals catcher Buck Martinez followed with a single to right. While Piniella headed home, cutting the lead to 4–3, rookie Scott Northey, inserted as a pinch runner for Adair, rounded second as if to go to third. As Oliva picked up the ball and saw Northey cross the bag, he rifled a perfect strike to shortstop Leo Cárdenas standing at second. The throw caught the rookie off base and removed the potential tying run from scoring position.

With two outs and Martinez at first, Worthington got Paul Schaal to slap a grounder to Killebrew near the first base bag. The slugger deliberately stepped on first to nail down the first AL West title. The Twins headed for the visitor's clubhouse, where they celebrated in typical fashion, laughing, joking, and dousing each other with champagne. As celebrations go, however, Goethel compared it to "a Saturday night at the Nickel Joint" with "no inkling of a rip-roaring all-night party." The difference from previous seasons, of course, was that a round of playoffs now stood between the Twins and a World Series date. Instead of the Fall Classic, they would be preparing for the Baltimore Orioles and the initial American League Championship Series.

EIGHTEEN

In a Game of Inches, Twins Swept Away

The New York Mets lost 120 games in 1962—their debut season—then lost at least 109 games in each of the next three summers. Early in the decade, if someone had told you that in 1969 the Mets would win the World Series and man would walk on the moon, you might have broken out in hysterical laughter. Certainly about the prediction that the lowly Mets would celebrate the last out in October.

But in a zany 1969, a year of the improbable, Buzz Aldrin and Neil Armstrong traipsed in the Sea of Tranquility, nearly a half-million young people gathered in upstate New York for a four-day music festival like none that had come before, and the Miracle Mets staged a stunning second-half surge to post their first-ever winning season and claim their first National League pennant.

The Mets had never finished higher than ninth, and 1969 seemed to augur more of the same when they opened the season by losing seven of ten games. They were based in the newly created NL East, where the Chicago Cubs—long the doormat of the league before the Mets—looked like the team to beat, winning ten of their first eleven. The Cubs, a veteran club built around future Hall of Famers Ernie Banks, Billy Williams, Ron Santo, and Ferguson Jenkins, held down first place from Opening Day into the second week of September. The Mets, who trailed the Cubs by ten games on August 13, engineered an inconceivable turnaround, led by a large contingent of kids in their mid-twenties and the budding lefty-righty combo of Jerry Koosman and Tom Seaver.

New York's surge began a few days later with two double-header sweeps of the expansion San Diego Padres. It was the weekend of the Woodstock Music and Art Fair, and youth made its mark that weekend at both Woodstock and Shea Stadium. In the first game of the Mets' doubleheader on August 16, the twenty-four-year-old Seaver pitched eight scoreless innings of a 2–0 victory that kicked off the club's 38-11 season-ending run. In his breakout season, Seaver won his last ten decisions and finished 25-7 with a 2.29 ERA. The twenty-six-year-old Koosman won the opener the following afternoon, going the distance in a 3–2 victory, starting an 8-1 finish by the hard-throwing southpaw.

The Cubs posted a losing record from that point on, perhaps in part because they played so many day games in the summer heat at Wrigley Field and manager Leo Durocher, who didn't believe in platoons, played the same eight regulars day after day. The Cubs led the Mets by just 2½ games when they arrived at Shea Stadium on September 8 for two key matchups with the surging Mets. On that Monday night, Koosman went the distance in a 3–2 win that moved the Mets even closer. When staff aces Seaver and Jenkins took the hill on Tuesday, the Mets scored early and often in a 7–1 romp that moved them to within a half game of the first-place Cubs.

That game is remembered most, however, for its symbolic moment involving a traditional omen of bad luck. A black cat crawled onto the field near the Cubs dugout, circled Santo in the on-deck circle, and then engaged in a lengthy stare-down with the fiery Cubs manager. The fate of the Cubs seemingly was sealed already, though, and the red-hot Mets took over first place by sweeping a doubleheader from the expansion Montreal Expos the following evening.

When the Mets clinched the NL East crown with a win over St. Louis on September 25, their long-suffering fans stormed the Shea Stadium turf as if the club had won the World Series. They celebrated wildly on the field, scaled the walls, climbed the scoreboard, and snatched nearly every souvenir from the park that wasn't tacked down. That included hundreds of square feet of sod, parts of the scoreboard, the netting on the team's portable batting cage, and the American flag. Luckily the Mets were off to Philadelphia after the game, because it took days to repair the damage.

Billy Martin and the Twins added to the summer's wackiness, executing triple steals and steals of home, as they hit, pitched, and ran their way to the first American League West crown. Even after the Twins clinched, however, several players had unfinished business before the American League Championship Series began on October 4. Although Rod Carew held a comfortable lead in the batting race, he lacked enough plate appearances to officially qualify for the title. Harmon Killebrew had the RBI crown sewn up, but the home-run race remained undecided. On the pitching side, Dave Boswell could join Jim Perry in the twenty-win club with two victories in his last three starts.

The night after the clinching in Kansas City, Boswell went seven innings and won his third straight start, a 6–2 victory good for his nineteenth win. Rather than wait until his final 1969 start to claim number 20, he made it four consecutive wins by beating Seattle on September 28. He worked seven innings of a 5–2 victory before blisters forced him to turn the game over to closer Ron Perranoski, who pitched two perfect frames for his Major League-leading thirtieth save. For the first time in their history, the Twins had two twenty-game winners in the same season.

After Leo Cárdenas made a sensational play to end the game, Boswell said he "went wild in the dugout" and "kissed the first four or five guys I saw." When the ecstatic starter retired to the clubhouse, the local press had a surprise for him. Writers had conspired to give him the silent treatment. Boswell watched as the press corps made its way around the clubhouse, talking to Carew about his three RBIS that day and Cárdenas about his game-ending glove work. Boswell picked up on the prank by the time the scribes moved on to Perranoski to discuss his thirtieth save, inspiring the twenty-game winner to retreat to the men's room. "If you clowns want to talk to me, you'll have to do it in here," Boswell barked. *St. Paul Pioneer Press* writer Arno Goethel wrote that he and his colleagues headed Boswell's way, where "they found their hero seated in the men's room with his trousers at half-mast."

Boswell, quick on his feet and always an entertaining interview subject, was in fine form. According to Mike Lamey of the *Minneapolis Star*, Boswell was cocked and ready when asked about going 8-2 down the stretch after his fight with Martin. "Well, if I lose a couple in a row, it looks like I'll have to get in another fight," Boswell replied. Martin overheard him and jumped in. "This time let me throw the first punch," Martin countered. Boswell fired back: "Are you that hard up?" Probably not. Martin might have been saving his best punches for a marshmallow salesman.

Carew secured the minimum number of plate appearances to qualify for the batting title in the season's penultimate game. He won his first batting crown with a .332 average, the first of fifteen straight seasons he cracked the .300 mark. He would go on to lead the league in hitting six more times before retiring after the 1985 campaign.

Although Killebrew had taken the Major League lead in homers in the clinching game against Kansas City, both Oakland's Reggie Jackson and Washington's Frank Howard homered over the next two days to make it a three-way tie at 47. The Twins slugger pulled in front again when he hit one out in Seattle on September 26 in a 4–3 extra-inning loss to the Pilots. Jackson wouldn't hit another home run the rest of the way, but Howard tied Killebrew with his forty-eighth in the opener of Washington's final series of the season on September 29.

On October 1, the Saturday on which Carew qualified for the batting title, Killebrew belted his forty-ninth to claim the AL home-run crown. He teed off on White Sox rookie Billy Wynne in the first inning with a two-run shot that scored Tony Oliva, though Wynne claimed Chicago's 4–3 victory. Killebrew matched his career high of 49 homers, his league-leading total in 1964, to take the sixth and final home run title of his Hall of Fame career. His 140 RBIS, 145 walks, and .427 on-base percentage were league-leading numbers as well, and all three were single-season highs. Killebrew and Carew shared the Triple Crown.

The 1969 season marked the fifth time Killebrew was among the top five vote-getters in MVP balloting, and this time he finished on top. In a 2010 interview, Killebrew took his typically modest tact about winning MVP honors: "We had César Tovar leading off. Carew was with us then. Tony hit third most of the time. We flip-flopped back and forth against left- and right-handed pitching. He had a great year. I drove in 140 runs and people said, 'Man, that's a lot of RBIS.' I said it should have been 240 with all those guys on the bases." Modesty aside, Killebrew was a clutch hitter in so many key situations; he slugged .686 in 217 plate appearances with runners in scoring position and delivered 20 game-winning hits.

Forty years later, Killebrew was more impressed that he played in all 162 games after rehabbing from a career-threatening injury the previous winter. "Nineteen sixty-nine was my best year," Killebrew recalled. "I don't know why because 1968 is when I got hurt in the All-Star Game and I missed half the season (with a ruptured hamstring muscle). Some of the doctors said I was through playing, that I wouldn't recover. I worked really hard that winter and came back and had the best year I ever had in baseball. Why? I don't know."

Oliva also had a sensational season. The penultimate game was memorable for him, too, as he reached an offensive milestone that had eluded him until 1969. After collecting his ninety-ninth RBI on September 22—and then going ten games without driving in a run—he singled home a run in the seventh inning against the White Sox to collect 100 RBIS for the first time. He had a similar take on the feat as Killebrew: "To have 100 RBIS, you have to have some people on base in front of you. We had César Tovar and Rod Carew."

The Twins won ninety-seven games and finished nine games in front of Oakland. Still, they closed with twelve fewer victories than the Baltimore Orioles, their American League Championship Series opponent. The 1969 Orioles, easily the best AL team that summer, were widely considered one of the best teams of all time, steeped in both power and pitching. "The key to winning baseball games is pitching, fundamentals and three-run homers," Baltimore skipper Earl Weaver often said. His 1969 club fulfilled that philosophy like few others.

Baltimore's two twenty-game winners, Mike Cuellar and Dave McNally, and up-and-coming right-hander Jim Palmer anchored an elite pitching staff. Although the twenty-three-year-old Palmer spent forty-two days on the disabled list, he won eleven straight decisions during the season and finished 16-4 in a breakout campaign. The 1969 Orioles also could slug with the best of them. Frank Robinson, who had struggled with his vision after a base-path collision in 1967, bounced back to hit .308 and club 32 home runs. First baseman Boog Powell had one of his best years, batting .304 and stroking 37 homers. The two combined for 221 RBIS. The Orioles also had Brooks Robinson, the defensive standout at third base, who delivered 23 homers and 84 RBIS.

The Orioles had won eight of twelve games against the Twins in 1969. Twins lefty Jim Kaat had been the most effective starter against the O's, claiming two of Minnesota's four wins and posting a 1.80 ERA in three starts. With Minnesota's two twenty-game winners, Jim Perry and Dave Boswell, ready to go, Kaat wasn't scheduled to start either of the first two games in Baltimore. The only question for skipper Billy Martin was whether to start Perry or Boswell in Game One of the best-of-five ALCS.

Martin wanted to beat one of the Orioles' twenty-game winners in Baltimore, where the ALCS kicked off and the O's had gone 60-21 during the regular season. If the Twins couldn't defeat Cuellar or McNally, they would face the nearly insurmountable task of having to win three straight against a team that rarely lost three in a row in 1969.

Perry got the Game One nod against Cuellar. Both twenty-game winners limited the opposition to a single through the first three frames, but the long ball decided the opener. In the fourth, Frank Robinson turned on a Perry pitch and dinged a hard liner off the left-field foul pole for a 1-0 Orioles lead. The

Twins quickly rebounded, as Tony Oliva led off the fifth and doubled to right field. He wheeled into third when Frank Robinson allowed the ball to get by him and came home to tie the score when Bob Allison lined a Cuellar offering to Orioles left fielder Don Buford.

Baltimore went back in front in the bottom half of the fifth, 2–1, when number eight hitter Mark Belanger lifted a 2-0 pitch from Perry into the first row of seats in left field. The Orioles shortstop had hit just two home runs all season, but to his credit, they had come off former Cy Young winners Jim Lonborg and Denny McLain. The Twins took a 3–2 lead in the seventh, when Harmon Killebrew walked with one out and Oliva tagged a four-hundred-foot home run to right-center.

Perry and the Twins were within three outs of beating the Orioles when Boog Powell opened the bottom of the ninth by jumping on a 3-2 pitch and lofting it into the right-field seats. Perry gave way to Ron Perranoski, who retired the O's to force extra innings, sailed through the tenth, then dodged trouble in the eleventh. The Twins loaded the bases in the twelfth, but reliever Dick Hall, replacing Marcelino López with one out, fanned Leo Cárdenas and induced catcher John Roseboro to fly out.

In Baltimore's half of the twelfth, Belanger led off with an infield single off Killebrew's glove at third base. After Perranoski retired the next two men, Belanger stood at third with two outs. Orioles center fielder Paul Blair, an excellent bunter, laid one down in the direction of third base, just beyond the playable range of Roseboro, and Belanger sped home with the winning run. In a postgame interview, Blair said he planned to take one cut at driving in Belanger, then bunt if he failed. After admittedly looking "pretty bad" on a swing, he laid down the game winner. For the Twins, the ALCS opener was a heartbreaker— and a testament that baseball is a game of inches. The Orioles scored on a home run that just caught the foul pole, another that barely cleared the wall, and a perfectly placed fifteen-foot bunt.

Game Two the following afternoon played out much the same. Boswell, a Baltimore native, squared off against the lefty McNally, and both pitched masterfully through ten scoreless innings.

Boswell allowed seven hits and walked five through ten innings, dodging occasional trouble, while the Twins managed just three hits and only twice advanced a runner to second. The most-costly walk was Boswell's sixth, opening Baltimore's half of the eleventh, when he put Powell aboard. Brooks Robinson bunted Powell to second, inspiring the Twins to intentionally walk second baseman Davey Johnson in order to face Belanger, who fouled out to Killebrew at third for the second out.

With left-handed-hitting catcher Elrod Hendricks due up, Martin called on Perranoski, his southpaw closer, and O's skipper Earl Weaver countered with right-handed-hitting bench player Curt Motton. On a 1-1 pitch, Motton slashed a liner that nicked the glove of a leaping Rod Carew and bounded into right field. Oliva charged the ball hard, backhanded it, and rifled a strong throw to the plate on what was a near-impossible play. The ball arrived just slightly up the line at the same time Powell reached home, and the Orioles slugger plowed into catcher George Mitterwald. Powell had missed the plate while sending Mitterwald sprawling, but the ball had skipped to the backstop and he had no trouble touching up to end the game.

Again Minnesota was on the wrong end of a one-run affair that could have gone either way—this time 1-0 in eleven innings. "We had a chance to win those first two games, but didn't have the clutch hit at the right time," Oliva said. "The pitching was there. I remember Boswell said, 'Give me one run,' but we didn't give it to him." Unfortunately for Boswell, his career took a tragic turn when he fanned Orioles star Frank Robinson with a slider on the final pitch of the tenth inning. "It felt like my shoulder went right into my jawbone," Boswell told the *Fort Myers News-Press* years later. "The arm would actually turn black and it ran all the way down the elbow." Boswell never was the same and retired two years later at age twenty-six. The hometown kid walked off the mound that October afternoon—not knowing that his career had taken a drastic downturn—to a standing ovation from the Baltimore crowd. It was a favorite memory of his injury-shortened career.

Trailing two games to none, the Twins returned home to the Met facing elimination. For Game Three, Martin chose to go with another right-hander, Bob Miller, instead of Kaat, who had allowed just six runs to the slugging Orioles and beat them twice in three starts. Martin held Miller in high regard for his pitching success in the heat of the pennant race, but Miller gave up singles to the first two hitters, Buford and Blair, and didn't survive the second inning. The Orioles tallied five hits and three runs before Martin replaced him with Dick Woodson, though two of the runs were unearned after Oliva slipped trying to catch a fly hit by Davey Johnson. It was all downhill from there, as the Orioles romped to an 11–2 victory.

It was an afternoon to forget for Oliva, who had injured his shoulder on his throw home on the final play of Game Two. The pain had started soon after the game, and by morning he had trouble lifting his arm and couldn't throw. After pressing Martin to play Game Three, Oliva was in the starting lineup because of its importance, but sat out pregame fielding drills, hoping to keep the Orioles in the dark about his sore shoulder.

Oliva played through the pain and collected two hits off winning pitcher Jim Palmer, but the injury was a factor in the ninth inning with the Orioles leading 9–2 and the game all but decided. Johnson led off the ninth with a single off Dean Chance and Hendricks greeted Ron Perranoski with a double down the right-field line. Oliva retrieved the ball and fired his relay throw directly into the grass in front of Carew, less than fifty feet away. The ball skipped past the second baseman, allowing Hendricks to circle the bases and score. The Metropolitan Stadium crowd of 32,735 unleashed its anger on Oliva, taking out its frustration for the team's failure in the ALCS. Then Belanger singled to right and Oliva made another throw to the infield with nothing on it. The boos grew louder. He was greeted with another Bronx cheer when he stepped into the on-deck circle in the bottom of the ninth with two outs, and the roar grew even louder after Carew grounded out to end Minnesota's season. Oliva, angered by the response, was the victim of his own desire to play at all costs. It was a frustrating end—for Oliva and the Twins—to an exciting 1969 season.

Minnesota's failure to push across runs was the real culprit in the ALCS. They scored just five runs and batted .155 against

Orioles pitching. The lack of punch, however, wasn't what had the media buzzing. It was Martin's decision to start Bob Miller in Game Three. The second-guessing began immediately. Why hadn't Kaat worked Game Three? Martin replied that Miller had been a stopper for the Twins all season. After Miller had pitched the clincher in Kansas City, Martin cited his pitching as "one of the main reasons" the Twins won the AL West title. "What if Miller had won today and what if Kaat had started and lost?" Martin retorted angrily at one point. Someone asked Martin what he thought the Twins needed to produce a better result in 1970. A new manager, he said, with a straight face.

That's what they got, as Calvin Griffith fired Martin during the World Series. The owner wanted Kaat to start Game Three, but the manager stuck with *his* choice. That decision may have been the last straw for the owner, though Griffith cited Martin's propensity to ignore organizational policies and guidelines when the firing was announced on the off day following World Series Game Two. Undoubtedly that included Martin's clash with Boswell, as well as some of the manager's loose rules governing his players and an angry mid-May confrontation between the manager and farm director George Brophy regarding the Minor League assignments of Twins prospects Charley Walters and Bill Zepp. When Brophy sent the two pitchers to Double-A Charlotte instead of Triple-A Denver, as Martin had preferred, the manager took his beef to the press.

"Brophy never played a game of pro baseball in his life, but he knows more than my pitching coaches," fumed Martin, who said his two pitching coaches, Art Fowler and Early Wynn, had helped the two hurlers to a point where they were better served testing their skills at the highest Minor League level. "I'm the farm director and he's the manager," Brophy responded. "He should handle his end and I'll handle mine." Griffith had the final word, defending his rookie manager: "There are only two people running the Twins—Billy Martin on the field and me in the office." But Griffith forced Martin to apologize to Brophy.

In the end, of course, Martin's confrontational style cost him his job, a firing that provoked widespread ridicule. *St. Paul Pio-*

neer Press sports columnist Don Riley weighed in, writing, "Griffith couldn't have done a more dastardly work of unpopularity if he turned down a reprieve for Joan of Arc—or got caught drilling holes in Washington's rowboat." The intense outcry by Twins fans was immediate. Telephones rang incessantly for days at Metropolitan Stadium. Angry callers also flooded the switchboards of the sports departments of local newspapers, and Griffith was hung in effigy on the University of Minnesota campus. Fans grabbed up more than ten thousand bumper stickers imploring the Twins to "Bring Billy Back." Thousands of Twins fans swore off the team—a common retort for years after Martin was gone—though the team's performance drop-off in the 1970s may have had more to do with the attendance decline that would come after the Twins quit competing.

While Martin's dismissal. wasn't a complete surprise to newspaper writers covering the team, most Twins players were shocked by it. "I was surprised because the most important thing was winning," Oliva said forty-five years after that ninety-seven-win season. Some spoke out against the firing, including Carew, who cited Martin for making a big difference in his career. Martin had spent so many hours with him, providing instruction and helping him refine his game to take advantage of his strengths. "He helped me tremendously on the field and off, giving me meaningful, fatherly advice when I needed," Carew wrote in his 1979 autobiography. "Billy and I also became good friends."

The Twins had won nearly one hundred games under a rookie manager, but they would defend their 1969 AL West crown with a new skipper who would be expected to win. More stunning even than Martin's firing was the New York Mets, who pulled off one of the biggest upsets in World Series history that October. The Orioles looked superior to the Mets in nearly every aspect of the game, and the Series outcome may have seemed apparent when Orioles leadoff man Don Buford, facing Tom Seaver, popped the second pitch of the Series into the bleachers for a home run. Mike Cuellar outpitched Seaver to secure Game One for the Orioles, 4–1, but then the Mets did what the entire American League could do only once all season: defeat the Orioles in four straight games.

The result had to have Twins players wondering what if *they* had advanced to play the underdog Mets. We'll never know, but Killebrew was prone to speculate when he ran into fellow Hall of Famer and longtime Orioles star Brooks Robinson. "Our club was as good as the Orioles," Killebrew said in 2010. "Even now I kid Brooks Robinson about losing to the Mets in the World Series. I said Brooks, 'Why couldn't the Orioles beat the Mets, for crying out loud. *We* would have beaten the Mets if we'd have played them.'"

The summer gathering at Woodstock in 1969 became an enduring symbol of 1960s youth culture, a high point of an era already slipping away. The moon landing and Miracle Mets also jazzed up an exciting year, but the political mood was shifting. Richard Nixon, who had criticized federal civil rights legislation and invoked images of burning cities during his run for the presidency, moved into the White House that year, intent on restoring "law and order" after a volatile decade of discontent and unrest.

When *New York Times* military correspondent William Beecher exposed the secret carpet-bombing of Cambodia in May 1969, nearly two months into the massive bombing raids, the public response was muted. The war's escalation, however, inspired the growing anti-war movement to intensify its opposition on a national scale. On October 15, 1969, the Moratorium to End the War in Vietnam drew Americans of all ages and walks of life to roughly three hundred U.S. colleges and universities. The largest crowd assembled in Boston, where South Dakota Senator George McGovern spoke to roughly 100,000 opponents of the war.

A month later, on November 15, a march on Washington attracted a crowd of 500,000. Events were held all weekend, beginning with Thursday night's March of Death, during which more than forty thousand people walked down Pennsylvania Avenue to the White House. For hours, they walked single file, each bearing a placard with the name of a dead American soldier or destroyed Vietnamese village. By then, nearly thirty-five thousand Americans had been killed in Southeast Asia.

With the civil rights movement in its final stage as a force for social and political change, "Black Power" was a logical extension of its original intent. What the late-1960s Black Power movement meant to active civil rights groups varied greatly. To many, it was the ongoing process to improve living conditions for African Americans in an integrated society. To some, it was a call for separatism. To others, it was a militant step forward to confront conditions that hadn't changed simply because civil rights legislation had been passed.

The Black Power movement was in full swing when Martin Luther King Jr. was assassinated on April 4, 1968, spurring tens of thousands of Americans to take to the streets. They responded with prayer vigils and peaceful marches, angry protests, and rioting. The rioting that broke out in dozens of American cities received the most media attention, of course, and whites commonly associated "Black Power" with violence.

On the night of King's assassination, hundreds filled the Sabathani Baptist Church in south Minneapolis. Hundreds more, including many University of Minnesota students, marched on City Hall the next day. The assassination not only incited anger and frustration in Black communities, but sorrow and fear as well. "I could hardly believe a man who had been preaching love and patience could be assassinated," Josie Johnson, the acting president of the Minneapolis Urban League at the time, told the *Minneapolis Star Tribune* in a 2018 interview.

Two days after the assassination, thousands of Minnesotans, in pelting rain, walked in peaceful marches across the Twin Cities to honor King. In poor communities, tensions ran high and anger boiled over. Fires were set and at times the threat of widespread violence appeared imminent, but Minneapolis-St. Paul largely stayed calm, avoiding the destruction that had plagued dozens of U.S. cities.

Stirring the most fear in white Americans were the Black Panthers, a revolutionary group that organized communities to create social service programs and taught militant self-defense for minorities. Its armed citizen patrols, intended to monitor and challenge police brutality, put it in direct conflict with law enforcement across the country.

The Panthers filled a void following King's assassination, advocating for self-determination through funding free medical clinics and free breakfasts for Black schoolchildren. Those programs made great inroads in the Oakland-San Francisco Bay Area, New York, Los Angeles, Philadelphia, and Chicago. In fact, the breakfast program was so successful that President Lyndon Johnson pushed for a federal equivalent after learning that the Panthers and affiliated groups were feeding more poor children than the U.S. government.

Fred Hampton, who as a twenty-year-old founded the Chicago chapter of the Black Panther Party in 1968, established a community service network that sustained a medical clinic and the breakfast program. As a teenager, he had recognized the need for youth education, recreation, and jobs and worked with the NAACP to start its West Suburban Youth Chapter, which attracted more than two hundred young people in its first year. A skillful speaker and negotiator, Hampton frequently organized protests against public policies that precluded fair living conditions for Black Chicagoans. He also convinced the city's Black street gangs to stop fighting each other.

Hampton, like most Black Panther leaders, was listed on the FBI's Key Agitator Index, a list of activists that FBI director J. Edgar Hoover had agents monitor closely. Chicago police also carefully tracked Hampton and the Panthers, who were headquartered on the city's West Side, the neighborhood where tensions between Black citizens and police ran highest. The neighborhood was a powder keg. Black Panthers were known to talk openly about "killing pigs" while Chicago police, under the direction of Mayor Richard J. Daley, had shown during the 1968 Democratic convention their penchant for administering punishing justice on the streets.

On December 4, 1969, fourteen Chicago police officers raided Hampton's apartment, killing him and fellow Panther Mark Clark. About one hundred bullets had been fired in the early morning raid, staged on the premise of searching for illegal weapons. Authorities claimed the Panthers opened fire on police, inciting a fierce gun battle, but ballistics experts later determined that all but one bullet had been fired from police weapons. They also concluded that "bullet holes" in the front door, which police cited as proof that the Panthers were shooting from inside the apartment, were nail holes created by police to cover up the attack.

Hampton was gunned down in his bed. While police insisted that the Panthers fired weapons first, in time, evidence eventually revealed that the FBI, the Cook County State's Attorney's Office, and the Chicago Police Department conspired to assassinate Hampton. No one in law enforcement was punished for the killings, or even for obstruction of justice in executing the elaborate cover-up.

NINETEEN

Four Dead in Ohio

At a time in which baseball didn't generate nearly as much off-season buzz as today, Billy Martin's firing kept Hot Stove talk on the front burner all winter. Twins fans were consumed with Calvin Griffith axing his manager after a ninety-seven-win season in 1969. The owner had to be thankful that the Minnesota Vikings provided the local sports scene with a pleasant diversion that winter, winning the NFL championship and advancing to Super Bowl IV.

The Vikings' opportunity to avenge the NFL's surprising loss to Joe Namath and the AFL's New York Jets a year earlier nearly didn't happen. On December 27, 1969, in the Western Conference title game at Metropolitan Stadium, an error-prone first half had put the heavily favored Vikings behind the Los Angeles Rams. They trailed 20–14 midway through the fourth quarter when quarterback Joe Kapp, a tough player inclined to run over defenders rather than avoid a hit, hurdled diving Rams cornerback Jim Nettles and stormed into the end zone from two yards out.

After kicker Fred Cox booted the extra point to give the Vikings a one-point lead, the defensive line, dubbed the Purple People Eaters, nailed down the victory. On the first play of the Rams' next drive, Carl Eller sacked quarterback Roman Gabriel in the end zone for a safety to put Minnesota up 23–20. In the final minute, with the Rams marching toward a game-tying field goal, Alan Page intercepted a Gabriel pass to secure the franchise's first playoff win. A week later, the Vikings made it two in a row with a 27–7 romp over the Cleveland Browns in the NFL championship game.

All four Purple People Eaters—Eller, Page, Jim Marshall, and Gary Larsen—were NFL Pro Bowl selections that year, when the stingy Vikings limited opponents to a league-low 9.5 points per game. The Vikings offense, led by Kapp, his favorite receiver, Gene Washington, and the running duo of Dave Osborn and Bill Brown, topped the NFL in points, averaging 27.1 per game. On January 11, 1970, in the final Super Bowl before the NFL-AFL merger, the Vikings were looking to cap a 12–2 season with a victory over the AFL champion Kansas City Chiefs.

The Vikings were double-digit favorites over the Chiefs, who many thought wouldn't even win the AFL title. More than a few Vikings anticipated they would be playing the Oakland Raiders that Sunday, but the Chiefs, with a complicated, multi-formation offense directed by coach Hank Stram, proved a formidable foe for Bud Grant's smash-mouth, straight-ahead Vikings. The Chiefs frequently changed their defensive alignment as well, constantly shifting their trio of talented, mobile linebackers, Willie Lanier, Jim Lynch, and former Gopher great Bobby Bell, to stifle the Vikings offense.

With chilly, mid-fifty temps at Tulane Stadium in New Orleans, the Chiefs shut down the Vikings offense until late in the third quarter, when Osborn dashed for a four-yard touchdown. By then, the Vikings were down 16–7, and their final three possessions ended with interceptions in a 23–7 defeat. Backup quarterback Gary Cuozzo threw the last pick after Kapp was knocked hard to the ground on a violent sack and suffered a shoulder injury. It was Kapp's last appearance as a Viking. He had played the 1969 season without a contract, an unusual but legal arrangement by NFL rules, which made him a free agent at season's end.

When the Vikings honored Kapp as the team's Most Valuable Player, he refused the honor: "There is no one most valuable Viking. There are 40 most valuable Vikings." The move was typical of the brash, rough-and-tumble Kapp, a respected leader on a talented team widely considered among the best to not win a Super Bowl. "I think the best thing that happened to us was when we got Joe Kapp," linebacker Lonnie Warwick told Pat Duncan, author of *Last Kings of the Old* NFL. "When he didn't return to us, I thought, 'Man, what a loss to our team.'"

Management had used a team option that allowed Kapp to play after failing to come to a contract agreement before the 1969 season. Despite being a Super Bowl quarterback months before, Kapp drew no interest from NFL clubs until the Boston Patriots finally signed him after the start of the 1970 season. The inability to get teams to negotiate in good faith with a free agent inspired Kapp to file a multimillion-dollar lawsuit against the Patriots and the NFL. In 1974, Judge William T. Seigert ruled that the NFL was in violation of antitrust laws, but a federal jury later decided that Kapp had not suffered damages. He wasn't compensated for lost income and never played football after that one season in Boston.

The Vikings' first Super Bowl appearance and Billy Martin's firing made for an atypical winter for Minnesota sports fans. It was a strange off-season for longtime Major League manager Bill Rigney, too. The fifty-two-year-old Rigney, whose managerial career began in 1954 with the Minor League Minneapolis Millers, was facing a familiar dilemma. He had the unenviable task of following the popular Leo Durocher as a manager of the New York Giants in 1956. After managing the expansion Los Angeles Angels for eight years, he arrived in Minnesota with the locals clamoring for Martin, whose popularity seemingly grew by the day.

Martin was another tough act to follow. "Bring Billy Back" bumper stickers were everywhere, spurring Rigney—the other, less-popular Bill—to quip that he thought the message was addressed to him. Luckily for Rigney, the backlash, as icy and bitter as a Minnesota winter, was directed at Griffith and not him. Beyond the bumper-sticker banter, Rigney avoided discussing the popular Martin.

Rigney brought with him Marv Grissom, who was his pitching coach with the Angels and had overseen Dean Chance's Cy

Young season in 1964. Chance was excited about being reunited with Rigney and Grissom, but before the winter was over, he was traded to Cleveland. He and fellow right-hander Bob Miller, highly regarded by Martin, were dealt with center fielder Ted Uhlaender and infield prospect Graig Nettles for veteran pitchers Luis Tiant and Stan Williams.

César Tovar had played sixty-one games in the infield in 1969, but with Uhlaender traded, he now was the full-time center fielder. The Venezuelan native responded with a career year in 1970, batting .300 and scoring 120 runs as the league's top leadoff man. In the American League, only Carl Yastrzemski crossed the plate more often. Tovar also showed considerable pop. He, Tony Oliva, and Kansas City's Amos Otis led the league with 36 doubles, though no one in the circuit matched Tovar's 13 triples. He also popped 10 home runs and again was a key catalyst for the offense.

Seemingly the only weakness in Tovar's game was his inability to remember the signs used by Rigney and the coaching staff. After Tovar had missed a few signs that spring, first base coach Vern Morgan pitched a solution to Rigney, noted Curt Smith in his book *Storied Stadiums*. "If you want Tovar to steal and I'm giving him the sign, why don't I call his last name three or four times and that'll signal him to go to second on the next pitch." Rigney was willing to give it a try. So, when Tovar reached base and Rigney flashed the sign, Morgan barked, "Tovar, look alive . . . c'mon Tovar, find your position . . . atta boy, Tovar, let's go!" Tovar asked the first base umpire for time and walked over to Morgan. "Vern, I've been with this club for five years," he said. "How come you don't call me by my first name?"

The newly acquired Williams and Ron Perranoski afforded the Twins a dominant lefty-righty combination in the bullpen. Like Perranoski, Williams had played against the Twins in the 1965 World Series as a Dodger, and both were critical to Minnesota's success in 1970. Rigney had a reputation for changing pitchers, and his quick hook meant the innings quickly accumulated for both hurlers. Working 113⅓ innings in 1970, Williams went 10-1 with a 1.99 ERA that ranked among the lowest posted by Major League relievers.

Tiant, a gregarious prankster who called the team's top slugger "Baby Killy," quickly settled into the Twins clubhouse. The
hard-throwing Cuban native had won twenty-one games in 1968
and led the American League with a 1.60 ERA, but was coming
off a disappointing season in which he had lost twenty games.
Amid reports that his fastball had lost some zip, Tiant struggled
for much of spring training. He played down the notion that his
fastball wasn't the same, though Rigney was convinced the right-
hander had lost confidence in the pitch after seeing him rely
on his off-speed stuff in camp. Tiant walked more than a batter an inning during spring training, and his control remained
problematic early in the season. It may have been affected by a
shoulder issue that eventually sabotaged his season in late May.

The 1969 Twins had lost their first four games under Martin,
but under Rigney, the 1970 club kicked off the season with four
straight wins. In the season opener, the Twins set the tone with
a 12–0 romp over the White Sox in Chicago. Jim Perry, a first-
time twenty-game winner in 1969, blanked Chicago on six hits to
jump-start a 24-12 campaign that culminated in Cy Young honors.

Leading the Opening Day onslaught was another off-season
pickup, left fielder Brant Alyea, acquired three weeks earlier
from Washington for two unproven pitchers, Joe Grzenda and
Minneapolis native Charley Walters. The Twins, shopping for
right-handed power after struggling against lefties in 1969, took
a chance on the twenty-nine-year-old Alyea, a one-time power
prospect who hadn't lived up to expectations. Senators manager Ted Williams had been hard on him and their relation-
ship wasn't the most cordial, but Alyea made quite an Opening
Day impression on his new teammates, going 4-for-4 with two
three-run homers and seven RBIS.

The Twins jumped on five White Sox hurlers for 15 hits. Tovar
kicked things off with a triple and scored one of three Twins runs
in the opening frame. Rod Carew and Oliva both had two hits
and combined to score five times. The front end of the Twins
lineup—Tovar, Carew, Oliva, and Harmon Killebrew—was on
its game right from the start and a difference-maker all season.
If they weren't setting the table for teammates further down the

order, they were delivering the clutch hit or game-winning RBI in the late innings.

While the Twins won eight of their first ten games to stake an early claim to first place in the American League West, the larger world provided more compelling storylines than did the early days of the baseball season. Three days after the Twins' opener, on April 10, 1970, Paul McCartney said in a press release that the Beatles weren't currently working and he didn't foresee a time he and John Lennon would collaborate again. He resisted saying it was a permanent split, but it was widely (and accurately) interpreted that the Beatles were no more.

It had been eight months since the group's last recording sessions—for *Abbey Road*, which featured two George Harrison classics, "Here Comes the Sun" and "Something." Frank Sinatra called "Something" the "greatest love song ever written" and Lennon considered it the best song on *Abbey Road*. An enduring highlight of the album were the song fragments woven together on the album's second side, beloved by many of the group's fans.

At the time of McCartney's announcement, the number one song on the *Billboard Hot 100* was "Let It Be," the Beatles' last chart-topping hit and the title track of their back-to-basics final album. *Let It Be* was released a month later in conjunction with a film of the recording sessions, which documented the fissures in the band members' relationships in the studio.

The breakup didn't happen overnight. When the Beatles gathered to record the white album, *The Beatles*, during the summer of 1968, Geoff Emerick, the group's longtime engineer, said the mood in the studio had turned morose. The Beatles had just returned from India, a spiritual journey that may have been a rewarding experience only for George Harrison. During several weeks of studio time defined by occasional outbursts, a two-week walkout by Ringo Starr, and the sudden constant presence of Yoko Ono, Emerick said it was apparent that the relationships the foursome shared had deteriorated markedly.

By then, according to Emerick, McCartney and Lennon were nearly incapable of working together. Harrison, who had come into his own as a songwriter, had become frustrated with not having more of his work appear on Beatles albums. And soon after the 1967 death of Brian Epstein, who had orchestrated the group's rise to stardom, McCartney assumed a managerial role. He pushed the others along at a time they were losing interest and it tested their patience. McCartney, who sometimes pushed too hard, might instruct Starr or Harrison on how he wanted a part played. When this happened with cameras rolling during the *Let It Be* sessions in early 1969, a frustrated Harrison snapped at McCartney: "I'll play whatever you want me to play. Or I won't play at all if you don't want me to play. But whatever it is that will please you, I'll do it."

The *Let It Be* recording sessions took their toll, and the recordings went unattended by the group for nearly a year before three of the four Beatles (without Lennon) returned to cut Harrison's "I Me Mine" in the early days of 1970. By then Lennon and the Plastic Ono Band had a hit with "Give Peace a Chance," in 1969, and "Instant Karma" would soon be climbing the charts. Harrison, with an abundance of unrecorded songs he had written, was busy preparing his triple album, *All Things Must Pass*, for release in November 1970. And McCartney's announcement that the Beatles were no longer working came as he was promoting his first solo album, *McCartney*, due out a week later.

Band members were going their separate ways, but there were memorable moments in the final months of the Beatles. One, during the *Let It Be* recording sessions, was when they took to the rooftop of Abbey Road Studios with keyboardist Billy Preston for their last live performance, in January 1969. Among the highlights of the forty-two-minute set were new songs "I've Got a Feeling," "Don't Let Me Down," and "Get Back," after which Lennon joked, "I'd like to say thank you on behalf of the group and ourselves, and I hope we've passed the audition."

The recording of *Abbey Road* in 1969 suggests the four put aside their differences, as they assembled what was arguably their warmest album, with a second side that was a remarkable collaboration of song pieces they had written. In the midst of recording *Abbey Road*, Lennon and McCartney cut "The Ballad of John and Yoko" without Harrison and Starr, with John on guitar and Paul on drums. At one point during the hastily arranged recording session, Lennon quipped, "A bit faster, Ringo." McCartney replied, "OK, George!"

The day after McCartney broke the hearts of Beatles fans, *Apollo 13* launched from Cape Kennedy, sending James Lovell, Fred Haise, and John Swigert on the third manned mission to the moon. Lovell, on his fourth and final space flight, and Haise were scheduled to board Aquarius, the lunar module, for a thirty-four-hour stay on the moon's surface. Swigert was named to the crew barely a day before launch, replacing Thomas Mattingly. The crew had been exposed to rubella, or German measles, and when it was discovered that Mattingly had never contracted rubella and wasn't immune, Swigert underwent two days of intensive training and proved he could pilot the command ship, *Odyssey.*

The moon landing had to be scrapped nearly fifty-six hours into the flight, however, when one of the two oxygen tanks aboard the command ship exploded and disabled the other tank as well. Two of three of its fuel cells were damaged, knocking out the *Odyssey's* primary source of electricity, power, and water. Thirteen minutes after the explosion, Lovell looked out a window and noticed something venting from the spacecraft. It was oxygen, as the exploded tank had been emptied and the other was depleting rapidly.

The loss of power forced the crew to all but shut down the *Odyssey* and crowd into the two-man lunar module, using its oxygen supply and its descent engine to occasionally provide an energy thrust on the long trip home. Because the explosion happened on the way to the moon, Mission Control had to devise a way—with a limited fuel supply—to slingshot around the moon with enough force to put the spacecraft in a position to reach Earth. With NASA staff computing the math, the crew, two hours after rounding the far side of the moon, executed a precise, well-timed, five-minute burn that put them on course.

The burn was executed under dire conditions. Without electricity, the temperature in the crew's cramped living space dropped close to freezing, making it nearly impossible to sleep. Water was in short supply and the astronauts became dehydrated, losing thirty-two pounds between them. Even as the astronauts limited their water intake to six ounces each a day, heavy condensation formed on the walls of the frigid spacecraft.

In time, carbon dioxide rose to dangerous levels in the lunar module, further imperiling the astronauts. Plenty of lithium hydroxide canisters were aboard to remove carbon dioxide from the air, but the square canisters from the command ship were incompatible with the round openings in the lunar module's environmental system. Mission Control in Houston, working with only the supplies aboard the spacecraft—plastic bags, cardboard, and tape—devised a way to attach the command ship's canisters to the lunar module's system.

As the *Odyssey* approached Earth, the astronauts faced one last potential threat. Had the explosion damaged the heat shield that protected them on reentry to the Earth's atmosphere? The command module, ice cold inside and filled with condensation, survived reentry and dropped safely into the South Pacific Ocean, but not before the crew experienced one final effect of their nearly disastrous mission. "The droplets furnished one sensation as we decelerated in the atmosphere," Lovell recalled years later. "It rained inside the CM."

A national tragedy had been avoided, but barely more than two weeks later, four American students, protesting the Vietnam War, weren't as fortunate. On April 30, President Richard Nixon announced that several thousand American soldiers had crossed the Vietnamese-Cambodian border for the first time to attack enemy positions. At the same time, the president escalated bombing raids over Cambodia and North Vietnam.

The decision to expand the American ground war into Cambodia spurred nationwide protests on college campuses. Just as the war had escalated, the protests escalated, turning violent at several schools. Police, some using tear gas and cattle prods, clashed with students, many of whom retaliated. At the University of Maryland at College Park, state police went head-to-head with one thousand students. At least twenty-five demonstrators and three policemen were injured in skirmishes. Students vandalized the ROTC building, overturning desks, heaving them and books out of windows, and causing $10,000 in damage. Twenty persons were arrested at Southern Illinois University in Carbondale, where three policemen were injured and two Molotov cocktails were thrown from dormitory windows.

On Saturday, May 2, police clashed with two thousand Kent State University students for more than three hours in northern Ohio. The wooden ROTC building on campus was set on fire and burned to the ground. Local authorities, looking to quell demonstrations, ordered an overnight curfew. Yet more than one thousand students were on the streets again Sunday, the third straight night of protests. They shared the streets with nearly one thousand Ohio National Guard troops, called in by Ohio governor James Rhodes to keep order.

Students were seen talking amicably with guardsmen on Sunday, but the mood on campus changed after the governor arrived in Kent and used a press conference to call protestors "the worst type of people that we harbor in America" and insisted that law enforcement would shut down demonstrations. Later, when students staged a mass sit-in at a downtown intersection in Kent, guard troops, with bayonets mounted on rifles, forced students back onto campus. At times, the two sides exchanged rocks and tear gas.

Each day, campus demonstrations across the country intensified, reaching a feverous pitch on Monday, May 4, and inspiring thirty college and university presidents to sign a telegram urging President Nixon to bring a rapid end to American involvement in Southeast Asia. More than five thousand persons attended a rally at the University of Minnesota, filling the mall in front of Coffman Memorial Union. They voted to strike the university immediately to protest the new ground war in Cambodia. Students picketed buildings, encouraging students and staff to boycott classes.

At Kent State, where the guard controlled activity on campus, a scheduled rally for Monday afternoon had been prohibited. But by noon, three thousand persons had gathered on the commons and refused to disperse when ordered by guard troops. When some in the angry crowd threw rocks at troops, Ohio Guard general Robert Canterbury ordered troops to load and lock their weapons; then guardsmen began to march across the commons as they fired tear gas into the crowd at the Victory Bell, an old brass railroad bell that is a campus landmark. Protesters walked up nearby Blanket Hill and down the other side into a fenced-in parking lot that bordered a football practice field. With guardsmen positioned on the practice field—and nowhere for either side to go—shouting and throwing rocks at troops intensified.

It seemed then that the confrontation might deescalate. Two Kent State professors, Jerry M. Lewis and Thomas R. Hensley, wrote "The May 4 Shootings at Kent State University: The Search for Historical Accuracy," a research study that appears on the Kent State University website:

> The Guard then began retracing their steps from the practice football field back up Blanket Hill. As they arrived at the top of the hill, twenty-eight of the more than 70 Guardsmen turned suddenly and fired their rifles and pistols. Many guardsmen fired into the air or the ground. However, a small portion fired directly into the crowd. Altogether between 61 and 67 shots were fired in a 13-second period.
>
> Four Kent State students died as a result of the firing by the Guard. The closest student was Jeffrey Miller, who was shot in the mouth while standing in an access road leading into the Prentice Hall parking lot, a distance of approximately 270 feet from the Guard.

The other casualties—Allison Krause, William Schroeder, and Sandra Sheuer—were more than 300 feet from the source of gunfire. Nine others were injured. It was Miller over whom fourteen-year-old Mary Ann Vecchio knelt, grief-stricken, with her arms raised. Kent State photojournalism student John Filo captured the Pulitzer Prize-winning photograph that made a lasting impression on the public. Such a powerful image that documented our own military shooting unarmed students turned more everyday Americans against the war.

In the wake of the Kent State shootings, campus unrest escalated further. Nearly five hundred colleges and universities were shut down or disrupted by demonstrations. A great majority of campus activity was peaceful, but clashes with police turned violent at the University of Wisconsin-Madison, Seton Hall in New Jersey, University of Texas-Austin, UCLA, American University in Washington DC, and University of Illinois at Chicago Circle. Protests took place at virtually every college in Minnesota, as thousands of students boycotted classes, engaged in marches, and attended rallies. At Macalester in St. Paul, most of the faculty joined the student strike.

On the Saturday following the four deaths in Ohio, thousands of protestors marched from the Minneapolis campus of the University of Minnesota to the State Capitol in St. Paul, picking up contingents of marchers along the way. By the time they reached the Capitol, roughly twenty thousand had assembled to voice their opposition to the war. Nearly 100,000 marched on Washington, with thousands standing in front of the White House, calling for the end of U.S. involvement in Southeast Asia. The Washington demonstration was the climax of a spontaneous, week-long response to the war's expansion and the killing of four Kent State students.

At Jackson State College in Mississippi a few days later, students at the predominantly African American school clashed with city and state police. Tensions between Blacks and whites ran high in Jackson. After students threw rocks at white motorists along the main street on campus and a truck was set on fire, police were called to campus. When students threw rocks and bricks at the officers, police advanced on the crowd near Alexander Hall, a women's dorm. In a tragedy widely forgotten, police opened fire on the dorm shortly after midnight on May 15, shooting roughly four hundred bullets or pieces of buckshot, according to an FBI investigation. Two young men, Jackson State junior Phillip Gibbs and high school senior James Earl Green, were killed by gunfire. Police officials claimed there was a sniper in the dorm, but investigators never found evidence to back up the charge.

Vice President Spiro Agnew, who served as President Nixon's hatchet man when it came to the administration's opposition, had ridiculed student activism since their days on the campaign trail. Following the Kent State killings, Agnew called the deaths "predictable" given the "traitors and thieves and perverts in our midst." A popular poster at the time—one which this writer had hanging in his bedroom—showed an opened roll of a Lifesaver-like candy and several of the round candies with holes in the middle scattered about. The roll was labeled "Spiro-Mints" and the candies had Agnew's image on them with the hole in his forehead. The poster's tagline: "It leaves you speechless!"

A tinge of unrest and counterculture came to baseball in 1970, though nothing as life altering or tragic as the unrest of the civil rights and anti-war movements. But in a sport run by staid, change-resistant owners, any change was significant, and that went for players, too. Long hair, mustaches, and beards had been in fashion for several years, but most ballplayers still looked like they'd just completed military duty. Sideburns and mustaches started to appear on 1970 baseball cards, though hardly anyone bought a Nehru jacket after Ken Harrelson wore one on the cover of *Sports Illustrated* in September 1968.

In January 1970, Curt Flood put a charge in the baseball establishment, filing suit to challenge Major League Baseball's reserve clause after the St. Louis Cardinals had traded him, as part of a multiplayer deal, to the Philadelphia Phillies. Under the reserve clause, a player was bound to his teams for life, a piece of property who could be traded but could never decide for himself where he would play.

Challenging the reserve clause meant going up against baseball's exemption from antitrust laws, granted in a U.S. Supreme Court ruling in 1921 and protected in subsequent legal challenges. "The courts were saying," noted longtime head of the players' union, Marvin Miller, "'Yes, you're an American and have the right to seek employment anywhere you like, but this right does not apply to baseball players.'" Flood didn't have legal precedent on his side—and might never play in the Majors again if he lost—but the thirty-two-year-old veteran, who had spent twelve years in St. Louis, was committed to the legal fight.

At trial, former owner Bill Veeck and onetime star players Jackie Robinson and Hank Greenberg were among those to testify on Flood's behalf. With active players fearful of being blackballed, however, none of Flood's peers appeared in court—and many of them sided with management anyway. His case reached the U.S. Supreme Court on appeal, but ultimately his legal challenge was unsuccessful. Still, Flood inspired solidarity among players and greater support for overturning the reserve clause.

The baseball establishment was nearly as upset with pitcher Jim Bouton, who chronicled his 1969 season with the expansion Seattle Pilots and Houston Astros in the book *Ball Four*, which hit the stores in June 1970. Bouton provided an insightful, humorous, but unvarnished look at the day-to-day life of Major Leaguers, including his own struggle as an aging pitcher trying to extend his career by learning the knuckleball. In humorously addressing survival in a twenty-five-man clubhouse, Bouton shared stories of widespread amphetamine use, players' salacious sexual humor and hijinks, and the late nights.

Most of the juicy stuff seems tame by today's standards, but Bouton played at a time when what took place away from the park was considered off-limits to sportswriters. Players resented him for violating the sanctity of Major League life, including telling tales of Yankee legends and former teammates Whitey Ford and Mickey Mantle. Bouton addressed Ford's mound techniques for doctoring the baseball late in his career. Mantle came off as a good-natured guy who might have had a longer career had he been more committed to rehabbing injuries and spent less time drinking and carousing with teammates after games.

Two weeks before *Ball Four* was published, commissioner Bowie Kuhn called Bouton into his Manhattan office after reading bawdy excerpts in *Look*. Kuhn, who said he had to remove the magazine issues from his home for fear his sons might read them, was looking for at least an apology. Bouton refused and stood his ground, insisting everything in the book was true and no harm was done by publishing it. After the June 1 meeting,

Kuhn and Marvin Miller, who attended with Bouton, haggled for two hours over the press release that would follow. Kuhn wanted to appear as though he had secured an apology or some sort of concession from Bouton, but had to settle with reporting that he had expressed his displeasure about the book, but no other action would be taken.

Apparently more than amphetamines were in play with players. On June 12, not long after Bouton had his sit-down with Kuhn, Pirates right-hander Dock Ellis tossed a no-hitter against the San Diego Padres. It wasn't a masterpiece; Ellis walked eight Padres and struck another with a pitch. But it's remarkable that he could pitch at all. He arrived in San Diego the day before the assignment. Ellis, who had developed a liking for LSD and Jimi Hendrix, took acid that day and partied. When he woke up the next morning, not fully conscious that an entire day had passed and thinking it was his off day, Ellis ingested LSD again. He still took the mound and had a day to remember, even if he couldn't. "I didn't know if I was facing Hank Aaron, Willie Mays or Mickey Mantle," Ellis said years later. "I was just out there throwing a baseball and having a great time."

For the Minnesota Twins, the 1970 season was a manic ride of highs and lows. Consistency wasn't the club's calling card. After winning eight of ten to start the season, the Twins went 19-7 in May and closed the month at 31-13, good for the highest winning percentage in the Majors. A June swoon followed, when the Twins were barely a .500 team, but they kicked off a 10-1 run on June 29, Harmon Killebrew's birthday. When the hot streak stalled on July 10, the Twins were 53-27 and five games up on the Oakland Athletics in the AL West. A nine-game losing streak in early August closed the gap markedly, setting up key series with Oakland down the stretch. When it was over the Twins had won ninety-eight games, one more than under Martin the year before, and finished nine games ahead of the A's.

An early taste of how Bill Rigney's first season as Twins skipper would play out may have been his team's walk-off win over the Detroit Tigers on April 25. The game took a strange twist in the seventh inning. Jim Kaat struck out Detroit starter Earl

Wilson to end the inning, inspiring catcher Paul Ratliff to roll the ball back to the mound as he headed for the Twins dugout. But Tigers third base coach Grover Resinger saw that Ratliff had trapped the ball in the dirt and had failed to tag Wilson, so he instructed Wilson to run to first base as Twins players left the field.

The pitcher took off running, easily reaching second and heading for third when Twins left fielder Brant Alyea approached the infield and realized what was going on. He dashed to the mound to retrieve the ball, but fumbled it as Wilson headed for home. Both Ratliff and Twins shortstop Leo Cárdenas had returned to the field and Alyea threw to Cárdenas at the plate. Wilson turned back toward third and Cárdenas threw back to Alyea, who tagged out the pitcher to complete the far-from-routine 7-6-7 putout. Wilson also pulled a hamstring muscle on the play and had to leave the game. After Minnesota's 4–3 win, decided by Killebrew's RBI single in the ninth, Tigers catcher Bill Freehan chastised Alyea for his role in the quirky seventh-inning strikeout: "If Alyea had been hustling, Wilson might have made it home. Tell him to start coming in and off the field a little quicker."

TWENTY

Dutch Treat Pays Dividends

After posting a 12-6 mark in April, the Twins headed to Baltimore to face the defending American League champions, who had executed a sweep of the first American League Championship Series six months earlier. Before the series opener on May 1, reserve outfielder Charlie Manuel and several teammates visited the Pimlico Race Course to play the horses. When Manuel discovered he had made a mistake in placing his bet, selecting a combination of horses that he didn't intend to wager on, he tore up his ticket. Soon after, to his surprise, he discovered that his ticket was a winner, good for $1,165—a significant sum at the time—and Manuel went to work taping his ticket together to claim his prize.

Manuel's good fortune didn't carry over to the game that night. With the Twins losing 5–2 in the sixth, the bases loaded, and two out, he pinch-hit for catcher George Mitterwald with a chance to put the Twins back into the game. Facing Orioles reliever Dick Hall, Manuel took a called third strike down the middle of the plate. In the clubhouse after the 9–3 loss, he referenced his track winnings when talking to *Minneapolis Star* writer Mike Lamey: "I would have given it all back, really, if I could have gotten a hit." But Lady Luck was still Manuel's friend off the field. For the Kentucky Derby the next day, Twins players put the names of the seventeen entries in a hat in a friendly wager. It was Manuel who drew the longshot Derby winner, Dust Commander. Sometimes it's better to be lucky than good.

The Twins, on the other hand, were good. Runs came in bunches in April and May as they surged to a 31-13 start and a 2½-game AL West lead over the California Angels. Leading the way was the foursome at the top of the batting order: César Tovar, Rod Carew, Tony Oliva, and Harmon Killebrew. Tovar hit safely in ten straight games in April and twelve straight in May. As Minnesota's leadoff hitter, he scored 45 runs in those first forty-four games and added some pop, stroking 10 doubles, five triples, and six home runs, good for a .503 slugging percentage through the first two months.

Carew, the defending American League batting champ, started fast, hitting safely in nine of ten games to open the season. He was batting a league-leading .432 in mid-May, following a 22-for-37 surge in which he became the first player in Twins history to hit for the cycle. On May 20 in Kansas City, Carew collected a first-inning single, a leadoff home run in the third, and a lead-off double in the fifth—all off Royals rookie Bob Johnson. After grounding out to end the sixth, Carew completed the cycle by drilling a run-scoring triple in the eighth off reliever Al Fitzmorris in a 10–5 victory.

The win was Minnesota's seventh straight, and in a happy clubhouse after the game, Carew was excited about his record-setting day. When *Minneapolis Tribune* writer Tom Briere asked him what it meant to him, Carew shot back, "Maybe I'll get a bonus. Do you think?" Not likely, but he may have deserved one. In late April, Carew pulled a rib-cage muscle and couldn't swing a bat. He missed eleven games, and when he returned, he still couldn't swing hard or turn on a pitch. So, he sprayed the ball more than ever, with great success. Carew continued to be bonus worthy, closing out May at a league-high .394.

Oliva hit safely in forty of forty-four games through May. Heading into June, he was batting .330, slugging .527, and had already recorded 40 RBIS. On May 5, a cool night in Detroit with temperatures in the forties, Oliva almost single-handedly secured an 8–5 victory, pounding a single, triple, and home run, and collecting six RBIS. Facing tough lefty Mickey Lolich in the opening frame, Oliva heated things up with a two-run homer into Tiger Stadium's upper deck. Oliva ended Lolich's day in the fifth by lining a bases-loaded triple over the head of center fielder Jim Northrup. Oliva piled up hits at a remarkable rate well into June, enjoying one of his patented long stretches of being nearly every pitcher's nightmare.

Killebrew, going the opposite way more frequently, posted impressive leadoff-type numbers in April—a .317 average and .434 on-base percentage—before his power spiked in May. During a nine-game hitting streak in early May, with the Twins playing in Baltimore, Detroit, and Cleveland, Killebrew homered in five straight games. The first of five was a two-run, ninth-inning shot off Baltimore's Jim Palmer on May 3. After Palmer had fanned him twice on breaking pitches earlier in the game, Killebrew abandoned his pull approach, jumped on a fastball on the outside corner, and lofted a fly that landed on the roof of the Twins bullpen in right field, giving the Twins a 4–3 victory over the AL champion Orioles.

The reigning league MVP popped 10 homers in May and closed the month with a bang in a 7–6 walk-off win over the New York Yankees. New York and Minnesota had split a pair of games at Metropolitan Stadium and were deadlocked at six after nine innings of the rubber game. When Killebrew came to the plate leading off the tenth inning, he had already powered one long ball off Yankees ace Mel Stottlemyre. This time Killebrew, facing relief specialist Lindy McDaniel, demonstrated why so many Twins fans, regardless of the score, were reluctant to leave the park if he might get a final at-bat in the late innings. Killebrew teed off on a 2-0 pitch and drilled a 421-foot blast into the left-field bleachers to secure the win. He began June batting a lofty .329.

After the first four hitters, the batting order was less potent. Although defensive whiz Leo Cárdenas had another solid season, first baseman Rich Reese, coming off a career year in 1969, wasn't as productive. At other positions, the Twins turned to untested players with mixed results. George Mitterwald and rookie Paul Ratliff took over catching duties when the Twins released aging veteran John Roseboro following the 1969 season. Brant Alyea, acquired from Washington in the spring, popped 16 home runs in just 290 plate appearances while sharing left field with left-handed-hitting rookie Jim Holt. Alyea was the most productive of the new arrivals.

While the Twins could push across runs, manager Bill Rigney had legitimate concerns about his pitching staff. Jim Perry was off to a solid start, but Jim Kaat had struggled in May after pitching effectively in the early going. Who should follow them was Rigney's biggest quandary. Luis Tiant was 5-0 heading into his final May outing, but his control remained problematic and he rarely worked deep into games. He had tossed a three-hit shutout over the Tigers in April at Met Stadium, but walked nine in 5⅔ innings at Tiger Stadium on May 5. He still earned the "W" with Oliva delivering six RBIS in that 8–5 win. Facing the Milwaukee Brewers on May 28, the twenty-nine-year-old right-hander heard a crack while delivering a pitch. He had suffered a hairline fracture in his right shoulder blade, a rare injury more likely to be suffered by a javelin thrower than a pitcher. El Tiante was told he might never throw again. He managed to return to the Twins in August, but the results suggested that he wasn't ready to pitch.

Dave Boswell, a twenty-game winner in 1969, had gone 2-5 with a 7.23 ERA in eight starts. After injuring his arm in his ALCS Game 2 start in Baltimore the previous fall, his fastball hadn't been nearly as good and his season was heading in the wrong direction. Rigney soon lost confidence in the right-hander, demoted him to the bullpen and rarely used him. Trade talks swirled for days involving Boston, with the Red Sox interested in Boswell. One rumored deal would have sent youngsters Reggie Smith and Sparky Lyle to Minnesota in return. The two teams never worked out a trade, and soon after talks died down, Boswell suffered a back injury. His season—and his career with the Twins—ended in late July. The elbow injury he suffered in the ALCS essentially ended his career. After pitching twenty-nine innings for the Tigers and his hometown Orioles in 1971, the twenty-six-year-old Boswell, a true character of the game, was through.

With Boswell and Tiant frequently making quick exits early in the 1970 season, relievers Ron Perranoski and Stan Williams shouldered a heavy workload. Over the first two months, they had been terrific in seventy-two combined innings, but Rigney was concerned about burning out his best relievers. The only other effective reliever was lefty Tom Hall, a candidate for the struggling rotation.

When Tiant was sidelined in late May, Rigney didn't turn to Boswell. Instead, the Twins recalled a nineteen-year-old right-hander who had yet to pitch a full year in the Minor Leagues, but had posted a 2.50 ERA and fanned 63 Triple-A hitters in fifty-four innings for Minnesota's Evansville affiliate. Bert Blyleven (born in the Netherlands as Rik Aalbert Blijleven) got the call and made his big league debut against the Washington Senators on June 5.

The 31-15 Twins, looking to bounce back from a pair of 5–1 losses at Fenway Park when they took the field at RFK Stadium, got on the scoreboard before the new kid took the mound on a pleasant Friday evening. Tovar opened the game by drawing a walk from Washington starter Casey Cox, then stole second and scored on Oliva's one-out single to left. Despite the early lead, Blyleven's Hall of Fame career got off to a rough start. He went 3-2 on Washington's leadoff man, Lee Maye, who turned on a pitch and drilled it into the right-field seats. The run was all Blyleven allowed over seven innings, as he scattered five hits, walked one, and fanned seven in a 2–1 victory. He opened up about the home run after the game.

"I wanted to crawl into a hole out there," the teenager, already quotable and entertaining, told *Minneapolis Tribune* writer Jon Roe. "I thought, 'Oh, no. Here we go.'" The rookie added that at that point, he was thinking about Frank Howard, the six-foot-seven slugger who was due up third in the inning and led the league in home runs. Blyleven, worried more about Howard touching him for a long one, retired him three times. The last time he faced the big man, he struck him out with a sharp-breaking curve. For good measure, after Frank Quilici led off the fifth with a single, Blyleven bunted him over, setting up Tovar to single home the game-winning run.

Blyleven, who said he was so nervous before the game that his legs were shaking, recalls looking toward the Twins dugout after giving up the blast to Maye. He caught sight of Rigney smiling, which he said helped settle him down. "I was going to go out to the mound after that homer," Rigney said later. "But I figured, why the hell should I? Am I going to go out to the mound every time this kid faces a batter? He's too good for that." And he was. After the game Rigney said it was the best debut by a starter he had seen in his fifteen years as a big league manager.

The rookie succeeded immediately with a stunning combination of poise and stuff, and his emergence solidified Minnesota's contender status. Over his first two months in the Majors, he allowed two runs or fewer in 10 of 13 starts and posted an impressive 2.78 ERA. Blyleven hit some rough spots in August, as might be expected for a rookie pitcher, but finished the season with 10 wins. Among Minnesota's top five starters, his 3.18 ERA at year's end was second only to Perry's 3.04.

With Blyleven in the mix, the pitching was better in June than May, but the lineup had provided so much run support in May that the Twins kept winning. The foursome at the top of the batting order couldn't sustain May's torrid pace—no lineup could be that explosive all season—and in June the Twins stumbled along at a .500 pace. Injuries had become a factor as well. Tiant was on the disabled list for the hairline fracture in his shoulder blade and wouldn't be returning anytime soon. Boswell was nearly finished and couldn't contribute. Perranoski, the Major League leader in saves, had a back ailment, but kept answering the call. With the holes in the rotation, he and Williams were taking on too many innings. Plus, Killebrew was playing with water buildup in one knee; he took cortisone shots to stay on the field and had yet to miss a game.

As June wound down, Oliva pulled a muscle in his thigh and developed a sore shoulder, the same one he had injured making a throw to the plate against Baltimore in Game 2 of the 1969 ALCS. He had been batting at a .395 clip over a ten-game stretch in mid-June, but his shoulder began to affect his swing. The injury was apparent when Oliva went hitless in three straight games for the first time all season, and he was finally forced to miss a few games. Cortisone shots were needed to get him back on the field.

In Milwaukee on June 22, playing the transplanted Pilots now known as the Brewers, the Twins' outlook and pennant hopes took a downturn. In the fourth inning of the series opener, Brewers first baseman Mike Hegan drew a leadoff walk. When right fielder Mike Hershberger chopped a Jim Kaat offering to Killebrew at third, the Twins were poised to turn an around-the-horn double play. After Carew took Killebrew's throw, pivoted and threw to first baseman Rich Reese, Hegan rolled into him and knocked him down. Carew's right knee took the brunt of the impact, causing the second baseman to suffer a torn ligament and cartilage damage, which required surgery a few days later. At the time, Carew led the American League batting race by a large margin at .376.

If the reigning American League batting champ was to return at all, it likely wouldn't be until September. The Twins could put a competent defensive player on the field. Initially Rigney went with veteran Frank Quilici, though in time, he gave rookie Danny Thompson most of the starts. Of course, no one on the roster or in the league could replace Carew's bat. That didn't trouble Oliva.

"Remember 1965," he told Tom Briere of the *Minneapolis Tribune*, when talk turned to how could the Twins survive without such a valuable piece of the offense. The '65 club lost Killebrew and Camilo Pascual to serious injuries in the middle of the championship season—and several other key players missed significant time—yet the Twins pulled away from the pack with two of the team's biggest stars sidelined.

In their first week without Carew, the Twins split four games in Milwaukee and did the same in Chicago to close a rough road trip on June 28 at 43-25. The Angels also had struggled for much of June, allowing the Twins to stay atop the division, but now the Angels were winning. So were the Oakland Athletics, who used a late-June 10-3 surge to make the AL West race a three-team affair. The Twins were just three games up on the Angels and five in front of the rejuvenated A's.

The Twins had had a tough time in June, but when they returned to the Met to begin a home stand on June 29—Harmon Killebrew's thirty-fourth birthday—American League president Joe Cronin was there to celebrate the club's 1969 award winners. In a pregame ceremony staged behind home plate, Cronin presented Killebrew the 1969 AL Most Valuable Player Award. The humble slugger doffed his cap when Twins fans gave him a warm ovation. Earlier in the day, Cronin had visited Fairview Hospital, where Carew was bedridden following knee surgery, to present the 1969 AL batting champ with a silver bat.

After the pregame ceremony, the Twins claimed the first of five straight victories in a successful home stand facing Kansas City and Chicago. In a 5–4 win over the Royals, César Tovar, in the midst of a fifteen-game hit streak, collected four hits and drove a Dick Drago pitch down the right-field line for a triple that scored the winning run in the sixth. Jim Perry recorded all but the final out on an extremely hot night with a game-time temperature of ninety-seven degrees. Perry gained a "W" but lost eight pounds.

He won the first and fifth games of the win streak to improve to 12-6. In between, youngsters Bert Blyleven and twenty-two-year-old Tom Hall turned in terrific outings. After Chicago ended the streak on July 4, the Twins won their next five—a surge that carried into an important West Coast trip to Oakland and Anaheim. When the Twins headed to Oakland for three games, the A's were 6½ games back.

Blyleven was scheduled to pitch the series opener on July 6. He had pitched with a tender elbow his last two times out, so manager Bill Rigney chose to rest the nineteen-year-old and went with rookie Bill Zepp. Making just his fourth Major League start, the twenty-three-year-old Zepp worked into the seventh inning, allowed a single run, and outdueled forkball specialist Diego Seguí. Tovar collected three hits, tallied the first Twins run, and singled home the clincher in a 2–1 victory.

In the second game, the A's jumped out to a 2–0 lead when Sal Bando stroked a fourth-inning, two-run homer off Hall, who was making just his third big league start. The Twins, however, erupted for four runs in their half of the inning to claim a 4–2 win. With the bases loaded, Killebrew delivered the decisive hit, drilling a four-hundred-foot, bases-clearing double off the center-field fence. Hall worked into the fifth before reliever Stan Williams took over, pitching five scoreless innings of two-hit ball for his sixth victory without a loss.

In the series finale on July 8, Perry and Catfish Hunter didn't pitch like staff aces. The Twins roughed up Hunter for six runs and took an 8–2 lead in the seventh—aided by a Rich Reese home run and a 4-for-4, four-RBI night from Oliva—but the A's tallied four ninth-inning runs off Perry before Ron Perranoski snuffed out the rally to secure the 8–6 win. Perry earned the win, Hunter took the loss, and both aces were 13-6 and shared the league lead in wins.

Next for Minnesota were the second-place Angels, who trailed by five games. The top two teams in the West were squaring off four times leading up to the All-Star break with the Twins riding a four-game winning streak. Blyleven, who grew up in Southern California, surprisingly returned to action, making his first-ever West Coast start on July 9 in front of a large contingent of family at Anaheim Stadium. The local kid pitched well, but left after six innings with Angels lefty Rudy May carrying a 2–1 lead into the seventh. The Twins scratched for the tying run that inning and the game was still tied when they came to bat in the ninth against Angels knuckleballer Eddie Fisher.

Extra innings may have seemed Minnesota's best chance to pull out a win when Fisher made quick work of the first two Twins hitters. Then a pair of slight, underweight Twins swung big bats. Hall, the rail-thin lefty reliever, slapped a pitch into left field for a single. The next batter, shortstop Leo Cárdenas, rarely known for home run dramatics, drilled a shot into the left-field bleachers to deliver a 4–2 victory. Hall pitched three perfect innings in relief of Blyleven and the Twins moved six games up on the Angels.

The following evening, Angels right-hander Andy Messersmith stalled Minnesota's winning ways and Tovar's fifteen-game hit streak. Tovar had batted .470 during his run and the Twins had won thirteen of fifteen games before Messersmith held them to six hits in a 2–1 loss. The Twins still had a five-game edge and nothing changed when the clubs split the final two matchups before the All-Star break. On Saturday, the Twins won behind another good outing from Zepp, who improved to 5-0 with six solid innings, followed by three scoreless frames from Hall and Perranoski in a 5–2 victory. In the Sunday finale on July 12, Perry lost for only the second time in nearly six weeks, not making it out of the fourth inning in a 6–2 defeat.

Tovar had scored a league-leading 71 first-half runs for the suddenly red-hot Twins, who boasted an AL-best 54-28 mark at the break. Oliva was now batting .327 and trailed Baltimore's Frank Robinson by only three points in the AL batting race. Killebrew, hitting .412 with eight homers in a fifteen-game surge, ranked among AL batting leaders at .322 and led the league with 26 homers and 72 RBIS in eighty-two games. Perhaps the best part of the prebreak push was that the starting rotation was coming around, aided by the trio of youngsters—Blyleven, Hall, and Zepp.

On July 14, 1970, Riverfront Stadium in downtown Cincinnati hosted the All-Star Game, just two weeks after the Reds opened their new home. Killebrew started at third base for the American League, and Jim Perry pitched two innings. Rod Carew had been selected, but he was in Minnesota rehabbing his surgically repaired knee. Remarkably, Tovar was bypassed despite a tremendous first half. Oliva, who had missed the annual affair in 1969 because of chicken pox, was chosen as a reserve and was on the field for the dramatic conclusion, which produced one of the Midsummer Classic's lasting memories.

The National League, in pursuit of its eighth straight victory, trailed 4–1 after Orioles third baseman Brooks Robinson drove a two-run triple to deep center off Cardinals ace Bob Gibson in the eighth inning. But Giants catcher Dick Dietz greeted Catfish Hunter with a home run leading off the bottom of the ninth. After singles by Bud Harrelson, Joe Morgan and Willie McCovey, the game was suddenly a one-run affair with runners on the corners and one out. Longtime Yankees ace Mel Stottlemyre got the call to face Pirates star Roberto Clemente, pinch-hitting for Gibson. Clemente lined a shot to right-center that Amos Otis tracked down, but the Royals outfielder could not throw out Morgan crossing the plate with the tying run.

In extra innings, the AL threatened three times before the game was decided in the twelfth. In the bottom half of the inning, after Angels right-hander Clyde Wright retired both Joe Torre and Clemente on ground balls, hometown hero Pete Rose slapped a single up the middle to keep the inning alive. Dodgers infielder Billy Grabarkewitz and Cubs outfielder Jim Hickman delivered consecutive singles, and Rose dashed around third as Otis fielded Hickman's hit to center.

Otis's throw and Rose reached Cleveland catcher Ray Fosse at the same time, a few feet up the third base line. The man called "Charlie Hustle" cemented his reputation as a hard-nosed player by bowling over Fosse. The ball popped loose and Rose scored to give the National League its eighth consecutive win. The collision also permanently altered the twenty-three-year-old Fosse's career. A serious shoulder injury suffered on the play sapped his power and contributed to an early retirement. The shoulder still bothers him today.

TWENTY-ONE

Baseballs and Bombs

The lilting Latin percussion of Santana's "Oye Como Va" enlivened the airwaves in the summer of 1970, a sign of how diverse the popular music scene had become in the six years since the British Invasion. Fronted by guitarist Carlos Santana, his group had made a big splash at Woodstock before releasing *Abraxas*, which featured the Tito Puente-penned song. In the summer's dog days, the funky, skiffle-tinged rhythms of Mungo Jerry's "In the Summertime" was a staple on Twin Cities radio. At the same time, rock continued to flourish and branch out. The Allman Brothers gave rock a Southern flavor with "Whipping Post" and "Midnight Rider." Creedence Clearwater Revival, the Grateful Dead, and Black Sabbath each released two albums in 1970, with Sabbath and Led Zeppelin at the forefront of the growing heavy metal genre.

Minneapolis-based Crow scored a national hit at the start of the New Year with "Evil Woman (Don't Play Your Games with Me)." Crow had landed a recording contact with Amaret, a subsidiary of Mercury Records, after winning a battle-of-the-bands event at the Bel Air Ballroom in Des Moines. Amaret soon released a single, "Time to Make a Turn," which had minimal impact. "A station in Seattle flipped it over and started playing 'Evil Woman,'" Crow bassist Larry Wiegand told Rick Shefchik, author of *Everybody's Heard about the Bird*, "and it just took off.

Everybody started playing it. That's the one we tried to push in the first place."

With the song's success, Crow spent most of the next three years on the road, performing at outdoor festivals and backing up dozens of musicians, including Janis Joplin; Jefferson Airplane; Vanilla Fudge; Eric Burdon; Three Dog Night; Chicago; Blood, Sweat, and Tears; the Allman Brothers; Iron Butterfly; Grand Funk Railroad; Steppenwolf; and the Steve Miller Band. "We were road dogs," Wiegand confessed to Shefchik.

Among rock bands, the psychedelic scene was in decline. British groups Pink Floyd and King Crimson were still building audiences, but the Beatles and Cream had broken up, and the music of groups such as Credence Clearwater Revival, Steppenwolf, and the Doors was more rooted in rock and blues by 1970. San Francisco had been the center of the rock universe, home to psychedelic pioneers Jefferson Airplane, but the group had been devastated by the death of teenager Meredith Hunter at a late-1969 outdoor festival dubbed "Woodstock West." The event at Altamont Speedway, thirty miles east of San Francisco, was dogged by logistical issues even worse than at Woodstock. In addition to inadequate access to food, restrooms, and health care, the performance stage stood just three feet off the ground and security was handled by a Bay Area branch of the Hells Angels motorcycle gang, which drank all day and began brawling with concertgoers. Violence broke out near the stage during Jefferson Airplane's performance, and Hunter was stabbed to death after the Rolling Stones began their set. Altamont took its toll on Jefferson Airplane, personnel changes soon came, and the band moved on from its psychedelic days.

Yet, psychedelia flourished among African American musicians, with Jimi Hendrix at the forefront. The Temptations had hits with "Psychedelic Shack" and "Ball of Confusion (That's What the World Is Today)." Sly and the Family Stone, the Chambers Brothers, and the 5th Dimension melded psychedelic elements into their music, and former Motown songwriter George Clinton soon took funk to new cosmic heights as the mastermind of two bands with debut albums, Parliament and Funkadelic.

Popular music was taking many new paths. Sly and the Family Stone, with a string of funky 1969 hits that included "Stand," "Hot Fun in the Summertime," and "Sing a Simple Song," were popular among Blacks and whites, rock and R&B fans. The Family Stone hit big again with "Thank You (Falettinme Be Mice Elf Agin)" and "Everybody Is a Star" in early 1970. Van Morrison, the prolific singer-songwriter from Northern Ireland, released two albums that year, *Moondance* and *His Band and the Street Choir*, earning radio play for "Moondance," "Crazy Love," "Blue Money," and "Domino." Genre-defying David Bowie, who had a 1969 hit with "Space Oddity," released his third studio album in 1970, *The Man Who Sold the World*.

Folk-influenced rock thrived at the end of the decade. Crosby, Stills, Nash, and Young had hits with "Teach Your Children," "Helpless," and "Woodstock," the festival anthem penned by Joni Mitchell, then Graham Nash's paramour. In the fall, Neil Young put out *After the Gold Rush*, which included his first Top 40 hit, "Only Love Can Break Your Heart," widely believed to be written for Nash following his breakup with Mitchell. Cat Stevens broke through in 1970 with his fourth album, *Tea for the Tillerman*, which garnered radio play for "Wild World" and "Father and Son." That year Simon and Garfunkel released their fifth and final studio recording, *Bridge over Troubled Water*. The Grammy Award-winning album featured two of Paul Simon's most beloved songs, its title track and "The Boxer."

Motown's newest discovery, the Jackson 5, dominated the Top 40 scene in 1970, topping the *Billboard Hot 100* four times with "I Want You Back," "ABC," "The Love You Save," and "I'll Be There." In early September, Edwin Starr's "War" had a three-week run as WDGY's number one hit. Written by Norman Whitfield and Barrett Strong for Motown, the song targeted the Vietnam conflict and became one of the most popular anti-war songs ever recorded. The Temptations recorded it first, but Motown executives feared it might alienate the group's more conservative fans, so Starr's funky version was released as a single. It held down the top spot on the *Billboard Hot 100* at a time when the anti-war movement was hard to ignore.

The militancy of anti-war groups stepped up markedly following May's Kent State shootings. Anger at the Nixon administration and the ineffectiveness of peaceful anti-war protests had fueled dozens of bombings in 1969, a way of violently targeting the Establishment without harming people, though some unexpectedly produced casualties. Such bombings didn't attract supporters, but they escalated in 1970 as political radicals saw few means to impact Nixon's expansion of what they perceived to be an immoral war.

In Madison on August 24, four young men orchestrated the bombing of the University of Wisconsin's Sterling Hall, home to the physics department and the Army Mathematics Research Center, which at the time was under contract with the U.S. Army. The militants detonated the bomb just before 4:00 a.m., when they thought no one would be there. But they were dead wrong; postdoctoral physics student Robert Fassnacht was killed by the blast and four others were injured. The intensity of the blast damaged twenty-six buildings on campus.

The wave of bombings had already come to the Twin Cities. A week earlier, in the middle of the night on August 17, fifteen to twenty-four sticks of dynamite exploded under the steps of the Old Federal Building in downtown Minneapolis. The blast rocketed chunks of granite as high as four hundred fifty feet into the air, shattered windows, and created enough debris to leave the building looking as though it had been struck in a wartime bombing raid. Located at Third and Washington Avenues South, the building had long housed a downtown post office but was then a military induction center. Although the explosion was heard as far away as nine miles and damaged several nearby buildings, there were no casualties. A security guard, who had checked the entrance from inside the building just minutes before the blast, suffered minor injuries.

Five days later, on August 22, an explosion ripped through a women's restroom in the Dayton's department store in downtown St. Paul. The blast blew the restroom's door off its hinges, shattered two toilets, and severely injured an English teacher from St. Louis Park. Standing just ten feet from the wastebasket containing the bomb, Mary Peek suffered injuries from metal fragments in her breast, abdomen, and legs, as well as burns to her lungs, which led to chronic pulmonary issues.

No one else was injured by the explosion, though fatalities could have resulted from a far more powerful bomb discovered in a nearby coin locker two hours later. An alert security guard noticed a piece of string hanging from the locker, connected to twenty pounds of dynamite that would have destroyed an entire side of the building and endangered dozens of police and firemen already on the scene. The bomb's timer was set to trigger a blast only twenty-seven minutes after it was found.

Bomb threats were common as well. In the days leading up to the Dayton's bombing, threats forced the evacuation of the St. Paul Pioneer Press-Dispatch building, the Donaldson's and Montgomery Ward's departments stores, and the downtown St. Paul Hilton on two separate occasions the same Saturday as the Dayton's attack. The First National Bank also received a threat, though the building was not evacuated. In Minneapolis, the Minneapolis Star and Tribune Building had to be vacated following a threat, and the Bureau of Printing and Engraving, a private company, twice was evacuated.

Even the Minnesota Twins were victims of a threat during a night game at Metropolitan Stadium on August 25. At 8:30 p.m., during the fourth inning of a scoreless duel between the Twins and Boston Red Sox, Bloomington police received a call that a bomb would explode at 9:30 p.m. Police determined that the call had been made from a phone booth inside the stadium, but a search failed to locate anything resembling an explosive device. At 9:15 p.m., with the Twins batting in the fourth inning, the decision was made to evacuate the stadium as a precaution and Twins public address announcer Bob Casey calmly told the crowd of eighteen thousand to evacuate the stadium until it was deemed safe to return.

While most fans headed for the exits, roughly one thousand joined Twins and Red Sox players who took refuge in center field. Soon after, vendors were hawking beer, soda, and hot dogs on the outfield grass. Small boys milled among their heroes, and in deep center field a crowd gathered to watch a card game between Red Sox slugger George Scott, Twins outfielder Brant Alyea, and Minnesota coach Bob Rodgers. After the search of the Met had been completed, fans were allowed to return at 9:45 p.m. and the game resumed.

Things weren't going well for the first-place Minnesota Twins even before the bomb scare. After securing back-to-back walk-off victories over the rival California Angels and Oakland Athletics in the first week of August, the Twins lost nine consecutive games, dropping three to the A's and then six more to the Washington Senators and Boston Red Sox. The Angels had struggled as well, but the A's were on a 16-6 surge when Minnesota's losing streak reached nine games after dropping both ends of a Sunday doubleheader at Fenway Park on August 15. Oakland had moved to within 3½ games of the Twins. The Angels were just four games back.

Minnesota's offense was sputtering, having failed to tally more than three runs over an eleven-game stretch. "I've never seen a whole lineup stop hitting at once," manager Bill Rigney told beat writers. "Everyone went flat at the same time." Futility at the plate peaked when Washington's best pitcher, Dick Bosman, tossed a one-hit, 1–0 masterpiece on August 13. Once again it was César Tovar who got the lone Twins hit to ruin a no-hit bid— this time a game-opening bunt single off Bosman. Tovar had stalled two other no-hitters in 1969, both times against Baltimore, and collected his team's only hit a Major League-record five times in a twelve-year career.

The Twins finally broke through in the win column on August 16, defeating the Red Sox, 9–6, in the final game of a dreadful road trip. The game was a seesaw affair until Tovar delivered the knockout punch to the losing streak—a two-out, three-run homer off Boston reliever Chuck Hartenstein in the eighth. After the game, a lighter mood permeated what had been a quiet clubhouse in recent days. Rigney was all smiles. "I'm 1-9 for the week," he said, "and you don't know how good I feel." Brant Alyea, George Mitterwald, and Harmon Killebrew also homered that day, but the home run barrage did not mark a major turnaround.

For the next two weeks, the Twins couldn't put together a lengthy winning streak, but the pitching was markedly better than it had been during the first half. By mid-August the Twins boasted the lowest team ERA in the league and would finish second to the Orioles' elite staff. Jim Perry had been dependable and effective, even when the team was losing. Bert Blyleven had been terrific and would have been the league ERA leader had he pitched enough innings. Although Jim Kaat was having an up-and-down season, Tom Hall and Bill Zepp had stepped in and made key contributions. Ron Perranoski and Stan Williams together posted 17 wins and a 2.21 ERA over 224⅓ innings that season—and saved forty-nine games.

The AL West race shifted again in late August, when Oakland lost nine of ten and the Twins showed signs of rebounding by taking two of three from the Red Sox at the Met. Blyleven worked the first of 60 career shutouts in the middle matchup on August 26, giving up just four hits in a 7–0 victory. He fanned eight Boston hitters, seven by expertly locating Uncle Charlie. "That first shutout tastes almost as good as winning your first one in the Majors," said the rookie. In the series finale the following day, Perry went the distance for his nineteenth win in a 5–2 victory.

The American League batting race, which had been a one-man affair until Rod Carew suffered his season-ending injury, heated up during the Boston series. Tony Oliva collected six hits in 12 at-bats against Boston to take the top spot on the batting leaderboard at .323. Not far behind were California's Alex Johnson (.320) and Chicago's Luis Aparicio (.318), followed by Red Sox teammates Reggie Smith (.318) and Carl Yastrzemski (.317). Yaz had gone just 1-for-12 against Twins pitching in the series.

Neither the batting race nor the AL West pennant chase were over. The Angels had inched to within three games of the Twins heading into September, setting up a potentially dramatic stretch run. The Twins would play California and Oakland early in the month, beginning with a stop in Anaheim at the end of a coast-to-coast road trip. It started poorly with three losses in the Bronx before the Twins headed to Milwaukee for three games with the Brewers, starting with a Tuesday night doubleheader on September 1.

Perry was on his game in the opener, blanking the Brewers on five hits to become a twenty-game winner for a second straight year. Killebrew stroked a three-run homer—his league-leading thirty-ninth—in the first inning of the 4–0 victory. But the big story was Perry, who had gone the distance in convincing fashion in consecutive starts and once again was at his best down the stretch. The Twins swept the twin bill, scoring six runs in the eleventh inning for a 7–1 victory in the nightcap. Killebrew put the exclamation point on the big inning with another three-run shot, giving him 40 homers on the season. After the Twins dropped the series finale in Milwaukee, they headed to Anaheim with a three-game lead.

With five wins in their last seven games, the Angels had to make a stand in the three-game set to stick around in the AL West race. It was a critical juncture for the Twins as well. In twenty-two games over the next twenty days of September, the Twins would square off thirteen times against the Angels and A's. With a strong showing, the two California clubs still had a chance to overtake them.

A crowd of thirty-eight thousand provided a playoff atmosphere to the opener of the Labor Day weekend showdown on September 4. Blyleven took the ball in the biggest game of his young career. If the Angels claimed the first game, they could gain a share of first place before the Twins left town. Alyea gave Blyleven a first-inning lead with a three-run shot off Angels lefty Rudy May. That was all the scoring the Twins needed, as Blyleven and closer Ron Perranoski combined on a 4–0 five-hitter. Perranoski rescued Blyleven in the sixth, entering with the bases loaded and one out. The thirty-three-year-old veteran, who fanned Billy Cowan and induced Tommie Reynolds to ground into a force play to end the threat, pitched 3⅔ scoreless innings to pick up his league-leading twenty-sixth save.

Perry earned his twenty-first win in the second matchup—a 4–3 Twins victory in which Kaat and Stan Williams worked 3⅔ scoreless innings in relief to put the Twins five games in front of the Angels. The lead expanded to six games when the Twins completed the sweep on Sunday. California right-hander Clyde Wright was looking to collect his twentieth win, but Tom Hall, auditioning for a rotation spot, outpitched the Angels ace and carried a shutout into the ninth. The Angels scratched for a run before Perranoski recorded the final three outs, but the Twins came away with a 3–1 win. The 150-pound Hall, who had expertly set up the final innings for Perranoski and Williams all season, secured his place in the rotation for the stretch run.

Minnesota's sweep sent the two contenders in opposite directions. After completing the road trip with three wins in Anaheim, the Twins returned home and won five of their next six games during a lengthy home stand that included visits by Oakland and California. The Angels, on the other hand, went on to drop nine straight, leaving Oakland as the lone remaining threat in the West.

The A's came to town for a three-game set that began on September 9. They had opened September with eight straight victories, though they still trailed by 5½ games when they arrived for their final 1970 visit to Minnesota. On a rainy Wednesday evening, Perry won for the twenty-second time, working eight innings of a 3–1 victory. A fourth-inning homer by former Twin Don Mincher kept the Twins ace from a shutout. Following the game, the Twins honored Bob Allison, who had announced he would retire at season's end.

Allison had exploded onto the scene in 1959. Powerfully built with speed and a strong arm, he stroked a league-leading nine triples and 30 home runs for the Washington Senators and won Rookie of the Year honors. In his first seven seasons, he averaged 28 homers and 88 RBIS per year—impressive numbers in a pitcher-friendly era—and he was a key contributor as the club became a contender in Minnesota. A series of wrist injuries in the mid-1960s slowly compromised his skills, and cranky knees forced Allison to face the retirement question by late in the decade.

Killebrew, Kaat, and Allison were the three remaining charter members of the Twins. Allison had hit the club's first home run on the day the Twins debuted at Yankee Stadium in 1961. Five days later on April 16, in a 10–5 win over the Baltimore Orioles, Allison set a single-game Twins record with seven RBIS, a record that Killebrew and Brant Alyea later tied but stood until part-time designated hitter Glenn Adams drove in eight in 1977. Among the many memorable moments generated by Allison in ten seasons in Minnesota were spectacular catches to save Jack Kralick's no-hitter in 1962 and Kaat's Game Two World Series victory in 1965. But the slugger also was appreciated for a decade of visiting hospitals, working charitable events, and serving as the honorary state chairman of the Minnesota Easter Seal campaign. Though articulate, the soft-spoken Allison pursued his profession and charitable work in a quiet manner, inspiring Twins beat writer Arno Goethel to once call him "the unknown outfielder."

At age thirty-six, with injuries taking their toll, Allison's power and production had dropped off markedly over the two previous years. Even as he played less, he didn't complain about the lack of playing time and often was the first guy to greet a home run hitter returning to the Twins dugout. Allison appeared in only forty-seven games during his final season, but provided a few key hits off the bench and saved a win in Cleveland on July 28, robbing Buddy Bradford of a grand slam with a leaping catch in right field in a 5–2 Twins victory. Allison batted just .208 with a single home run, though the postgame tribute provided another memorable moment in a thirteen-year career.

On what was being called BAT Day—Bob Allison Tribute Day— Allison was lavished with an assortment of gifts, including a shotgun and case presented by Killebrew and Kaat on behalf of the team. Owner Calvin Griffith gave the longtime slugger a recreational vehicle to spice up his retirement. Even the two other Major League teams in town honored him. Minnesota North Stars forward J.P. Parise and Minnesota Vikings fullback Bill Brown presented gifts, including a portable television set "to watch Vikings games," noted Brown. Standing in a steady rain, Allison, with his voice cracking with emotion, thanked the crowd for making Minnesota a great place to live and received a standing ovation. The tribute was to take place between games of a scheduled twin bill, but the rain continued falling and canceled the second contest. By then, a few tears had been shed as well.

The Oakland series ended with a doubleheader the next evening. The second-place A's needed a sweep to stay in Minnesota's rear-view mirror. Catfish Hunter, stuck on 16 wins for more than a month, pitched the first game, and didn't make it out of the third inning. Leadoff man César Tovar led the assault, collecting three hits and igniting a four-run rally in the third for a 6–1 victory. Hall, who had pitched brilliantly in consecutive starts and limited the Angels to a run over eight innings in his last outing, went the distance and fanned eleven. In the second game, Kaat and Williams combined on a 7–2 victory.

Twins pitching was terrific throughout the team's 10-2 surge to start September, which featured sweeps of both California clubs. The surge allowed the Twins to move 8½ games up on the second-place A's. It had been a memorable few days for the Perry clan as well. Jim had beaten the A's for his career-best twenty-second win on Bob Allison Tribute Day, putting the Twins firmly in the driver's seat in the AL West. And while Jim's team was taking both ends of its doubleheader with Oakland the following day, his younger brother Gaylord of the San Francisco Giants pitched his second of *four* consecutive shutouts. Scattering four harmless singles in an 11–0 romp, he won for the twentieth time, making the brothers the first siblings to win twenty games in the same season.

There was one key difference in their milestone appearances. During Gaylord's outing, the Houston Astros accused the future Hall of Famer of using a foreign substance. Second base umpire Augie Donatelli went to the mound and executed the search. The thirty-year-old Perry had a reputation for doctoring the ball, a covert skill to which he admitted after his retirement, but the palm of his right hand turned up clean. He retired the final eight Astros and secured his second of five twenty-win seasons.

TWENTY-TWO

Twins Claim Second AL West Crown

With the American League West race all but decided, the Twins gained a split of a mid-September, four-game set with the California Angels when Jim Perry secured his twenty-third win in the finale. The 4–3 victory, at the end of an eleven-day home stand, kicked off a four-game winning streak that pushed the Twins to the brink of the division title. They inched closer with three wins in Chicago, where, in the September 20 finale, nineteen-year-old Bert Blyleven worked a three-hitter for his tenth win. Following the 8–1 win, the Twins traveled to Oakland, needing to beat the Athletics just once to clinch the AL West.

Tony Oliva, putting on a late-season push for his third American League batting title, collected three hits in Blyleven's Chicago outing. He collected his 102nd RBI, a new personal high, then stroked three hits twice more in Minnesota's next three games to close within a percentage point of California's Alex Johnson in the batting race at .324. But in the opener with the A's on September 21, Oliva was held hitless.

So were the rest of the Twins. They had dominated the season series with Oakland, winning eleven of fifteen games to that point, and had the A's on the ropes. For one final day, however, the A's had reason to celebrate. On a Monday night at Oakland-Alameda County Stadium, twenty-one-year-old Vida Blue, making just his eighth big league start with two career wins to his credit, no-hit a red-hot club on a 14-5 run. He retired the first eleven Twins before allowing a fourth-inning walk to Harmon Killebrew, the only blemish on his pitching line. "I threw him a curve on a 3-and-1 pitch," Blue said after the game. "We were just trying to keep the ball away from him because the score was still 1–0 then. He can hit it out of the ballpark."

One of the few hard-hit balls was catcher George Mitterwald's liner at A's shortstop Bert Campaneris, which ended the fifth frame. Blue, who struck out nine, fanned both second baseman Danny Thompson and pinch hitter Bob Allison to open the ninth. He went up two strikes on César Tovar, who had made a name for himself breaking up no-hitters, before inducing a lazy fly that Don Mincher caught in short right field to complete the no-no.

Twice Blue thought the no-hitter was gone, both times at the hands of Mitterwald. On the line shot, Blue turned to see Campaneris leap to make the backhanded grab. In the eighth, with the score still 1–0, Mitterwald hit a hard grounder that third baseman Sal Bando fumbled but recovered in time to record the out. "I thought Mitterwald's grounder would get past him, but he got his glove on it and made a great play," Blue explained to reporters. After Minnesota's 6–0 loss, Perry called Blue from the Twins clubhouse to congratulate him. Manager Bill Rigney sent the rookie southpaw a bottle of champagne, on hand in anticipation of a division-winning celebration in Oakland.

The following morning Jim Kaat and Ron Perranoski made the two-hour drive from Oakland to Pebble Beach Golf Course before the second game of the series with the A's. Kaat wasn't scheduled to pitch and Perranoski wasn't likely to face a heavy workload, so it seemed like a perfect day to squeeze in a round of golf. The two left-handers enjoyed their day overlooking Monterey Bay, but a surprise awaited Kaat when they returned to the ballpark late that afternoon. "We walk in the visitor's clubhouse and there's two baseballs in my glove. That meant you were the starting pitcher," Kaat explained in a 2020 interview with the *Minneapolis Star Tribune*. "I said to our pitching coach, Marv

Grissom, 'What's this?' and he told me (Dave) Boswell had a sore back and they moved me up a day."

Luckily for Kaat and the Twins, on that Tuesday night, September 22, the wait for Minnesota's first hit off the A's Chuck Dobson was brief. Tovar, the last Twin retired by Blue the night before, walked to open the game. One out later, Oliva turned on a 3-1 breaking pitch and drove it into the right-field bleachers for a quick 2–0 lead. When Oliva crossed the plate on Rich Reese's two-out double in the seventh, the Twins were up 5–2 and needed only nine more outs to claim the West crown. Kaat, who had pitched the pennant-clincher against Washington in 1965, managed to work the first five-plus innings and allowed just a single run before Perranoski came on to record the final 11 outs. The A's scratched for a ninth-inning run to close the gap to 5–3, but with two down, Perranoski induced a weak grounder from Felipe Alou, which Cárdenas carried across second base for the final out. "Pebble Beach. Win the division. That was a good day," Kaat told the *Star Tribune*.

The Twins stormed onto the field to congratulate one another before retreating to the clubhouse, where they broke open several cases of champagne. Luis Tiant, who had battled arm woes much of the season, unloaded a quart on Rigney in the manager's private dressing room. The title was Rigney's first as a big league manager. It didn't come easy. The Twins gave him their most inconsistent performance as a contender, inflaming a chronic ulcer that was at its worst down the stretch.

The season had been filled with peaks and valleys. The Twins played like World Series champs the first two months, before a June swoon and a dreadful nine-game losing skein in August. Injuries were another source of concern. Rigney's club lost Rod Carew for three months. Tiant, who was expected to be a key addition to the rotation, missed much of the year, and Boswell won just three times after posting his only twenty-win season.

But twenty-two-year-old lefty Tom Hall and nineteen-year-old rookie Bert Blyleven combined for twenty-one victories. Blyleven arrived in June and became a rotation fixture. Hall, after excelling in relief and in a few spot starts, ascended to a starting role. He came through repeatedly down the stretch and went 7-1 with a 2.12 ERA in 11 starts. Staff ace Jim Perry closed strong for a second straight summer, going 6-1 with a 2.62 ERA in his final nine starts of 1970. The thirty-four-year-old Perry finished with 24 wins, four more than in 1969, and was named the AL Cy Young Award winner.

Reliever Stan Williams gave the Twins five hurlers with double-digit wins, as he went 10-1 with 15 saves and a stellar 1.99 ERA in 113⅓ innings. The off-season trade that brought him to Minnesota from Cleveland was widely seen as a Tiant-for-Chance deal with Williams thrown in, but the veteran reliever was easily the most productive of the three. At thirty-four, Perranoski wasn't as dominant as he had been in recent seasons, but led the AL in saves for a second straight year—the first two seasons that saves were an official statistic.

The Twins offense wasn't as potent in 1970. Killebrew delivered 41 homers and 113 RBIs, placing him among the league leaders, though his totals dropped from those of his MVP season. The Twins also lost the run production of Carew, who returned to the Twins with a pinch-hitting appearance in the clinching game against Oakland, exactly three months to the day he suffered the injury. After going 0-for-5 over the final days of the campaign, Carew finished with a .366 average in 204 plate appearances. A second consecutive batting title had seemed reasonable before that takeout slide by Milwaukee's Mike Hegan. At season's end, however, Carew still was unable to play regularly and missed the postseason.

Tovar and Oliva had career years during Rigney's first season, a 98-64 campaign that rated one win ahead of Martin's 1969 club. Tovar was the lineup's catalyst, batting .300 with a .356 OBP, and finishing second in the league in runs (120) and third in hits (195). For the fifth time in seven seasons, Oliva led the American League in hits with 204, and once again was in the thick of the AL batting race. He was firing on all cylinders in the final weeks. Batting .398 over his final twenty-seven games, Oliva finished at .325, the highest single-season average of his career.

Such a September surge normally would be enough to secure a batting title, but both Johnson and Carl Yastrzemski torched AL pitching down the stretch. Yaz batted .406 over his last twenty-one games and closed the season with a six-game hitting streak in which he went 12-for-20. He finished four points ahead of Oliva at .329. Johnson hit safely in twenty-eight of his final thirty games and batted .468 in a season-closing twelve-game hit streak. Even with 22 hits in those twelve games, he trailed Yaz by a single point going into the Angels' final game on October 1. With Yaz and the Red Sox having finished their season a day earlier, Johnson went 2-for-3 in a 5–1 win over the White Sox to close at .329 and take the batting title by four-tenths of a percentage point.

After Kaat, Williams, and Perranoski combined on a three-hit shutout of the Kansas City Royals in the season finale, the Twins focused on their return engagement with the formidable Baltimore Orioles in the American League Championship Series. The defending AL champions had won their final eleven games of the season and posted a 108-54 record, best in the Majors. All that after winning 109 games in 1969. Boog Powell had another big season for the Orioles, leading the club with 35 homers and 114 RBIS. He and Frank Robinson again led a balanced attack that featured six regulars with 17 or more homers. The Orioles also had three twenty-game winners. Southpaws Mike Cuellar and Dave McNally tied Perry for the league lead in victories with 24, while twenty-four-year-old Jim Palmer became a twenty-game winner for the first time. Palmer would win twenty-plus games in seven of the next eight seasons.

Avenging Baltimore's sweep in the 1969 ALCS would be a difficult task for the Twins. The pitching staff would have to quiet Baltimore's bats and Twins hitters would have to solve the O's dominant starters. The upstart New York Mets had shown it could be done the previous fall, shocking the baseball world by upsetting the heavily favored Orioles in a five-game World Series.

On the eve of the 1970 ALCS, there was reason for optimism. The Twins had taken seven of twelve games in the season series, and this time the showdown for the AL pennant opened in Minnesota. Although two twenty-four-game winners took the hill at the Met in Game One, Cuellar for the Orioles and Perry for the Twins, the bats won out on a blustery Saturday afternoon. Neither Cuellar nor Perry survived the fifth inning in Baltimore's 10–6 win, but before he departed, Cuellar lifted a fourth-inning fly ball into a strong wind, which carried it into the right-field bleachers for a grand-slam homer. The stiff breeze not only blew the ball beyond the fence, but kept it from going foul.

Orioles shortstop Mark Belanger, who was standing on first when Cuellar put the ball in play, was well positioned to track the ball's path. "When the ball went by, it was 15 feet foul," Belanger told *St. Paul Pioneer Press* writer Patrick Reusse. "The wind blew it back in." Baltimore starter Dave McNally was in the clubhouse watching the game on television when his rotation mate made contact, and he told Reusse that NBC broadcaster Jim Simpson's immediate response was, "There's a long foul ball to right."

That long foul ball to right went for a home run recorded at 330 feet, the same distance supposedly separating home plate from the wall down the right-field line. Thinking it was foul, Perry didn't even follow the flight of the ball. Cuellar didn't start running until it had tucked inside the foul pole. Oliva watched the ball blow back toward the field as he drifted toward the right-field corner. He thought he had a play on it at the last second, but it dropped into the seats behind him.

Baltimore scored seven runs in the inning to take a 9–2 edge. Coming back was a tall order, though the Twins immediately chipped away at the deficit. Tovar singled home a run in Minnesota's half of the fourth, and the gap closed to 9–6 when Killebrew homered and Mitterwald delivered a two-run single in the bottom of the fifth. But that's as close as the Twins would get. They managed 11 hits, but only one after their three-run uprising in the fifth.

Forty-year-old reliever Dick Hall worked the final 4⅔ innings for the Birds, allowing just a seventh-inning single by Oliva to earn the Game One victory. Oliva's hit provided Minnesota its last glimmer of hope. He was perched on first with one out when left fielder Brant Alyea jumped on a Hall offering and drove it to deep center. Center fielder Paul Blair initially turned the wrong way on the ball, which the wind then began to carry deeper. Blair sprinted in pursuit and made a stunning over-the-head catch at the fence, juggling the ball for a second before recording the key out. Hall then set down the final seven hitters.

On Sunday, a perfect October afternoon with temperatures in the seventies, the two clubs were back at the Met with two left-ies, McNally for the Orioles and Hall for the Twins, taking the mound for Game Two. The Orioles jumped on Hall for four runs before Rigney yanked him in the fourth with the Twins down, 4–0. Minnesota tallied three runs off McNally in its half of the inning, however, when Cárdenas drew a leadoff walk and Kille-brew and Oliva powered back-to-back home runs into the left-field bleachers. With the Orioles leading 4–3, the pitching staffs took over. McNally settled down and Williams worked three per-fect innings for the Twins, keeping both teams off the score-board. The score was still 4–3 going into the ninth.

For a second time in the series, though, Baltimore scorched Twins hurlers for a seven-run inning. Perranoski had nothing in the ninth, retiring only one of the six batters he faced. And once again Baltimore's starting pitcher played a key role in the onslaught. McNally, who had singled home a run earlier in the game, started the seven-run rally with a double. Powell's bases-loaded double down the left-field line put the Birds up 6–3. The slugging first baseman, 5-for-10 with five RBIS in the first two games, stroked a Perranoski offering that landed on chalk and kicked up a cloud of white dust as it headed into the left-field corner. The big blast came two batters later on Davey Johnson's three-run homer off Tiant, who relieved Perranoski and relin-quished two more runs. The Twins, down by eight runs, went quietly in their half of the ninth. The final was 11–3.

The win was Baltimore's thirteenth straight and put the Twins on the brink of elimination. The AL West champs didn't have long to ponder their predicament, as there was no off day for travel and the series resumed in Baltimore on Monday after-noon. The Orioles called on Palmer, their third twenty-game winner, to pitch Game Three. Palmer, who had won the decid-ing game of the ALCS the previous fall, squared off against

Kaat, bypassed by Billy Martin in favor of Bob Miller for Game Three in 1969.

Mimicking the first two games of the series, the Orioles scored early and often, quickly forcing the Twins starter from the game. Powell kicked off the scoring in the first inning with a run-scoring single, his sixth RBI of the ALCS. The Twins couldn't afford to fall further behind the defending AL champions, but two Twins errors soon doomed them to another lopsided loss. With one out in the second, Palmer slapped a lazy fly into short center field. Jim Holt in center came charging in and second baseman Danny Thompson ran into the outfield in pursuit. Holt called Thompson off the ball at the last second before the ball deflected off his glove for a two-base error. Blair made the Twins pay for the miscue with a run-scoring single that stretched the lead to 2–0.

The Orioles blew the game open in the third with another error figuring prominently in the scoring. Brooks Robinson opened the inning with a double to left and scurried to third on Davey Johnson's single. With no outs and the O's threatening, Rigney lifted Kaat for Blyleven. The rookie right-hander induced Andy Etchebarren to hit a grounder to short. Cárdenas's throw home arrived before Robinson, but Twins catcher Paul Ratliff dropped the ball making the tag.

Continuing the offensive onslaught by Baltimore hurlers, Palmer doubled home a run off Blyleven. Don Buford then delivered a sacrifice fly to left for the third unearned run of the inning, putting the Orioles up 5–0. The Twins threatened against Palmer in the fourth and fifth frames, but he settled down, fanning twelve Twins in a 6-1 series-clinching victory.

Palmer's win was the Orioles' fourteenth straight, and the AL champs stayed on a roll. They opened the World Series in Cincinnati and returned home with a pair of one-run decisions to go up two games on the Reds. The O's winning streak reached seventeen games when they clobbered the Reds, 9–3, in Game Three at Memorial Stadium in Baltimore. The winning streak stalled as Cincinnati salvaged Game Four, but with Cuellar on the hill for Game Five, the Orioles claimed another 9–3 victory and their first World Series title since sweeping the Dodgers in 1966.

Despite a loss in the final game for a second consecutive October, the future looked promising. Tovar had been terrific at the top of the batting order, and Carew would return at full strength from knee surgery when the Twins gathered again in Florida the following spring. Both Oliva and Killebrew were still getting it done, as they had combined for 64 homers and 220 RBIS in 1970. On the pitching side, twenty-four-game winner Perry and Kaat would be back to anchor the rotation, and youngsters Blyleven, Hall, and Bill Zepp would come to camp fortified by their September success. Plus, the bullpen would have both Perranoski and Williams to close out wins.

The key players were still in place after back-to-back AL West crowns. Claiming a third consecutive division title in 1971 was a strong possibility, but that wouldn't be enough for the Twins after losing twice in the ALCS. They would be looking to finally secure a return trip to the World Series, something that had eluded them over the previous five seasons. Unfortunately for Twins fans, it would take another seventeen seasons before the Twins made that return trip.

At the same time the Minnesota Twins were heading home for the winter, American troops were returning home from Vietnam in large numbers. More than 500,000 Americans were stationed there when President Richard Nixon moved into the White House in January 1969. He soon began bringing them home and stepped up the cutbacks in late 1970. By year's end, the total had dwindled to 280,000, and on January 4, 1971, President Nixon announced, "The end is in sight."

Yet, even as troops came home, the bombing raids over Vietnam, Cambodia, and Laos continued for years, carried out to disrupt enemy supply lines along their borders. They were executed with little regard for life. Laos was the most heavily bombed country in the war. Nearly 600,000 bombing raids dropped more than 2 million tons of explosives on Laos, most of which did not detonate; the residual explosives have killed roughly twenty thousand Laotians since the war's end. Cluster bombs, of which 270 million were dropped on Laos, continue to kill Laotians today.

To expose enemy positions, U.S. warplanes also dropped millions of gallons of Agent Orange, an herbicide containing dioxin, which defoliated forests and caused serious health problems—tumors, birth defects, psychological symptoms, and cancer—in both U.S. soldiers and Southeast Asians. The cost of attacking supply lines—raids that weren't particularly effective—came at great cost, destabilizing friendly regimes in both Cambodia and Laos and fueling staunchly anti-American revolutionary movements that succeeded once U.S. troops left. The extensive bombing raids didn't win the hearts or minds of those who endured them.

Southeast Asians didn't frame the war in Cold War terms, as the two presidents who waged it did. After rabid anti-communism fueled the witch hunts of Wisconsin Senator Joseph McCarthy in the 1950s, U.S. politicians remained fearful of being seen as soft on communism. President Lyndon Johnson applied those political and military tensions to the Third World, fearing a communist sweep across Southeast Asia, from Vietnam west to Thailand and Burma, and to the south to Indonesia. Which, of course, did not happen.

Perceiving Vietnam as a larger battle between the United States and the Soviet Union, or between the United States and China, ignored conditions that spurred revolution in Vietnam, conditions which neither the French nor the Americans could overcome. The Vietnamese were more apt to view the conflict as a homegrown political movement fighting a colonial conflict against world powers that had waged war on their soil for decades. Overplaying the role of the Soviet Union or China vastly underestimated the Vietnamese desire for change and a new mandate to rule their own nation.

The truth is, the United States had lost the Vietnam War long before it ended—perhaps even before getting involved in the ground war—and a failure to understand Vietnamese cultural history doomed the U.S. military to nothing better than a stalemate. Military strategy and firepower couldn't bring legitimacy to the U.S.-supported, anti-communist regimes in South Vietnam. When the United States stepped up its role in Vietnam in the early 1960s, the South Vietnamese leader was Ngo Dinh Diem, a ruthless and brutal dictator who imprisoned, tortured, and killed hundreds of his political adversaries. During a state dinner in South Vietnam in 1961, then vice president Lyndon Johnson called Diem the "Winston Churchill of Southeast Asia." Two years later Diem was overthrown in a military coup—orchestrated by the CIA before he was executed by his own officers—and each new military junta brought a new corrupt leader, none of whom gained popular support among civilians.

From the Vietnamese standpoint, the South Vietnamese government lacked the "Mandate of Heaven," noted Frances Fitzgerald in *Fire in the Lake*, her look at the cultural differences of the Vietnamese and American experiences during the war. The U.S.-backed regimes had lost the moral and political legitimacy to rule, and according to traditional Eastern belief, the will of Heaven, or *Tianming*, manifests itself, with a person's leadership skills a more important attribute than political system or doctrine. When the mandate is lost, revolution will burn away corruption and vice. When the mandate is restored, society can rebuild and begin anew.

The fate of the American war effort became more apparent in 1971, when former U.S. military analyst Daniel Ellsberg gave the *New York Times* and *Washington Post* access to a top-secret study documenting the history of American involvement in Vietnam. Known as the Pentagon Papers, the government study revealed that every postwar administration, dating to the Truman presidency, had misled Americans about the level and specifics of U.S. involvement in Indochina. As early as 1954, U.S. personnel orchestrated acts of sabotage and terrorism in North Vietnam in coordination with France's war effort there. Perhaps the most stunning revelation was that by 1965, the year American troops were first sent off to fight the ground war, U.S. military and intelligence officials had widely concluded that neither fighting nor negotiating would achieve the desired result.

After seventy years of French colonial rule, Vietnam faced massive challenges and rapid change as it worked to move a largely traditional society into the modern world. When the United

States followed the French into the fray in the early 1960s, success at winning hearts and minds depended on more than military solutions. The various U.S.-supported military regimes failed to address numerous domestic issues to the satisfaction of the Vietnamese people.

By the time all American troops had left Southeast Asia and the last helicopter departed the flat roof of the U.S. embassy in Saigon in April 1975, some 58,200 Americans had been killed in the war. The civilian deaths in Vietnam, Cambodia, and Laos ran in the hundreds of thousands—perhaps millions. According to the Vietnamese government, more than three million soldiers and civilians from the region died in twenty years of war with France and the United States.

EPILOGUE

What Happened to the Twins?

Despite retaining the talented core of players that had won back-to-back division titles, the Minnesota Twins slumped to 74-86 in 1971 and didn't finish higher than third place in the American League West for thirteen consecutive seasons. They finished with a winning record only four times before winning the 1987 World Series. After Frank Viola was masterful in Games One and Seven to bring the first championship to Minnesota, the Twins won ninety-one games in 1988, their first ninety-win season since 1970. The string of futility through the 1970s and into the 1980s wasn't unusual for a small-market team—owned by a family and run on a shoestring budget—but for much of the 1960s, the Twins were an elite team.

During the franchise's later years in Washington, it benefited greatly from an influx of Cuban prospects, courtesy of Joe Cambria, the prolific scout who signed hundreds of players and provided the Griffith family a nearly exclusive and inexpensive source of talent from the island. The Twins gained a critical advantage with Camilo Pascual, Zoilo Versalles, and Tony Oliva on the roster as the team became competitive in the 1960s.

In addition to Cambria playing an important role in the Twins' early success, Twins owner Calvin Griffith was an astute judge of talent and his staff was remarkably successful at developing cornerstone players. The Senators had struggled for years, but the franchise's fortunes would soon turn after Griffith signed Harmon Killebrew in 1954 and Bob Allison a year later. The scouting acumen became apparent when a run of rookies had an immediate impact in the Majors, beginning with Allison, who powered 30 homers as the 1959 AL Rookie of the Year. Harmon Killebrew also blossomed that summer, breaking out with an AL-best 42 homers and 105 RBIS at age twenty-three.

In 1961, the first year in Minnesota, the 150-pound Versalles emerged as a skilled defensive shortstop with pop, delivering 25 doubles and seven homers at age twenty-one, at a time when home runs didn't come cheaply. Two more rookies settled into the Minnesota infield in 1962. Third baseman Rich Rollins produced 16 homers and 96 RBIS and made the AL All-Star team. Second baseman Bernie Allen contributed 27 doubles, 12 homers, and 64 RBIS, and finished third in Rookie of the Year voting.

Then power-hitting outfield prospects joined the Twins in consecutive seasons. In 1963, Jimmie Hall popped 33 homers, slugged .521, and also finished third in the AL rookie vote. A year later, Tony Oliva had a debut season for the ages, becoming the first AL rookie to win the batting title by hitting .323. He also led the league in runs (109), hits (217), doubles (43), and total bases (374)—and delivered 32 homers and 94 RBIS to boot. Oliva won Rookie of the Year honors, as did Rod Carew, the last impact hitter developed by the Twins in the 1960s. He batted .292 as the AL's top rookie in 1967.

It all came together in 1965, when the Twins deposed the five-time defending AL champion New York Yankees with a deep and dangerous lineup and an underrated pitching staff that excelled at hitter-friendly Metropolitan Stadium. The Twins had led the league in scoring for three consecutive seasons beginning in 1963—and in home runs in '63 and '64, when they recorded the second- and third-highest, single-season team totals in Major League history. So, it was easy to overlook the 1965 pitching staff, which posted a 3.14 ERA that was the third-lowest in the league.

All five Twins hurlers with double-digit starts posted a lower ERA than the league's 3.46 mark. Three starters—Camilo Pascual, Jim Grant, and Jim Kaat—were twenty-game winners in the middle of the decade. Youngsters Jim Merritt and Dave Boswell, age twenty-one and twenty respectively during the 1965 season, were highly regarded prospects who would win twenty a few years later. With Boswell and Merritt on the roster, Jim Perry mostly worked in relief before surfacing at the end of the decade as the staff ace and Cy Young Award winner.

Pascual was thirty-one on Opening Day 1965; Allison and catcher Earl Battey were thirty. The rest of the batting order and pitching rotation were in their twenties. So, even though the 1965 club fell to Sandy Koufax and the Los Angeles Dodgers in the 1965 World Series, the Twins seemed poised to be a dominant force in the American League, capable of making multiple trips to the World Series. But the budding dynasty never materialized.

So, what happened? Several factors helped snuff out hopes of multiple pennants and a World Series title. One is that a few players, for reasons often difficult to explain, could not sustain their early success. Among them were Allen and Rollins, 1962 rookies who were expected to be productive regulars for a long time, but neither of whom developed into a consistent run producer. They were, to an extent, victims of circumstance.

The power surge of 1961, led by Roger Maris and Mickey Mantle, fueled a notion that home runs were coming cheaply after the American League expanded by two teams that season. After the 1962 campaign, baseball owners—worried about the increase in homers—voted to expand the strike zone from the armpits to the top of the shoulders at the high end, and from the knees to the bottom of the knees on the low end. Hitting a ninety-mile-per-hour fastball at the shoulders is a nearly impossible task, so perhaps it shouldn't have been surprising that the changes had a substantial impact. Adopted for 1963, the new strike zone slashed not only power numbers, but offense in general; roughly two-thirds of all big league regulars saw their batting average drop that season.

Baseball historian Bill James studied how the change affected hitters. His findings suggested that players like Allen and Rollins, as well as former Twins first baseman Vic Power—those who hit close to .300 with medium power—were affected the most by the tweak to the strike zone. Both Allen and Rollins drew a lot of walks as rookies, but with the strike zone expanded markedly, walked far less frequently in subsequent years.

Rollins was still productive in 1963, but his first two big league seasons were his best. After the 1965 championship season, he rarely was a regular, moved to the Seattle Pilots in the 1969 expansion draft, and retired a year later. Allen, after posting most of his single-season highs in 1962, suffered a career-altering injury in 1964. As Allen covered second base on a ground ball to shortstop Zoilo Versalles during a June contest with the Washington Senators, Don Zimmer threw a cross-body block into him. Allen suffered severely torn ligaments, missed nearly all of 1965, and could only fashion a career as a journeyman with the Senators, Yankees, and Expos before retiring in 1973.

Injuries compromised or shortened the careers of other early-1960s cornerstones. Earl Battey, the All-Star catcher, was a defensive stalwart who stroked a career-high 26 home runs in 1963 and ranked among the best-hitting catchers in the first five years of Twins baseball. Despite suffering thirteen different ailments in 1965, he remained productive through the championship season. By then Battey was bothered by chronically sore knees, goiter, and weight issues, forcing a surprisingly early retirement after the 1967 season. A key contributing factor came during the 1965 World Series, when Battey ran neck first into a railing while chasing a foul ball. He finished the Series, but was hospitalized and treated after Game Seven. He later said the neck injury was difficult to recover from and a factor in his early retirement.

Allison battled the injury bug as well. In 1963, he suffered the first of four wrist or hand injuries in four seasons. During the 1965 pennant race, Allison was struck on the right wrist by a pitch from Boston's Jerry Stephenson in July. He missed only ten days with a fracture, but struggled on returning. He fractured a bone in his left hand the following season, hit by a pitch from Boston's Jim Lonborg. Then, in 1967, Allison suffered a knee injury that would bother him the rest of his career. He required regular cortisone shots to stay on the field, and after being reasonably productive in 1967 and 1968, he became a part-time player and retired following the 1970 campaign, not long after turning thirty-six.

Following his remarkable rookie campaign in 1963, Hall remained productive for two more seasons. He never hit 30 homers again, but was a key contributor to the 1965 pennant push. The left-handed-hitting center fielder was beaned by Angels southpaw Bo Belinsky in 1964, which forced him out for a week and seemingly had long-term effects. Some of his teammates thought he was not the same hitter after the beaning. Facing lefties going forward, Hall hit for a markedly lower average and demonstrated virtually no power, while striking out far more frequently. Twins skipper Sam Mele started right-handed-hitting rookie Joe Nossek in center down the stretch in 1965, and Nossek got the starts against lefties Sandy Koufax and Claude Osteen during the World Series. Hall's production dropped off steadily, and by 1968, at age thirty, he was a part-timer.

During the 1965 pennant race, Pascual sustained a career-altering injury: a torn muscle at the back of his shoulder. He returned before season's end and made a World Series start, but after seven years as the staff ace with two twenty-win seasons and three strikeout crowns the first three years in Minnesota, Pascual was never the same. Shoulder soreness persisted in 1966, and after a disappointing year in which the Twins finished 89-73 and were never in the AL race, Griffith felt compelled to make changes to a club that a year earlier looked built for the long term. Griffith retooled, dealing Pascual and Allen to Washington for relief specialist Ron Kline. To replace Pascual, Griffith sent Hall and Don Mincher to the California Angels for Dean Chance.

In 1967, Chance turned in a terrific twenty-win season in the thick of one of the American League's greatest pennant races. Four teams competed into the final days of the season, and the Twins probably wouldn't have been there at the end without Chance. Still just twenty-six years old, he came back the next spring and once again pitched like an ace, though he went 16-16 for a Twins club that struggled to score runs as it had in 1967. He suffered a back injury while training for the 1969 season and spent fifty-four days on the disabled list. He was never the same pitcher and retired in 1971, two months after he turned thirty.

After Chance's injury-plagued 1969 season, Calvin Griffith dealt him to Cleveland. Luis Tiant, who came over in the trade, filled Chance's rotation spot, but soon suffered a hairline fracture in his right shoulder blade, a rare and career-threatening injury. The Twins let him go after one season. Griffith thought Tiant was finished; Tiant thought his release was simply a cost-cutting measure.

With the thirty-year-old veteran's mid-to-high nineties fastball gone, no Major League team was interested in him the following spring. But he adjusted his pitching style to accommodate the loss of velocity. A revamped delivery provided more deception and Tiant learned how to succeed by changing arm angles and speeds. He enjoyed three twenty-win seasons in the mid-1970s with Boston and posted two victories in the unforgettable 1975 World Series between the Red Sox and Cincinnati Reds.

As the 1967 club lost the AL pennant to the Red Sox on the last day of the season, Versalles endured his worst season as an everyday player. Just two years earlier, Versalles had led the league in runs, doubles, triples, and total bases, winning AL MVP honors. His performance declined dramatically in 1966 and the slide continued during the dramatic '67 pennant race. Winning MVP honors was the high point of his career, and perhaps its downfall. "It literally destroyed Zoilo's career," says one former Twins teammate, "because the next year he tried to become a player that he really wasn't. And he felt all the pressure and tried to live up to what he did the year before."

The Twins lost more than the pennant on the final weekend of the 1967 season. Jim Kaat, Minnesota's best pitcher down the stretch, departed the first of those two critical games against the Red Sox with an elbow injury. Kaat said the injury would have required Tommy John surgery had the procedure been developed then. At the time elbow surgery rarely was successful, and because he could pitch without pain, Kaat bypassed surgery and kept pitching. He wasn't as effective for several years—including the last few of Minnesota's window to compete—but he eventually returned to full heath and won twenty games for the Chicago White Sox in 1974 and 1975.

The biggest "what if" regarding Kaat's injury is whether he would have pitched the Twins to the 1967 pennant on that final weekend. Needing just one victory to advance to the World Series, he was at his best that September—his absolute best in a twenty-five-year career—and was cruising along with a 1–0 lead that afternoon until throwing strike three past Red Sox starter José Santiago leading off the third inning. He was forced to leave, and the Twins fell both days to finish a game behind Boston.

Griffith retooled again following the disappointing 1967 finish, sending Versalles and Jim Grant, cornerstones of the 1965 team who had failed to repeat their success, to the Los Angeles Dodgers for catcher John Roseboro, Battey's replacement, and relievers Bob Miller and Ron Perranoski. The Twins claimed division titles in 1969 and 1970, winning with an entirely new group of regulars surrounding Killebrew and Oliva in the batting order. Before Minnesota's run to the first AL West title in 1969, Griffith added veteran shortstop Leo Cárdenas by trading homegrown lefty Jim Merritt to the Cincinnati Reds.

Whereas the 1965 championship team was built with mostly homegrown talent—perhaps the best in the game for a few years—the late-1960s clubs called on veterans acquired from other organizations. After the Twins lost the 1970 ALCS to Baltimore, Allison and Frank Quilici retired and the injured Boswell no longer fit into the Twins' plans, leaving only Oliva, Killebrew, Kaat, and Perry remaining from the 1965 club. By then, of course, the Cuban connection had dried up, the victim of Cuban-U.S. relations reaching a low point following the Bay of Pigs fiasco in 1961. Borders closed soon after, making Oliva the last key player to join the Twins from Cuba. Plus, the Twins weren't nearly as successful at finding impact talent. The amateur draft began in 1965, and the team's draft record didn't produce everyday players and rotation fixtures as Griffith's signings often had over the previous decade.

The Twins drafted and signed just two impact players in the first seven years of the draft (1965–71). The first was San Diego State third baseman Graig Nettles, a fourth-round pick in the inaugural draft. Nettles went on to have a stellar career—but with the Cleveland Indians and New York Yankees after the Twins dealt him and Chance to Cleveland to acquire Tiant and reliever Stan Williams. The other impact selection was Bert Blyleven, the Dutch-born high school pitcher from California, chosen in the third round in June 1969. Barely a year later, at age nineteen, he began a Hall of Fame career, sparking the Twins to make their last successful run at October baseball in that era.

Blyleven wasn't the only young pitcher to emerge during the 1970 push to the AL West crown. The rotation's outlook suddenly was promising as twenty-two-year-old Tom Hall and rookie Bill Zepp replaced injured starters and pitched big games down the stretch. Hall had been terrific as both a starter and reliever that season, but wasn't as effective in that swingman role in 1971, when the Twins fell from contention. Looking for an established reliever to help get the club competitive again, Griffith dealt Hall to Cincinnati for veteran Wayne Granger after the '71 campaign. Meanwhile, Zepp, in the course of making a name for himself during the 1970 pennant chase, asked to be traded closer to his Michigan home. The Twins accommodated and traded him to Detroit after his rookie season, a deal that didn't have a payoff for either club. Minnesota acquired two Minor Leaguers who had little Major League impact and Zepp was injured the next season and retired at twenty-four.

There were other Twins picks from the first seven years of the draft to surface in Minnesota, including Rick Dempsey, Danny Thompson, Steve Braun, Steve Brye, Eric Soderholm, Rob Wilfong, and Glenn Borgmann. None became long-term cornerstones, and Dempsey and Soderholm enjoyed their best years with other big league clubs. The Twins did score big with outfielder Lyman Bostock, a twenty-sixth-round pick from Cal State, Northridge in 1972, and catcher Butch Wynegar, a high school prospect from York, Pennsylvania, chosen in the second round in 1974. By that time, however, the golden years were history and the Twins were struggling to play .500 baseball.

For the Twins, their final bids for another World Series berth ended with consecutive ALCS losses to the Baltimore Orioles.

Although the Orioles stumbled and lost the 1969 World Series to the upstart New York Mets, they were the best team in the Majors in both '69 and '70. In fact, those clubs are widely considered among the best in Major League history. They were the kind of team that the 1965 Twins seemed destined to become.

Expectations ran high heading into the 1971 season, but age and injuries suddenly caught up to the Twins. The franchise's outlook took a dramatic downturn that June, when Oliva suffered the devastating knee injury that robbed him of his power and compromised what was left of an outstanding career. He never played the field again when he returned in 1973, taking over the brand-new position of designated hitter. Killebrew, increasingly bothered by an old football knee injury, saw his power decline, beginning in 1971, and his run production dipped steadily. After averaging 45 home runs and 115 RBIS per 162 games over a twelve-year span with Washington and Minnesota, he never reached 30 homers again. By 1972, when Killebrew turned thirty-six and Oliva thirty-four, the Twins' top run producers for most of a decade were each playing on one healthy leg.

The prospects arriving from the Minor Leagues couldn't sustain the success of recent seasons, and suddenly the Twins were contenders no more. Although they celebrated only one American League pennant and failed to win a World Series title, those Twins teams, in a remarkable and challenging time in our nation's history, provided an abundance of excitement and joy to baseball fans.

BIBLIOGRAPHY

Allen, Maury. *Bo: Pitching and Wooing*. New York: Dial Press, 1973.

Armour, Mark L., and Daniel R. Levitt. *Paths to Glory: How Great Baseball Teams Got That Way*. Dulles VA: Brassey's, 2003.

Aschburner, Steve. *Harmon Killebrew: Ultimate Slugger*. Chicago: Triumph Books, 2012.

Barrow, Tony. *John, Paul, George, Ringo, and Me: The Real Beatles Story*. New York: Thunder's Mouth Press, 2005.

Brackin, Dennis, and Patrick Reusse. *Minnesota Twins: The Complete Illustrated History*. Minneapolis: MVP Books, 2010.

Butler, Hal. *The Bob Allison Story*. New York: Julian Messner, 1967.

Carew, Rod, with Ira Berkow. *Carew*. New York: Simon & Schuster, 1979.

Carlos, John, with Dave Zirin. *The John Carlos Story*. Chicago: Haymarket Books, 2013.

Caro, Robert A. *The Years of Lyndon Johnson: Master of the Senate*. New York: Alfred A. Knopf, 2002.

Creamer, Robert W. *Stengel: His Life and Times*. New York: Simon & Schuster, 1984.

Davis, W. Harry. *Overcoming: The Autobiography of W. Harry Davis*. Edited by Lori Sturdevant. Afton MN: Afton Historical Society Press, 2002.

Duncan, Pat. *Last Kings of the Old NFL: The 1969 Minnesota Vikings*. Self-published, CreateSpace, 2014.

Emerick, Geoff, with Howard Massey. *Here, There and Everywhere: My Life Recording the Music of The Beatles*. New York: Gotham Books, 2007.

Farrell, John A. *Richard Nixon: The Life*. New York: Doubleday, 2017.

Fitzgerald, Frances. *Fire in the Lake: The Vietnamese and the Americans in Vietnam*. New York: Little, Brown, 1972.

Glasmeier, Amy K. *An Atlas of Poverty in America: One Nation, Pulling Apart 1960–2003*. New York: Taylor & Francis, 2005.

Golenbock, Peter. *Dynasty: The New York Yankees, 1949–1964*. Lincolnwood IL: Contemporary Books, 2000. First published 1975.

Haas, Jeffrey. *The Assassination of Fred Hampton: How the FBI and the Chicago Police Murdered a Black Panther*. Chicago: Lawrence Hill Books, 2010.

Halberstam, David. *The Best and the Brightest*. New York: Random House, 1992. First published 1969.

Hall, Richard H. *The UFO Evidence—Volume 2: A Thirty-Year Report*. Lanham MD: Scarecrow Press, 2001.

Hamilton, Neil, A. *Eyewitness History: The 1970s*. New York: Facts on File, 2006.

Hauser, Thomas. *Muhammad Ali: His Life and Times*. New York: Simon & Schuster, 1991.

Hill, Tim. *John, Paul, George, and Ringo: The Definitive Illustrated Chronicle of The Beatles*. New York: Fall River Press, 2008

Kaat, Jim, with Phil Pepe. *Still Pitching*. Chicago: Triumph Books, 2003.

Kearns, Doris. *Lyndon Johnson and the American Dream*. New York: Harper & Row, 1976.

Kruth, John. *This Bird Has Flown: The Enduring Beauty of Rubber Soul, Fifty Years On*. Milwaukee: Backbeat Books, 2015.

Kusch, Frank. *Battleground Chicago: The Police and the 1968 Democratic National Convention*. Chicago: University of Chicago Press, 2008.

LaFeber, Walter. *The Deadly Bet: LBJ, Vietnam and the 1968 Election*. Lanham MD: Rowman & Littlefield, 2005.

Leavy, Jane. *Sandy Koufax: A Lefty's Legacy*. New York: HarperCollins, 2010.

Lewis, Jerry M., and Thomas R. Hensley. "The May 4 Shootings at Kent State University: The Search for Historical Accuracy." *Kent State University: Ohio Council for the Social Studies Review* 34, no. 1 (Summer 1998): 9–21.

Magan, Christopher. "Minnesota's Worsening Racial Disparity: Why It Matters to Everyone." *St. Paul Pioneer Press*, April 29, 2016.

Makower, Joel. *Woodstock: The Oral History*. New York: Tilden Press, 1989.

Mantle, Mickey, and Mickey Herskowitz. *All My Octobers: My Memories of Twelve World Series When the Yankees Ruled Baseball*. New York: HarperCollins, 1994.

Martin, Billy, and Peter Golenbock. *Number 1*. New York: Dell, 1980.

McWatt, Arthur C. *Crusaders for Justice: A Chronicle of Protest by Agitators, Advocates, and Activists in their Struggle for Civil and Human Rights in St. Paul, Minnesota, 1802–1985*. St. Paul: St. Paul Branch of the NAACP, 2009.

Mikan, George, and Joseph Oberle. *Unstoppable: The Story of George Mikan, the First NBA Superstar*. Indianapolis: Masters Press, 1997.

Miles, Barry. *The British Invasion*. New York: Sterling, 2009.

Miller, Jeff. *Down to the Wire*. Dallas: Taylor, 1992.

Mona, Dave, and Dave Jarzyna. *Twenty-Five Seasons: The First Quarter Century of the Minnesota Twins*. Minneapolis: Mona Publications, 1986.

Nathanson, Iric. *Minneapolis in the Twentieth Century: The Growth of an American City*. St. Paul: Minnesota Historical Society Press, 2010.

The 1960s Chronicle. Lincolnwood IL: Publications International, 2004.

Pappu, Sridhar. *The Year of the Pitcher: Bob Gibson, Denny McLain, and the End of Baseball's Golden Age.* New York: Houghton Mifflin Harcourt, 2017.

Phinney, Kevin. *Souled American: How Black Music Transformed White Culture.* New York: Billboard Books, 2005.

Pluto, Terry. *Loose Balls: The Short, Wild Life of the American Basketball Association.* New York: Simon & Schuster, 1990.

Remnick, David. *King of the World.* New York: Random House, 1998.

Roseboro, John, with Bill Libby. *Glory Days with the Dodgers and Other Days with Others.* New York: Atheneum Books, 1978.

Rosh, B. Joseph. "Black Empowerment in 1960s Minneapolis: Promise, Politics, and the Impact of the National Urban Narrative." Master's thesis, St. Cloud State University, March 2013.

Runtagh, Jordan. "Beatles' 'Sgt. Pepper' at 50: How George Harrison Found Himself on 'Within You Without You.'" *Rolling Stone.* May 25, 2017.

Sandbrook, Dominic. *Eugene McCarthy: The Rise and Fall of Postwar American Liberalism.* New York: Alfred A. Knopf, 2004.

Schaffner, Nicholas. *The British Invasion: From the First Wave to the New Wave.* New York: McGraw-Hill, 1982.

Schumacher, Michael. *Mr. Basketball: George Mikan, the Minneapolis Lakers, and the Birth of the NBA.* New York: Bloomsbury, 2007.

Selvin, Joel. *Altamont: The Rolling Stones, the Hells Angels, and the Inside Story of Rock's Darkest Day.* New York: HarperCollins, 2016.

Shea, Stuart. *Calling the Game: Baseball Broadcasting from 1920 to the Present.* Phoenix: Society for American Baseball Research, 2015.

————. *The 1960s' Most Wanted.* Dulles VA: Potomac Books, 2006.

Shea, Stuart, and Robert Rodriguez. *Fab Four FAQ: Everything Left to Know about the Beatles.* New York: Hal Leonard Books, 2007.

Shefchik, Rick. *Everybody's Heard about the Bird: The True Story of 1960s Rock 'n' Roll in Minnesota.* Minneapolis: University of Minnesota Press, 2015.

Showers, Bob. *The Twins at the Met.* Edina MN: Beaver's Pond Press, 2009.

Smith, Curtis. *Storied Stadiums: Baseball's History through Its Ballparks.* New York: Carroll & Graf, 2001.

Smith, Tommie, with David Steele. *Silent Gesture: The Autobiography of Tommie Smith.* Philadelphia: Temple University Press, 2007.

Solberg, Carl. *Hubert Humphrey: A Biography.* New York: W. W. Norton & Company, 1984.

Stark, Steven D. *Meet the Beatles: A Cultural History of the Band That Shook Youth, Gender, and the World.* New York: HarperCollins, 2005.

Sullivan, Denise. *Keep on Pushing: Black Power Music from Blues to Hip-Hop.* Chicago: Lawrence Hill Books, 2011.

Swensson, Andrea. *Got to Be Something Here: The Rise of the Minneapolis Sound.* Minneapolis: University of Minnesota Press, 2017.

Thielman, Jim. *Cool of the Evening: The 1965 Minnesota Twins.* Minneapolis: Kirk House, 2005.

Thornley, Stew. *Holy Cow! The Life and Times of Halsey Hall.* Minneapolis: Nodin Press, 1991.

Turner, Steve. *Beatles '66: The Revolutionary Years.* New York: HarperCollins, 2016.

Welter, Ben. *Minnesota Mayhem: A History of Calamitous Events, Horrific Accidents, Dastardly Crime, and Dreadful Behavior in the Land of Ten Thousand Lakes.* Charleston SC: History Press, 2012.

Williams, Jakobi. *From the Bullet to the Ballot: The Illinois Chapter of the Black Panther Party and Racial Coalition Politics in Chicago.* Chapel Hill: University of North Carolina Press, 2015.

Wolf, Gregory H., James Forr, Len Levin, and Bill Nowlin, eds. *A Pennant for the Twin Cities: The 1965 Minnesota Twins.* Phoenix: Society for American Baseball Research, 2015.

Worthington, Allan, with V. Ben Kendrick. *I Played and I Won: The Al Worthington Story.* Maitland FL: Xulon Press, 2004.

Wyman, Bill, with Richard Havers. *Rolling with the Stones.* New York: DK Publishing, 2002.

Yastrzemski, Carl, and Al Hirshberg. *Yaz.* New York: Viking Press, 1968.

INDEX

284